PRAGUE

ARTĚL STYLE

ARTĚL Books
Prague – New York
www.artelglass.com

PUBLISHER
Karen Feldman

EDITOR
Scott Ross

GRAPHIC DESIGN
Beverly Joel, pulp, ink.

COPYEDITOR, ENGLISH
Scott Ross

COPYEDITOR, CZECH
Kristýna Dvořáková

CARTOGRAPHER
© Draughtsman Ltd., Dorest, England. All rights reserved

FACT CHECKING
Lucie Fialová & Kateřina Bratršovská

TEL
+420 271 732 161
EMAIL
info@artelglass.com

Printed in the Czech Republic

Second Edition: May 2013
(Original Edition 2007)

ISBN 978-0-9792856-1-5

Second Edition

SPECIAL THANKS
Scott Ross, Beverly Joel, Lucie Fialová, Jamie Fisher, Kateřina Bratršovská, Daniela Beer, Kristýna Dvořáková, and Michaela Vaculik.

PHOTO CAPTIONS & CREDITS
Cover (background, top): Old Town Square, c. 1930; (background, bottom): Charles Bridge, c. 1955; (bottom): Porcelain Wellies with Czech Blue Onion Motif, photo by David A. Land, 2006

p. 22: Bellhop (Source: Depositphotos.com)

p. 48–49: Czechoslovakian World War II Commemorative Painting, 1945

p. 50: Astronomical Clock in Old Town Square, c. 1953

p. 76: Toy store window in Nové Město, 1962; (Source: ČTK / Czech News Agency)

p. 144: State Organized Hairdressing Show, Lucerna Palace, 1966 (Source: ČTK / Czech News Agency)

p. 152: Prague's "House of Nourishment," 1958 (Source: ČTK / Czech News Agency)

p. 190: Tros Sketos (Jaroslav Róna, František Skála a Aleš Najbrt), c. 2008 (Photo by Adam Holý)

p. 212: Boy Reading Newspaper, c. 1950

p. 222: Book cover ("Around the World in 44 Days"), 1929

p. 240: Prague telephone directory archive, 1939 (Source: ČTK / Czech News Agency)

Back cover: Škoda Felicia Convertible at Karlštejn Castle: 1959 (Source: Archive of the History of the Škoda Auto Company)

Table of Contents

Introduction

In October of 1994, I moved from San Francisco to Prague to oversee production at a startup shampoo company owned by an American—a position I was 100% unqualified for, other than basically being a trustworthy person. This was the start of my love affair with Prague. Four years later, I founded my own luxury crystal company, ARTĚL Glass. I've been in Prague ever since, and I now wholeheartedly think of this foreign capital as home. My decision to move here permanently was a most unexpected twist in my life, as I'd originally planned to stay for only a year.

Over the nearly two decades that I've lived in Prague, the flow of visitors has been constant. Many have been people I know; others, friends of friends; and more than a handful have been people who simply managed to get my email address through the very vaguest of connections. Each inquiry, however, brought the same request: a list of my personal must-see-and-do suggestions for their visit to Prague. Each time I answered an inquiry, I'd add some new information to a file I kept containing an ever-expanding list of shops, restaurants and often-overlooked sights, which I would send as an email attachment to my correspondent.

Eventually, I began to ponder the idea of wrapping up all of my Prague recommendations into a book that might fill a much-needed niche in the existing guidebook market. And that's exactly what I ended up doing! The first edition of *Prague: ARTĚL Style* was published in 2007. It quickly became one of the top-selling Prague guidebooks on Amazon and ultimately required three print runs (6,500 copies in all!) in order to keep up with demand.

Not surprisingly, Prague has changed quite a bit in the six years since the first edition came out. Several beloved shops and restaurants have closed, while many exciting newcomers have arrived on the scene,

and I ultimately realized that the time had come to produce the updated and expanded 2013 edition that you now hold in your hands.

This time, I collaborated with an old friend and Prague aficionado, Scott Ross, who helped me out with editing and organization, and together we have made lots of positive changes. In addition to dozens of up-to-date recommendations for places to stay, eat, shop, and play, the 2013 edition has improved maps, new fun facts, a guide to Czech beer and local pubs, and lots of cross-referenced information that should make it easier for you to find what you're looking for.

Like the 2007 edition, this book is *not* intended to be a general "tourist" guide to Prague, as those are easy to come by (and you prob-

ably already have one). Instead, my goal is to provide you with the kind of "insider" info I give my visiting friends. I hope you'll find it to be a fun complement to the stodgier (and perhaps less materialistic) guidebooks out there as you plan your trip and during your stay.

Prague is an ever-evolving city, so I'm always more than receptive to comments and feedback that will help this guide stay up to date. I've included a survey form on the ARTĚL website (*www.artelglass.com/are-you-satisfied*), which I hope you will use to let me know what worked well for you and where more improvement is needed. I will personally read every form that is submitted, and I thank you in advance for your input!

Just To Clarify...

I personally visited *all* the shops, hotels (where I stayed for at least one night), restaurants, cafés, and sights in this book (OK, except for the helicopter and hot air balloon rides). That is, every entry in this book is something I personally recommend, based on my own experience.

I did *not* receive any discounts, payments, or kickbacks in exchange for inclusion or a positive review in this book. Not that I wasn't offered any – because I most certainly was – but I turned all of them down in order to maintain objectivity, and I think it's important to share this fact with my readers.

A GUIDE TO THE LISTINGS

To make the listings as useful and user-friendly as possible, each entry includes the following:

• English name
• Czech name (when applicable)
• Street name and number (e.g., "Vinohradská 64")
• Neighborhood number and name (e.g., "Prague 1, Staré Město")*
• Reference to street map at the end of the book (e.g., "Map C")
• Website address (when applicable)
• Telephone number
• Metro information, including stop name and line color**
• Tram information, including line number(s) and stop name**

* See p. 17–19 for information on neighborhood names and numbers.
** See p. 13–17 for metro and tram information.

Most of the hotels, sights, restaurants, and shopping destinations listed in this book are located within the city center (the neighborhoods of Staré Město, Nové Město, and Malá Strana – see p. 17–18). However, there are a few listings in each section for places that are somewhat "further afield" – these will be clearly labeled, and will also include approximate travel times from the center of town.

I've tried to make each listing as comprehensive and up-to-date as possible, but if you need additional information, here are a few things to keep in mind:

WEBSITES

Many Czech websites, especially those for newer or fancier establishments, offer an English option (typically represented by a small British flag button); but MANY do not. I have found that the best way to deal with this is to use the Google Chrome web browser (www.google.com/chrome), which automatically translates *most* Czech websites to English – super handy!

PHONES

By and large, unless you are calling a hotel or sit-down restaurant, it's a waste of time to contact most local establishments by phone, as you can typically expect neither a prompt answer nor an English speaker. If you absolutely need to contact a business by telephone, it's usually best to ask your hotel concierge to do so on your behalf.

BEFORE YOU GO

When To Go

Spring and autumn are my two favorite times of year in the Czech Republic. So, if at all possible, try to plan your trip for April/May or September/October. During the spring, the weather is ideal and the countryside is bursting with fruit-tree and chestnut blossoms, as well as amazing yellow fields of rapeseed. The autumn brings ideal temperatures along with the changing leaves. Summer, on the other hand, can be oppressively hot, which is especially unpleasant since most of the city does not have air-conditioning. Perhaps worse is the endless sea of other summer tourists. And while a snow-dusted Prague can be extremely charming if you're lucky enough to catch it, the days of winter are terribly short (with darkness falling around 4 pm), so there's not too much bang for your sightseeing buck.

National Holidays

When planning your trip to Prague, you may want to factor in the dates of the national holidays listed below, as they can impact hotel rates and availability, store opening hours, and the overall 'vibe' of the city (in terms of festivals, parades, etc.). See p. 205 for more information.

January 1: New Year's Day. Anniversary of the establishment of the Czech Republic in 1993.

March/April: Easter Monday (Yes, Monday!). In the Czech Republic, Easter is celebrated on Monday, not on Sunday, as in other countries' traditions.

May 1: International Workers' Day (also known as *May Day*). A celebration of the international labor movement, May 1 is a national holiday in more than 80 countries and celebrated unofficially in many other countries.

May 8: Liberation Day. Commemorates Prague's liberation from German occupation in 1945.

July 5: Cyril and Methodius Day. These Greek missionary brothers from the ninth century created a new alphabet that was used to translate the Bible into the Slavonic language, thereby introducing literacy to this region. They were declared Patron Saints of Europe in 1980 by Pope John Paul II.

July 6: Master Jan Hus Day. Hus (1370–1415) was a famous religious reformer whose teachings helped shape the Protestant Reformation.

September 28: Saint's Day of St. Wenceslas. Known as the "chief patron of the Czech lands" and the symbol of Czech statehood, Wenceslas (903–935) founded St. Vitus

CHARLES BRIDGE IN AUTUMN, 1953

Cathedral at the Prague Castle. That's him on horseback in the huge sculpture at the top of Wenceslas Square, which, of course, was named after him. Note: the Czech name for Wenceslas is Václav, and the square is known locally as *Václavské náměstí*.

October 28: Establishment of the First Republic of Czechoslovakia, the first democracy in Europe, which lasted from the end of World War I in 1918 through 1938 (when significant parts of the nation were annexed by Germany).

November 17: Commemorating the Velvet Revolution (Nov. 17–Dec. 29, 1989), when student-led demonstrations led to the collapse of the Communist Party of Czechoslovakia and the subsequent conversion from Czech Stalinism to parliamentary republic.

December 24: Christmas Eve

December 25: Christmas Day

Everyday Items and How Much They Cost in Prague

ITEM	PRICE IN CZK	PRICE IN USD
Grande Latte at Starbucks	85 CZK	$3.50
Bottle of Coke	22 CZK	$1.10
Bottle of Mineral Water	11 CZK	$0.55
Beer (.5 liters)	30 CZK	$1.50
The *International Herald Tribune*	100 CZK	$5.00
Public Transport Ticket	32 CZK	$1.60
Movie Ticket	179 CZK	$8.95
1 Liter of Gas	36 CZK	$1.80
1 Gallon of Gas	136 CZK	$6.80
McDonald's Cheeseburger	20 CZK	$1.00
Pint of Häagen-Dazs	160 CZK	$8.00
Snickers Bar	12 CZK	$0.60

Betcha Didn't Know

1. In 1823, fingerprints were first recognized as a form of identification by Jan Evangelista Purkyně, a Czech.

2. In 1841, the sugar cube was invented in the Czech Republic by Jakub Kryštof Rad.

3. In 1892, Daniel Swarovski, a Czech, revolutionized the costume jewelry industry when he invented an electric device for machine-cut faceted beads and stones resembling precious gems, resulting in extremely sharp edges on each facet that create rainbow-colored refractions.

4. In 1907, classification of human blood into four types (A, B, AB & O) was initiated by Jan Janský, a Czech.

IVANA TRUMP, CZECH NATIVE, C. 1990 (SOURCE: WWW.CZSK. NET/SVET/CLANKY/OSOBNOSTI/ TRUMPOVA.HTML)

5. In 1913, Baťa Shoes, the largest shoe manufacturer in the world, was started in the Czech Republic by Tomáš Baťa. They now have nearly 5,000 international retail locations and service over a million customers per day. If you want to visit the Baťa museum, however, you'll have to go to Canada, as the founder emigrated there before World War II.

6. Until WWII, Czechs drove on the left side of the street, just as in Great Britain. When Hitler invaded in 1939 he changed it to the right side. After the war ended, the Czechs never bothered to change it back again. As a result, if you go to the National Technical Museum (see p. 59) you'll see several cars with steering wheels on the right-hand side.

7. In 1949, Ivana Trump (maiden name Zelníčková) was born in the industrial town of Zlín. As an alternate member of the Czechoslovakian Olympic ski team in 1968, she defected to America and went on to marry "The Donald" in 1977 – and to famously divorce him in 1992.

LOOK, HE'S ON THE WRONG SIDE! (TATRA 77 ADVERTISEMENT, C. 1930)

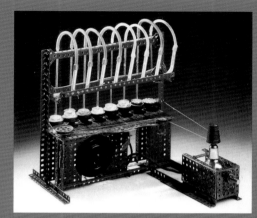

THE FIRST CONTACT LENS MACHINE, MADE FROM MERKUR TOY SET, 1963 (SEE P. 136)

8. In 1961, the first modern gel-based contact lenses were invented by Otto Wichterle, a Czech, on a homemade apparatus using a child's building set.

9. In 1966, the plastic explosive Semtex was invented by Stanislav Brebera, a Czech.

10. The Czech Republic boasts the largest per capita beer consumption in the world, at 132 liters (about 35 gallons) in 2010. That's far more than the runner-up, Germany (107 liters), and almost twice that of the US (78 liters) and the UK (74 liters). The average Czech beer is usually served by the half-liter, so that works out to about 264 individual beers per person — and actually quite a bit more, since the overall figure includes a significant portion of the population who are too young to drink beer. Believe it or not, the annual consumption rate has *dropped* considerably since 2006, when Czechs consumed 163.5 liters (about 43 gallons) per person!

BEER JUROR, 1963
(SOURCE: ČTK / CZECH NEWS AGENCY)

December 26: St. Stephen's Day, commemorating the first Christian martyr. This is an official public holiday in many countries throughout Europe.

Time Zones

Prague is on Central European Time, one hour ahead of GMT (Greenwich Mean Time).

London:	1 hour behind
New York:	6 hours behind
Los Angeles:	9 hours behind
Hong Kong:	7 hours ahead
Sydney:	8 hours ahead

CZECH AIRLINES, C. 1955
(PHOTO COURTESY OF CZECH AIRLINES)

GETTING TO PRAGUE

BY AIR

Prague's Airport, *Letiště Václava Havla Praha* (Václav Havel Airport Prague) is 19 km (12 miles) northwest of the city center. There are two terminals, so if someone is meeting you at the airport, be certain to specify *which* terminal you will be arriving at.

The good news is that the airport is small, efficient and modern. There are few airports in which you can land, go through passport control, collect your baggage and go through customs control in 30 minutes or less; happily, Prague is one of them. Both passport control and customs clearance are very informal, so you should ease through both without any problem. The only time I've ever been stopped at customs I was carrying large boxes, and even then it was easy to talk my way through it. If they do stop you they will request to see your passport.

The easiest and quickest way to get into town is by taxi. There are two firms at the airport that provide taxis: Airport Taxi (white cars) and Taxi AAA (yellow cars). I prefer Taxi AAA. Either firm should be able to quote you an approximate price in advance. A taxi ride to the center should be no more than 550 CZK, and an absolute maximum of 600 CZK.

If you need local currency, there will be three *bankomats* (ATMs) after you have exited the sliding glass doors just beyond customs control. You will see them to your left (KB, Česká spořitelna, and ČSOB, any of which are fine to utilize).

BY TRAIN

Neither of Prague's main train stations is charming, welcoming, or easy to navigate. If you do plan to arrive by train, I would *highly* recommend that you have someone from your hotel meet you at the station for a direct transfer.

On the upside, trains do run on time, are comfortable, and often provide a cheaper option than flying when traveling to nearby cities such as Berlin, Dresden, Munich or Vienna.

Train Times to Other Cities

COUNTRY	CITY	JOURNEY TIME	TRAINS DAILY
Austria	Vienna	4.5 hours	8
Germany	Berlin	5 hours	8
	Dresden	2.5 hours	8
	Frankfurt	9.5 hours	1
	Hamburg	7.5 hours	4
	Munich	6 hours	6
	Nuremberg	4 hours	9
Hungary	Budapest	7 hours	6
Poland	Krakow	10.5 hours	1
	Warsaw	10 hours	4
Slovakia	Bratislava	4.5 hours	9

For longer trips to cities such as Budapest and Krakow that usually call for overnight trains, I recommend that you fly. ČSA (Czech Airlines) has daily flights to both cities. Overnight trains tend to arrive at an ungodly hour in the morning, and you're unlikely to score a good night's sleep, as the train starts and stops throughout the night with frequent passport checking. In short, it simply is not worth the money saved unless you happen to love trains, have a lot of time on your hands, or find yourself on a tight budget.

The easiest place in Prague to purchase train tickets and inquire about options is at the former state-run travel agency (and still the biggest one), Čedok.

TRAIN STATION POSTER, C. 1952

■■■■■■■■■■■■■
Čedok
Na Příkopě 18, Prague 1, Nové Město (Map A)
www.cedok.cz
TEL 224 197 264
HOURS Mon–Fri: 09:00–18:00
METRO Můstek ● ○
TRAM 5, 8, 14, 26 to Náměstí Republiky

INTERNATIONAL TRAIN STATIONS
■■■■■■■■■■■■■
Hlavní nádraží (Main Station)
Wilsonova 8, Prague 2, Vinohrady (Map C)
METRO Hlavní nádraží ●
TRAM 5, 9, 26, to Hlavní nádraží

■■■■■■■■■■■■■
Nádraží Holešovice
Vrbenského 39, Prague 7, Holešovice (Map F)
METRO Nádraží Holešovice ●
TRAM 5, 12, 14, 15, 17 to Nádraží Holešovice

What To Take With You

1. Your Passport! Once you're here, leave your passport in a safe place within your hotel room. Never carry your passport around town; it's simply unnecessary, and the risk far outweighs the need. It's also a really good idea to scan a copy of your passport and driver's license and send the scans in an attachment to an email address you can access from anywhere. This way, should any unfortunate incidents occur, you'll have something to work with. As with all things travel-related, it's better to be safe than sorry.

2. Any Necessary Visa! Be certain to check your country's particular travel requirements for visiting the Czech Republic well in advance of your departure. Countries within the European Union vary on requirements. Please do not assume that if you're fine to travel in Germany the same will necessarily hold true in the Czech Republic, or you may find yourself being turned away.

3. Electrical Adapters! If you bring a laptop computer or other appliances, you will need an adapter. The power supply in the Czech Republic is 220 volts and the sockets require a two-pin plug.

4. Comfortable Walking Shoes! These are absolutely essential; cobblestones can be killers if you're not used to them.

5. A Small Travel Umbrella! You never know when it might rain, and it's always best to be prepared.

Money

The currency in the Czech Republic is the Czech crown (*koruna česká*) and you will see this abbreviated as either Kč or CZK. For the purposes of this book, we will use the latter (CZK).
• Notes are available in the following denominations: 100, 200, 500, 1000, 2000, and 5000 CZK.
• Coins are available in the following denominations: 1, 2, 5, 10, 20, and 50 CZK.

CZECH CURRENCY, 1989

EXCHANGE RATE

At the time of printing (May 2013), the exchange rate was as follows:

- 25 CZK to €1
- 20 CZK to $1

Although the Czech Republic is a member of the European Union, it is not yet using Euros. Some stores, hotels and restaurants will accept Euros, but this is not at all the norm. The currency of everyday use remains the Czech crown.

If you have an ATM card, there is really no need to exchange money before you arrive – there are *bankomats* (ATM machines) located at the airport and the train stations, so you can easily withdraw cash upon arrival. However, if you'll feel safer having some of the local currency on hand when you arrive, get about 2,500 CZK, as this will certainly cover all of your initial expenses.

CREDIT CARDS AND DEBIT CARDS

Credit cards and debit cards are widely accepted in Prague, so many of your expenses can be handled this way. MasterCard and Visa are the most widely accepted cards, so be sure to have at least one of these if you plan to use credit cards as a method of payment.

ATM MACHINES

Known in the Czech Republic as *bankomats*, ATMs are available throughout the city with an English language option, and you should have little difficulty using them for cash withdrawal. As noted above, they can be found at the airport and train stations, so you can simply withdraw cash upon arrival and then 'top up' your cash supply as needed during your stay in town. Be sure to check with your bank regarding transaction fees.

CURRENCY EXCHANGE

Throughout Prague there are numerous options for the exchange of currencies, including banks, hotels, Bureaux de Changes, and random individuals on the street. None of these are wise choices – that is, unless you're a fan of unfavorable exchange rates, exorbitant fees, or the possibility of actual danger. Your best bet is simply to use one of the many *bankomats* (ATM machines) located throughout the city.

PICKPOCKETING & CRIME

Although Prague is basically an incredibly safe city to walk around in, a recent insurance report found that it has the highest number of claims from travelers who have been pick-pocketed of any city in Europe. Where do you need to be especially vigilant? Just about anywhere, to be perfectly honest – in trams, in the metro, on the Charles Bridge, in museum gift shops, or even at that really sweet café. Should luck not be on your side, I've listed several police stations in Prague 1 and 2 (see p. 219), which will come in handy.

LOST / STOLEN CREDIT CARDS

In case of emergency, here are the local telephone numbers for three major credit card companies:
Master Card / Visa:
+001 880 826 2181
American Express: 222 800 222
Diners Club: 255 712 712

Tele-Communications

If you can't live without your mobile phone, it might make sense to purchase one in the Czech Republic when you arrive. This is cheaper and easier than renting one from abroad. There are three main providers in the Czech Republic and Vodafone, for now, is the cheapest. You will need to purchase a phone (prices start at 700 CZK) and a SIM card including credit for 200 CZK, 500 CZK or 1,000 CZK. All told, you will be connected for about $45. The same phone can be used when you travel to other European countries; simply purchase a new local SIM card providing you with a local number and credit. See p. 221 for information on local telephone service providers.

GETTING AROUND PRAGUE

Prague is a very small city, and to be honest the most charming way to get around is on foot. Don't be fooled by all the metro stops, they are actually extremely close together. However, as you'll be doing *lots* of walking in Prague, there are definitely times when you'll want to utilize public transport (especially when going up the hill to the Prague Castle), and luckily, Prague has an excellent public transport system. As in New York City, it's the easiest, quickest and least expensive way to get around town. The system includes the metro, trams, buses,

and even a funicular, but you'll probably only need to utilize the metro and trams during your visit. The systems are extremely simple, and with a bit of common sense you should not experience any problems.

I've included the names of the nearest metro and/or tram-stop for every listing in this book to make finding your destination as simple as possible. If you do plan to use public transport during your visit, I highly recommend that you get a Travel Pass for either 24 hours or 3 days (see below), as it will save you lots of time fiddling with single tickets or seeking them out.

SINGLE TICKETS

24 CZK: Single journey up to 30 minutes or 5 stops on the metro (no transfers).
32 CZK: Travel on whole system up to 90 minutes, including transfers.

See p. 221 for information on local telephone service providers.

TRAVEL PASSES

24 hour	110 CZK
3 day	310 CZK
1 month	670 CZK

Where to purchase single tickets and one-day passes

Single tickets or a one-day pass can be purchased from machines at all metro stations and some tram stops, *tabáks* (tobacco /news stands throughout the city), hotels, and city information centers.

Where to purchase travel passes longer than one day

These can only be purchased from windows at metro stations or information offices; I find it easiest to pick them up at the Muzeum metro stop, which is open daily. The Můstek metro stop is another good option, but this is open on weekdays only. Look for the window in the section of the station labeled *Můstek B* (not *Můstek A*).

POSTCARD SENT BY A CZECH PRISONER TO HIS LOVER IN PRAGUE, C. 1931

SOKOL POSTER, 1912

13

STATUE OF ST. WENCESLAS,
OVERLOOKING WENCESLAS
SQUARE

NOTE: Your name and date of birth must be written on the back of the pass.

Muzeum
HOURS Daily: 07:00–21:00
TEL 222 623 777
Beneath McDonalds entrance

Mŭstek B
HOURS Mon–Fri: 06:00–20:00; Sat: 07:00–14:00
TEL 222 646 350
Beneath Jungmannova entrance

VALIDATING TICKETS
Tickets are only valid once you have inserted them in the yellow validating machines that are visible as you pass into the metro station (not on the train itself) or board a tram. Be sure to insert them face-up in the direction the arrow is printed. These machines will then stamp your ticket with the date and time. For single tickets and travel passes, you will only need to do this the very first time you use it. After that, simply keep it with you in case you're asked to show it.

For the metro, the machines will be on the platform immediately before you descend the escalator.

On trams and buses, the machines will be located close to the doors, and, should you be carrying a fresh ticket or pass, you will validate it once you're already onboard.

Public transport in Prague is based on a trust system, but from time to time, especially at metro stops like Mŭstek and Malostranská or on the #22 tram, plain-clothes

EDUCATIONAL POSTER: *SAFETY IN THE STREETS*, 1939

inspectors with metal badges in hand will ask to see your validated ticket. If you fail to show one, you will be required to pay a fine (currently 800 CZK). If you refuse to pay this fine, the police will be called, and if you don't have money they will bring you to a *bankomat* so you can withdraw the cash to make the payment.

Metro

Hours: 05:00–24:00
Departures: During rush hour, every two to four minutes; during off-peak hours, every four to ten minutes.

The Prague metro opened in 1974, and is made up of three lines designated by letters and colors:

Line A: Green
(Depo Hostivař–Dejvická)
Line B: Yellow
(Černý Most–Zličín)
Line C: Red
(Letňany–Háje)

Colors are far more memorable than letters, so moving forward I'll simply refer to them as the

Green ●, Yellow ● or Red ● lines. A map showing all three lines can be found on the back cover flap.

Transfers are possible at three stations:
Muzeum: Green + Red Lines
Můstek: Green + Yellow Lines
Florenc: Yellow + Red Lines

PRAGUE METRO C. 1978
(SOURCE: ARCHIVE DP)

MALÁ STRANA, C. 1971

Trams

Hours: 04:30–24:00
Night trams: 24:00–05:00

Part of Prague's urban landscape since 1900, trams are still the backbone of the public transport system. Not only are they incredibly efficient (they cover every nook and cranny of the city), they also give visitors the opportunity to sightsee along the way. The #22 tramline is famous for the sights and vistas along its route; if you take it to the Prague Castle, try to get a seat on the right side so you can enjoy the panoramic view of Prague on your way up the hill.

Although you'll see plenty of new trams, the bulk of Prague's fleet (thank goodness) dates back to a design that was introduced in 1961 and manufactured through 1973. Their wonderfully rounded design is now iconic, and my favorite feature is the fiberglass seats mounted directly on heaters, a big plus during the blisteringly cold winter months. No trip to Prague would be complete without taking at least one ride on these classic (and sadly, soon to be extinct) tramcars.

Which side should I be on?

Simply knowing what number tram you need to take is *not* enough; you must know which direction you need to go in as well, as every tram stop will have two directions to choose from. To determine which side you should be on, you will need to look at the tram route list posted just under the sign showing

Throughout the city, metro stations are indicated by the following logo:

After you've decided where you want to travel and what color line you need to use to get there, you'll descend what is often a very steep and quick escalator to the platform, which will have two sides. You will need to determine which side of the platform is correct for your destination. Signage clearly marks the station you're at, and by determining whether the stop you want to go to is to the right or left of the current station, you can establish which side to stand on.

NOTE: **Due to construction, the Národní třída metro station (on Line B) will be closed until sometime in mid-2014. For more information, visit the Prague Public Transit website: www.dpp.cz/en/narodni-trida-b-temporary-metro-station-closure/**

which tram numbers are available at a given stop.

- The sign will list all the stops that the tram will make.
- The stop you're at will be highlighted.
- If the stop you want to go to is *below* the highlighted stop, you're on the correct side.
- If the stop you want to go to is *above* the highlighted stop, you're on the wrong side and must change.

To the left of your listed stop there will be a number signifying how many minutes it will take you to reach your destination. Shockingly, this information is almost always dead-on accurate. Don't ask me how they do this...

How long do I need to wait for my tram?
Once you have found your tram and the right direction, you can check the timetables, which are divided into weekdays (*pracovní den*), Saturday (*sobota*) and Sunday (*neděle*) to see when the next tram will come. As noted above, this information is remarkably accurate.

Facts about the metro and tram:
- On some trams and all metro trains, the doors do *not* open automatically; you will need to push a button to enter / exit the car.
- You are expected to offer your seat to pregnant women or the elderly.
- Children under 6 ride for free.
- Pets require a ticket unless they are in a bag.
- Luggage, if large, requires a 16 CZK ticket.

Taxis

Prague has a terrible reputation for surly taxi drivers grossly over-charging foreigners. If you hail a taxi, that reputation will be proven 100% accurate. A word to the wise: DO NOT HAIL A TAXI! It will likely not go well. Instead, you should *call* a taxi – the firms listed below speak English and are trustworthy:

AAA Taxi
TEL 14014

City Taxi
TEL 257 257 257

If you're at a restaurant, by all means ask them to call you a taxi; they will not be put off by the request. It is also possible to request a taxi via SMS (text messaging), but this is best done in Czech – so you may need to ask a friendly local to help you out...

If you don't have a phone and desperately need to take a taxi, your next best bet is to seek out one of the "Fair Place" taxi stands located throughout the city, which you can identify by their orange 'thumbs-up' signs. Taxis at these stands are required by law to honor a maximum fare amount set by City Hall (currently 28 CZK per kilometer), so although fares might vary among the different firms using these stands, they will never exceed the maximum – so this is a much better choice than hailing a cab.

If you're without a phone, not near a Fair Place stand, and desperate to take a taxi *right now*, make sure to agree on a price *before* entering the cab. If you're in the center of town and going to

another location within this area, the cost should not exceed 200 CZK.

PRAGUE NEIGHBORHOODS

A User's Guide

Like many cities, Prague is composed of several distinct neighborhoods, each with its own history, look, and feel. Here's what you need to know...

MALÁ STRANA
Lesser Town
(see Map B on p. 228–229)

Located just below the castle, this is the oldest part of the city. Quaint, charming and historic, it's packed with Baroque and Renaissance architecture. Lots of hotels, restaurants, small shops and very expensive real estate (mostly inhabited by expats) fill this quarter, so there are very few businesses based here.

HRADČANY
Castle District
(see Map D on p. 232–233)

An outgrowth of Malá Strana, this is the crown jewel of Prague. The Prague Castle (Pražský hrad) presides over the neighborhood, along with several smaller palaces (most of them now serving as museums) and beautiful gardens.

STARÉ MĚSTO
Old Town
(see Map A on p. 226–227)

This is the pulse of the city center, full of businesses, shops, department stores, restaurants, and expensive real estate; it's also where Czechs gather when a hockey championship is won.

JOSEFOV
The Jewish Quarter
(see Map A on p. 226–227)

This part of Old Town is where you'll find most of the Jewish sights, as well as magnificent turn-of-the-20th-century Art Nouveau buildings. These serve as apartments for rich Czechs and expats, as well as a few lucky Czechs who have lived there since the Communist era and enjoy rent control. One family I know lives in a 110 sq. meter (1184 sq. ft.) apartment on Pařížská (the fanciest street in town) and pays a mere 3,550 CZK ($178) for rent, not counting 3,600 CZK ($180) per month in utilities (it's such a *trial* having to heat a place with four-meter [13 ft.] ceilings...).

NOVÉ MĚSTO
New Town
(see Map C on p. 230–231)

This section of town borders Old Town but is definitely a bit grittier and less touristy. The real estate is generally more affordable here, and you'll find lots of businesses, restaurants, and shops.

VINOHRADY
Vineyard District
(see Map E on p. 234–235)

A residential and business district that borders Nové Město. Both Czechs and expats choose this area to live in, as it's much more "real" than downtown and has a neighborhood feel, yet you're only one or two metro stops from the city center. The buildings are primarily Art Nouveau (although less glamorous than downtown) and Functionalist.

BOHEMIAN COUNTRYSIDE, 1953

FREQUENTLY ASKED QUESTIONS

What is the history of the name "ARTĚL"?
The company takes its name from an early-20th-century collective of Czech artisans whose dedication to preserving traditional methods of handcrafts-manship led them to reject industrial production techniques. ARTĚL carries on the spirit of these artisans and their commitment to producing – entirely by hand – lasting objects of impeccable quality, design, and functionality. For more information, visit *www.artelglass.com*.

What and where is Bohemia?
Bohemia is a historical region occupying the western two-thirds of what is now the Czech Republic. It is culturally distinct from Moravia, which occupies the eastern third.

Can I drink the water?
Yes, and you'll be absolutely fine, as was officially confirmed for me on a recent visit to the Prague Water Works. That said, you will not be able to order tap water at a restaurant, so try my two local favorites: Mattoni (I find it superior to both Perrier and San Pellegrino) or Bonaqua. Be sure to

clarify whether you want it with bubbles or not, as flat water is not the norm. In most grocery stores you will also find Aquila, another favorite of mine. If you purchase water in a store, you will need to be familiar with the following terms:

Perlivá: Sparkling; cap usually red

Neperlivá: Still; cap usually blue

Jemně perlivá: Medium sparkling (my personal favorite); cap usually green

How much should I tip taxi drivers?
10%

How much should I tip at restaurants?
10%

Can I negotiate prices in stores?

In antique stores absolutely, and I encourage you to try. In general you can expect to get about 10% off the marked price, especially if you pay cash. However, for general merchandise, is it not normal to negotiate for a better price.

What is the difference between the blue and red numbers on the buildings, and which one should I reference to find an address?

The numbering system dates back to 1805:

Blue numbers are for street addresses. These are the numbers you care about.

The lowest numbers are always closer to the river, a fact I only recently learned. **Red numbers** are used by the cadastre office (land registry) in each district in Prague. Each building or house has a specific number in its district.

What is the significance of the city numbers that appear in address listings (e.g., "Prague 2")?

Prague is made up of ten districts, and the number signifies the district. Most of the tourist sites – and the recommendations on the pages that follow – are located in Prague 1 (which includes the Malá Strana, Staré Město, and Nové Město neighborhoods), while many of the "further afield" listings are in Prague 2 (Vinohrady).

What is the local tax rate?
- Value Added Tax (VAT): 15% and 21%
- Corporate Tax: 19%
- Personal Tax: 15%
- Mandatory social and health insurance payments are based on an employee's gross salary; both the employer and employee contribute.
- Employer contributes social tax of 25% and health insurance of 9%
- Employee contributes social tax of 6.5% and health insurance of 4.5%

How much do you pay for your apartment? How big is it?

I pay $635 (12,700 CZK) a month for a very comfortable one-bedroom apartment that is 75 sq. meters (807 sq. ft.). My rent represents what a Czech would pay versus what a foreigner generally

BLUE & RED BUILDING NUMBERS, KOŽNÁ STREET, 1910

would – a real bargain in comparison with New York City or London, but it's important to remember that the average salary in the Czech Republic is only $1,216 (24,319 CZK) a month; in other words, in proportion to salaries, rents are actually very high in Prague. This is somewhat resolved by rent control. For example, I am the only foreigner in my building; all of the other tenants have been there since before the fall of communism, and their rent for the same size apartment is approximately $171 (3,410 CZK) per month. Currently, this is a big issue between landlords and government. It's almost impossible to make capital improvements (desperately needed after 50 years of neglect) when the income from rent does not even begin to cover the apartment itself, let alone the building.

Where do all the Czechs disappear to on spring and summer weekends when the city seems so empty?
Virtually every Praguer has a country house (whether a modest *chata* or a more substantial *chalupa*), where they escape on spring and summer weekends. It was one of the few things under communism that the government was not interested in controlling. East Hampton it is not! However, there are advantages: roosters wake you in the morning, fresh farm eggs from the chicken coop across the way, apple and cherry blossoms each spring with a bounty of fruit soon to follow, and *most* importantly, one of the most picturesque

and unspoiled countrysides I've ever seen.

How did people get jobs under communism? Were they able to change jobs? Did people get fired? Did everyone earn the same amount?
There was zero unemployment under communism, so getting a job was not a big accomplishment. High schools were specialized for particular trades – carpentry, glassmaking, hospitality, etc. – and coursework included on-the-job training at a local firm; after graduation, it was typical that one would work for that same firm.

Firing, as such, did not exist. This perhaps is not surprising, given that the goal was 100% employment. However, it was possible to be put in a lower position with less pay. There were only two reasons someone would ever be let go: either for "political reasons" (i.e., being foolish enough to express anti-communist views), or for stealing "too

much" from the company (everyone stole). As my Czech friend Kristýna noted, "Everyone stole under communism. I don't think anyone bought a single brick. If you look at people's *chatas* (country houses), you can tell where they were working at each point in their building process – the railways, say, or the glass industry – based on the various materials utilized in the construction."

Job-hopping was not possible, so if you were unhappy at work you were basically out of luck. Salaries were not equal, but the differential was not based on talent or efficiency. If someone was a member of the Communist party, they could be paid more than double what a non-member in the same position would receive. Interestingly, manual laborers such as coalminers were among the highest paid people in the country – which makes sense if you consider the philosophy behind communism.

CHATA, C. 1974

I Only Have One Day In Prague, So What Should I Do?!

- Start early!

- Have breakfast at **Café Savoy** (see p. 158).

- Take tram #22 to the **Prague Castle** area; sit on the right side to get a great view of the city when the tram goes up the hill to the castle. Get off at Pohořelec.

- Go see the ceiling fresco at **Strahov Monastery Library** (see p. 56) – this is simply amazing.

- Stroll around Prague Castle. Definitely pop into **St. Vitus Cathedral** (see p. 56).

- Have lunch at the **Lobkowicz Café** (see p. 171) and take in the view.

- Check out the collection at **Lobkowicz Palace** (see p. 52).

- Follow the steep **Prague Castle Stairs** (see photo above) down toward the metro, but stop along the way at

Villa Richter – **Terra** (see p. 165) for a glass of wine and yet another view.

- Take the metro from Malostranská to Staroměstská—you can certainly walk, but the metro is very cool...

- Head to the **Jewish Quarter** (see p. 18) and check out the **Spanish Synagogue**.

- Take a break – a gelato at **Angelato** (see p. 166) is certain to hit the spot.

- Check the time at the **Clock Tower** in Old Town Square. For a fantastic view of Old Town, take the glass elevator to the lookout on top of the tower (see p. 72).

- Walk down Celetná to **Obecní dům** (the Municipal House – see p. 64). Once inside, be certain to look at all the public spaces, including the pub and bar in the basement.

PRAGUE CASTLE STAIRS, C. 1920

- Drop by the flagship **ARTĚL Design Shop** (see p. 116), located just around the corner, to check out our collection of handmade Bohemian crystal and vintage Czech items.

- Have a drink at the **Grand Café Orient** (see p. 169) and be amazed by the highly stylized Czech Cubist décor.

- Head to the Aria Hotel for dinner on the rooftop terrace at **Coda** (see p. 159), which offers a sublime view.

- Alternatively, dine at **Bellevue** (see p. 155), which has an exquisite riverside location and a view of Prague Castle.

- After dinner, stroll over the **Charles Bridge** (see photo on left); no visit to Prague is complete without it. My favorite time is at night when the city is lit up and the bridge is less crowded.

- Go home; you must be exhausted!

CHARLES BRIDGE, C. 1955

Hotels

There is no one hotel that I consider the "must stay" location in Prague; what I *can* tell you is that *each* hotel listed below is a place I have stayed myself—some for the purposes of this book, and others simply as a means of escaping my apartment and my cats (to whom I'm allergic) for a night of peaceful sleep—and I would recommend all of them to friends without hesitation.

Hotels are listed alphabetically. Room prices are subject to availability, and I recommend that you go online to find Best Available Rates – the rates I have provided are the standard Rack Rates, which include breakfast and VAT (Value Added Tax) of 15%, unless stated otherwise.

For all hotel listings, I've included what I like to call the "Linen Factor," wherein I list one of three classifications:
• So nice you want to steal the sheets
• Lovely – almost as nice as my own bed
• Perfectly adequate

As I use my own bed as a point of reference, I thought it would be useful to let you know what I sleep in at home: 400 thread-count custom-made bedding with embroidery. My pillow and duvet are goose-down and made locally. It's the 400 thread-count that is key to my bedding happiness, as my sheets are silky and buttery to the touch. Needless to say I can't wait to get into them every evening!

■ ■ ■ ■ ■ ■ ■ ■ ■ ■ ■

Archibald at the Charles Bridge

Na Kampě 15, Prague 1, Malá Strana (Map B)
www.archibald.cz
TEL 257 531 430
METRO Malostranská ●
TRAM 12, 20, 22 to Malostranské náměstí

Located on picturesque Kampa Island, this hotel enjoys one of the most exceptional riverside locations in town, including a beautiful view of the Charles Bridge and the cityscape of Old Town. Housed in a building dating back to the 16th century, the charming yet simple rooms feature Art Nouveau wall stenciling and period wood furnishing. With that said, I must point out that the bathrooms are small and in need of renovation, the towels are worn and definitely not plush, and the orange "juice" leaves much to be desired – but if you are willing to relinquish such luxuries, in return you will be able to stay in one of the most charming locations in all of Prague. Many of the rooms have river views that are nearly as spectacular as those at the Four Seasons for a fraction of the price. What's more, although you will be staying in the heart of the city, you will have a feeling of being in a very remote and private location.

DESIGN
16th-century building with Art Nouveau accents in bedrooms.

STATS
Rooms: 33, including 14 with river views.
Rates: Start at €69 Low Season / €109 High Season, including breakfast.
Check-in: 14:00
Checkout: 12:00
Gym: No
Free Internet: Yes – plus one computer in the lobby.
DVD Player: No
Nightly turndown service: No
Linen Factor: Perfectly adequate, but it's borderline.
Bath Products: Bring your own – trust me!
Daily Newspaper: No

As I mentioned in the Basics section (p. 6), I did not receive any discounts, payments, or kickbacks in exchange for inclusion or a positive review in this book. That being said, there were occasions where hotel managers insisted that my room be "comped" (i.e., no charge), while others accepted my money happily. The good news for my readers is that in each case where the hotel's Public Relations Director or General Manager knew why I was there, the staff never seemed aware of who I was or the purpose of my visit. In other words, in each hotel, I was definitely left with the impression (for better or worse) that I was treated just like any other guest would be.

Pets: Yes – no charge (small pets only).
Parking: 500 CZK per day.

ROOM RECOMMENDATIONS

Room 11: This room is by no means the largest in the hotel, but it's definitely one of the coziest, and its second floor location offers a wonderful view the Charles Bridge and Vltava River.

Room 23: This intimate and romantic room, located on the top floor, features a wood-beamed ceiling, as well as a fabulous view of the Charles Bridge and the Vltava River.

Room 8: Although this room is situated on the first floor, which is not my favorite, it does feature a small terrace that overlooks the Charles Bridge and Vltava River as well as the inner courtyard – a real bonus in the warmer months.

EATING IN

Breakfast: 07:30–10:00 Buffet.

Lunch & Dinner: 11:30–23:30 The hotel's restaurant, U Karlova mostu, offers a menu filled with Czech classics at slightly inflated prices.

Table Request: Ask to sit in the back corner, facing the restaurant, as this will allow you to fully appreciate the exposed vaulted brick arches.

Room Service: No

STAYING IN

Should you be lucky enough to have a riverside room, remove the quintessential Czech lace curtains obstructing your view, open your windows, and enjoy an evening gazing out your window at the stellar view – I did! In the morning, the birds

---

Not On Any Kind of Budget? Here Are Four Hotel Rooms That Are Sure to Satisfy:

One Night and It Must Be Perfect (Spectacular View from a Spectacular Room)
Four Seasons Hotel – Room 701 (see p. 30).

Can I Stay Forever? (Spectacular View from the Best Private Terrace in Town)
Mandarin Oriental – Presidential Suite (see p. 37).

Summer Garden View (Five Windows Overlooking the Most Beautiful Baroque Garden in Prague)
Aria Hotel – The Dvořák Suite (see p. 75).

Cozy Winter Retreat – (Fireplace in Your Room, NOTHING Is More Cozy than That...)
Romantik hotel U raka – Room 6 (see p. 41).

---

will be singing, too. Just delightful.

In the warmer months, the hotel opens an outdoor restaurant on the cobble-stoned riverbank, so be sure to spend an evening having dinner and/or a few beers almost literally on the river...but be careful not to drink too much – you don't want to fall in!

ALSO WORTH NOTING

Rooms with a river view command a €15–€20 premium depending on the season. In my humble opinion, this is money well spent.

Avoid the new garden rooms. The windows face the courtyard and are visible from all of the riverside rooms, so privacy is limited.

FUN & FABULOUS FEATURE

As the hotel is literally adjacent to Kampa Park, you'll want to enjoy a stroll in one of the most picturesque locations in Prague. In the morning it will be virtually empty, so you can have the park all to yourself; in the evening, you can enjoy a riverside

view of the illuminated downtown skyline.

■ ■ ■ ■ ■ ■ ■ ■ ■ ■ ■ ■ ■ ■ ■

Aria Hotel

Tržiště 9, Prague 1, Malá Strana (Map B)
www.ariahotel.net
TEL 225 334 111
METRO Malostranská ●
TRAM 12, 20, 22 to Malostranské náměstí

Blessed with a brilliant location in the heart of Malá Strana, the Aria Hotel overlooks Vrtbovská, a fantastic Baroque garden (see p. 25). Absolutely request a room overlooking the garden! The hotel can also arrange for rental of the garden and can assist with catering, be it a romantic dinner for two or a wedding for 200. Everything about this place is top-notch, and the owner clearly cut no corners in creating a polished, bold impression. The lobby even has several prints and sculptures from his personal art collection. The visually appealing rooms are modern in décor, with a color palate that varies

VRTBOVSKÁ GARDEN, MALÁ STRANA
(PHOTO COURTESY OF ARIA HOTEL)

from floor to floor. The hotel is dedicated to several musical genres – jazz, opera, classical and contemporary – and each of the 52 rooms celebrates an individual artist or group who was of particular influence to their genre.

DESIGN
Contemporary building with Art Deco accents throughout.

STATS
Rooms: 52 rooms, including six with garden views.
Rates: Start at €264 Low Season / €298 High Season, including breakfast.
Check-in: 15:00
Checkout: 13:00
Gym: Yes – small but

suitable, including a view of the garden! Turkish steam baths in locker rooms. Massages and La Prairie spa treatments are available, including twelve different facials.
Free Internet: Yes – and all rooms include a desktop computer.
DVD Player: Yes – plus a library of 5,000 DVDs (and 4,000 music CDs).
Nightly turndown service: Yes
Linen Factor: Lovely – almost as nice as my own bed.
Bath Products: Molton Brown
Daily Newspaper: Wide selection available in Winter Garden.
Pets: No
Parking: 700 CZK per day.

ROOM RECOMMENDATIONS
Room 411: The Mozart Suite has five windows facing the garden and an extra bedroom with twin beds, making it perfect for a family of four. The living room is large and has a kitchenette, which could prove very handy.
Room 311: If the Mozart Suite is not available but you'd still like a two-bedroom suite, the Beethoven Suite is the other interesting option. It has a very homey feel (including a kitchenette), but the living room is a bit smaller and the first-floor view of the garden is less interesting.
Room 313: The Tchaikovsky

Room has two windows facing the garden. The room isn't huge, but it is very romantic and has one *enormous* benefit: it's the only room in the hotel from which you can sneak out the window at night and take a romantic stroll in the fabulous gardens. Shhh... don't tell them it was me who told you!

Room 309: The Dvořák Suite includes one bedroom and a wonderful view of the bottom-most section of the garden, which happens to be the most beautiful.

EATING IN

Breakfast: 07:00–11:00
Buffet plus an extensive à la carte menu, served in the lovely Winter Garden.

Lunch & Dinner: 11:30–23:30
Aria's restaurant, Coda, is a perfect spot for lunch, dinner or a simple mid-day coffee break (see p. 159).

Table Request: The green table for six is my absolute favorite, although you really can't go wrong with any choice. The dining room was recently redone using fabulous Art Deco furniture from the owner's extensive personal collection.

Room Service: 24 hours

STAYING IN

Private Screening Room: The room seats up to 40 people, and is rumored to feature the same electronic equipment Steven Spielberg has in his home. Hotel guests are welcome to use it when it's not booked.

"The Music Box": A private entertainment room with a plasma TV screen and super-comfy sectional sofa. Perfect for kids; set them up with a video while you enjoy dinner, or as a rainy day activity.

From 19:00–23:00 each evening, the hotel has a local pianist playing the grand piano in the lobby.

ALSO WORTH NOTING

The suites (e.g., the Mozart and Beethoven) are a "bargain" in relation to comparable suites at the Four Seasons and Mandarin Oriental.

The Jazz Floor is in the attic, so if you don't like slanted ceilings, avoid it.

Ivana Stehlíková, the hotel's music director, is rumored to be the go-to source for impossible-to-get tickets to live shows in town.

FUN & FABULOUS FEATURE

All rooms feature an iPod preloaded with 500 songs.

From April through October, hotel guests have direct access to the Vrtbovská Garden, free of charge, from 09:00–22:00. After closing to the public at 20:00, the garden remains open two extra hours exclusively for the hotel, which is happy to serve cocktails there should you desire a nightcap or pre-dinner drink.

■ ■ ■ ■ ■ ■ ■ ■ ■ ■ ■ ■ ■ ■
Augustine Hotel

Letenská 12/33, Prague 1, Malá Strana (Map B)
www.theaugustine.com
TEL 266 112 242
METRO Malostranská ●
TRAM 12, 18, 20, 22 to Malostranská

The Augustine is the newest luxury property in Prague, and if you're a design connoisseur or architecture aficionado, this is where you will want to stay, as it's easy to see that an incredible amount of thoughtfulness and care went into the design of

this property – even the hallways are exceptionally beautiful! As for service, although I would not describe it as being on the same level as the Four Seasons or the Mandarin Oriental, I would still call it gracious. The rooms are beautifully appointed with parquet floors, to-die-for hand-embroidered curtains, Czech Cubist ceramics, as well as a thoughtful selection of books and prints – all of which give the feeling of spending the night in a very stylish home rather than a hotel. The bathrooms, with polished marble, heated floors, plasma screen TVs, and my favorite terrycloth bathrobe in town, are large and breathtakingly refined – they completely fulfill the fantasy of what you dream of having at home. The Augustine's spa also happens to be among the best in Prague. Need I say more?

DESIGN

Contemporary classic with Czech Cubist accents, housed in a beautiful 13th-century Augustinian monastery (hence the name).

STATS

Rooms: 101 rooms, including 16 suites.
Rates: Start at €330 Low Season / €502 High Season, including breakfast.
Check-in: 14:00
Checkout: 12:00
Gym: Yes – large and well equipped.
Free Internet: No (Wi-Fi service is available, but fees apply; however, two computers in the Business Center are available free of charge.)

DVD Player: Only in suites.
Nightly turndown service: Yes
Linen Factor: So nice you want to steal the sheets (the linen is by Pedersoli).
Bath Products: REN – Clean Bio Active Skincare
Daily Newspaper: *The International Herald Tribune* or *Wall Street Journal* (or whatever you wish) delivered to your room upon request.
Pets: No
Parking: 950 CZK per day.

ROOM RECOMMENDATIONS

Tower Suite: Imagine a 360-degree panoramic view of Prague from your bed. That is precisely what you will find in the three-floor Tower Suite. This suite provides one of the all-time great views of Prague, overlooking the Prague Castle, Malá Strana, Staré Město and more. Be forewarned, there are *lots* of steep stairs involved in making it to bed, but if you're up for the challenge (and the exercise), the view is absolutely worth it.

Suite 224: This spacious suite is my favorite. Featuring several rooms, including a living room, a study, a library (with working fireplace, of course), a kitchen, a large dining room, a super-deluxe bathroom, and a bedroom to match, it would be ideal for a movie star staying for a month or two, as the 150 square meters (!) gives you plenty of room to spread out and make yourself very much at home.

Room 233: I loved this Executive room, which looks out onto the monks' garden, with a picturesque view of a pine tree in the foreground and the

steeples of St. Thomas Church in the background. The room, as with all the rooms in the hotel, is so thoughtfully appointed: The curtains are to die for, Cubist-era prints decorate the walls, and porcelain Czech knickknacks and books are subtly placed throughout the room, leaving one with the impression of being a guest in a very nice home in the Bohemian countryside, rather than a hotel room in downtown Prague.

EATING IN

Breakfast: 07:00–11:00; 07:00–14:00 on weekends and bank holidays.

Lunch & Dinner: 12:00–15:00 & 18:00–23:00
Litchfield, the Augustine's restaurant, is certain to hit the spot for virtually any palate, day or night, as the brasserie-style menu offers a little something for everyone.

Table Request: Ask for a banquet table overlooking the main courtyard. In summer, dining on the terrace is a must.

Room Service: 24 hours

STAYING IN

Augustine Spa: 09:00–21:00
See p. 146 for a complete description.
Litchfield Coffee & Bar 11:00–24:00

AUGUSTINIAN MONK-IN-RESIDENCE (WITH BUNNIES)
(PHOTO COURTESY OF AUGUSTINE HOTEL)

Possibly the chicest bar in town; they make fabulous cocktails, and it's quiet enough that you can actually have a conversation. In the warmer months, I love indulging in an aperitif or two on the cloister terrace, with its beautiful vaulted ceilings.

ALSO WORTH NOTING
Slippers are available only by request, which is a bit odd as the rooms feature wood floors and you will *definitely* want slippers. Once requested, they arrive promptly.

FUN & FABULOUS FEATURE
There are currently five monks-in-residence living at the property, so don't be surprised when you see them walking by in their handsome brown robes!

Be sure to request a tour – given by one of the monks – of the monastery's library, which is filled with lots of old medical books. The tour is 500 CZK per person, and booking must be made at least three weeks in advance.

■ ■ ■ ■ ■ ■ ■ ■ ■ ■ ■ ■
Dům u velké boty
Vlašská 30/333, Prague 1, Malá Strana (Map B)
www.dumuvelkeboty.cz
TEL 257 533 234
METRO Malostranská ●
TRAM 12, 20, 22 to Malostranské náměstí

Nestled in a little square in the steeply sloped Malá Strana neighborhood, Dům u velké boty is an old family residence that dates back to the Renaissance period, when it was built for workers at nearby Wallenstein Palace. In 1926, it was acquired by the family of the current occupants (and your hosts), Mr. and Mrs. Rippl, and the charming interior design appears to have changed very little since then. The pension is a wonderful place to stay – and very ARTĚL style – as it is filled with personal design touches and fabulous vintage finds that I wholeheartedly approve of. So if you prefer intimate hotels where you feel like you are staying in a friend's house (especially one decorated by their Bohemian grandmother), I think you will love this place – I did.

DESIGN
Renaissance building with a Baroque façade; the circa 1910–25 interior design features original antiques and artwork.

STATS
Rooms: 10, including 2 suites.
Rates: Start at €80 Low Season / €135 High Season, including breakfast.
Check-in: 15:00
Checkout: 12:00
Gym: No
Free Internet: Yes – plus one computer in the cellar.
DVD Player: No – and no TVs either!
Nightly turndown service: No
Linen Factor: Perfectly adequate
Bath Products: Relax Refresh Revive
Daily Newspaper: No
Pets: Yes – no charge.
Parking: €13 per day.

ROOM RECOMMENDATIONS
Room 26: This room is easily my favorite. Although it is not the largest in the hotel, it is without a doubt the most charming and interesting. Facing the courtyard and featuring a spacious balcony with a view of the Prague Castle, as well as some very picturesque Malá Strana buildings, this enchanting room also features a rather unusual bathroom with a ceramic tile kitchen stove from the late 19th or very early 20th century built into the wall. The bedroom has wonderful veneered furniture from the 1920s, as well as a somewhat curious selection of original artwork from the same period.
Room 33: Like Room 26, this spacious room also features a lovely ceramic tile stove from the late 19th or very early 20th century, as well as fabulous brass beds from 1915; the beds won me over immediately as I happen to own the exact same kind! The view looks out across the street and offers a perfect view of the German Embassy, housed in a Baroque Palace once owned by the Lobkowicz family (see p. 52).
Room 34: This street-side room is also quite spacious and happens to be one of the only three rooms in the property to offer a bathtub.

EATING IN
Breakfast: 08:00–10:00 Small buffet with eggs made to order by your hosts!
Table Request: Anywhere with a view of the stove, so you can watch them cook your breakfast.
Room Service: No – but there is a self-serve (honor system) refrigerator in the lobby with drinks at very affordable prices.

STAYING IN
Pack a good book and a deck of cards, as there are no TVs in the rooms.

ALSO WORTH NOTING

The staff is not only able to recommend concerts, activities and restaurants, they are also happy to arrange the tickets or make reservations for you. Refreshingly, their recommendations are very sincere and they go out of their way to suggest things they really think you will like and to steer you away from things they view as excessively touristy or a rip-off, etc.

The hotel does not have an elevator, and rooms on the ground floor are not recommended, as they face the street, so be sure to keep this in mind if climbing stairs is an issue for you.

FUN & FABULOUS FEATURE

Geraniums! Your host, Mr. Rippl, happens to have a very green thumb, and visitors from April through the first frost will benefit as the hotel features the most fabulous and picturesque geranium flowerboxes on every street-facing windowsill.

■ ■ ■ ■ ■ ■ ■ ■ ■ ■ ■ ■ ■ ■
Four Seasons

Veleslavínova 2a, Prague 1, Staré Město (Map A)
www.fourseasons.com/prague
TEL 221 427 000
METRO Staroměstská ●
TRAM 17, 18 to Staroměstská

The riverside location at the Four Seasons simply cannot be beat – nor can the service. No request is too big, too small, or too obscure for them, so if you're dying to, say, take a helicopter ride over Prague, they will not let you down. The flowers in each room are lovely, the bathrooms are big, and the "cheap" rooms are actually quite spacious. They also have deliciously comfortable beds and linens to match. If you love a safe bet, put your chips on the Four Seasons; whenever my mother's friends visit Prague, they inevitably stay here and it always gets rave reviews.

DESIGN

Baroque, Neo-Classical, Neo-Renaissance and Modern buildings, with unique interior designs that complement each building's architectural style.

STATS

Rooms: 162 rooms, including 32 with river views and 20 suites.
Rates: Start at €325 Low Season / €479 High Season, including breakfast
Check-in: 15:00
Checkout: 12:00
Gym: Yes – small but well equipped. Each workout station has its own TV and headphones. A very nice environment to work out in, but often overcrowded. Even though they don't have a formal spa, massages, manicures and pedicures are available and the setting is utterly relaxing.
Free Internet: Yes; in-room broadband service is also available (fees apply), and there are two computers in the Business Center.
DVD Player: Yes
Nightly turndown service: Yes
Linen Factor: So nice you want to steal the sheets.
Bath Products: L'Occitane, Asprey in rooms with a river view, and Aqua di Parma in Suite 701 and the Presidential Suite
Daily Newspaper: The International Herald Tribune or Wall Street Journal delivered to your room.
Pets: Yes – no charge (small pets only).
Parking: €32 per day.

ROOM RECOMMENDATIONS

Room 701: I immediately fell for this Premier suite. Both the oak-paneled living room (which is massive and even includes a dining room table) and the bedroom offer expansive and unobstructed views of the Prague Castle; you can look directly at the castle while lying in bed! Better yet, you can see the reflection of the castle in the bathroom mirror while lying in the tub for a soak. This is the pied-à-terre *everyone* who stays there will *wish* they owned! It speaks perfectly of the magic of Prague. Not only will you not need to leave your room, you won't *want* to!
NOTE: The suite includes a small kitchenette off the living room and a second bedroom is possible.
Room 501: This one-bedroom suite is a wonderful backup if Room 701 is simply too expensive (or not available), as it's about half the price. This suite features floor-to-ceiling windows offering a fabulous view of the Prague Castle across the river. I'm confident that you will not be disappointed.
Room 414: With soaring ceilings creating an atmosphere true to Prague's architectural and decorative grandeur, the décor of this Renaissance room is very romantic, to say the least. Although there are a handful of rooms with the same designation throughout

the hotel, this one is absolutely the best, as it is situated on the corner of the building and thus has three windows.

EATING IN
Breakfast: 07:00–11:00 À la carte.
Lunch & Dinner: 12:00–24:00 CottoCrudo, the Four Seasons Hotel restaurant (see p. 159), will satisfy even the most discerning gourmand, and the menu is surprisingly affordable (by Four Seasons standards).
Table Request: Ask to sit by a window or a railing for a great river and castle view; the terrace is lovely if the weather is good.
Room Service: 24 hours

STAYING IN
CottoCrudo Bar: 11:00–01:30
Summer Terrace: 11:30–22:00 A perfect mid-day retreat from the bustle of touristy Prague. Perfect for lunch or even just an afternoon coffee or ice cream. With a cool summer breeze coming in off the river, this is the perfect way to re-energize before heading out to your next activity.

ALSO WORTH NOTING
Monika, the pedicurist at the spa, is among the best in town, but the bill will be as princely as the service (see p. 150).

The hotel is happy to arrange a private tour of Karlštejn Castle. Even better, take a vintage car ride to the Bohemian countryside to see Nelahozeves Castle and indulge in a picnic, as well as a test drive of the car!

Traveling with children? There is no better hotel in town to accommodate your young tykes than the Four Seasons. They seem to have thought of everything and their list of services and activities for your little ones is mind-bogglingly impressive.

FUN & FABULOUS FEATURE
How about a morning run led by a hotel concierge? It is most certainly possible, and not surprisingly, the staff will be happy to cater it to suit your interests. Jogging maps are also available for solo runners. Or how about cycling with a biking aficionado from the hotel's purchasing department? It can be arranged, and the Four Seasons will, of course, provide all the necessary equipment.

■ ■ ■ ■ ■ ■ ■ ■ ■ ■ ■ ■ ■ ■
Golden Well Hotel
U Zlaté studně 166/4, Prague 1, Malá Strana (Map B)
www.goldenwell.cz
TEL 257 011 213
METRO Malostranská ●
TRAM 12, 20, 22 to Malostranské náměstí

Nestled high in the hills of the steeply sloped Malá Strana neighborhood and housed in a building that dates back to the 16th century, the Golden Well is a real gem and a true find. With a bit of luck and advance planning you will be rewarded with a location that is literally next door to the castle gardens and has an all-encompassing panoramic view of the city. Request (and pay extra for) a room with a view, it's absolutely worth it! Every aspect of the hotel is top-notch, and it's clear that the owner, who also owns the Aria Hotel, understands what clients want and expect. The hotel staff also stood out as exceptional – both in their professionalism and friendliness – which was particularly unexpected for a property of this size.

DESIGN
16th-century building with an Old World-style interior that is full of antique replicas.

STATS
Rooms: 19, including two suites.
Rates: Start at €240 for 1 night, €180 for 2 nights or €161 for 3 or more nights in Low Season / €292 for 1 night, €248 for 2 nights or €234 for 3 or more nights in High Season, including breakfast.
Check-in: 14:00 (includes hotel tour and welcome drink.)
Checkout: 12:00
Gym: No
Free Internet: Yes – plus one computer in the lounge.
DVD Player: Yes – plus DVD library at reception.
Nightly turndown service: Yes
Linen Factor: Lovely – almost as nice as my own.
Bath Products: Molton Brown
Daily Newspaper: Yes, delivered to your room.
Pets: No
Parking: €25 per day.

ROOM RECOMMENDATIONS
Room 35: This Grand Deluxe room is a favorite among guests and would be my hands-down first choice. It is not only very charming and cozy, but it also offers big windows with a view to the castle gardens and the city, including St. Nicholas Cathedral. The very large bathroom with a corner Jacuzzi bathtub is an added bonus. Loved it!
Room 34: This Deluxe room is large and spacious. It

features two big windows overlooking the rooftops of Malá Strana, as well a small window over the bed with a panoramic view of the city. I loved looking out of it at night and seeing the cityscape illuminated – especially Petřín Hill (see p. 74). With the window open, I could hear the church bells ringing; the whole experience was utterly charming. This room also features a very large bathroom with a corner Jacuzzi bathtub.

Room 23: This suite can sleep up to four people, so it is great choice for families. From the living room there is a terrific view of the cityscape, and the bedroom also features nice views to the castle gardens and the city. This room also includes several original architectural details from the building – check out the ceiling!

EATING IN

Breakfast: 07:00–11:00
Buffet, plus an extensive à la carte menu at no additional fee. Even if you're not staying at this hotel, I would definitely consider having breakfast here. I can't think of a better location to enjoy a cup of coffee and plan one's day in Prague. Breakfast is 600 CZK per person, which is quite fairly priced as the food and service is excellent and the location cannot be beat – plus, from April through October, after breakfast you can walk directly into the castle gardens from the secret door on the upper terrace.

Lunch & Dinner: 12:00–23:00
Terasa U Zlaté Studně, the Golden Well Hotel's award-winning restaurant (see p. 164) is the perfect retreat for lunch, dinner or a mid-day coffee break. There has been a restaurant in this location since 1924, and it's definitely worth a visit.

Table Request: Ask to sit on terrace next to the railing; if eating inside, request the second-to-last table at the far end of the dining room, next to the window.

Room Service: 18:00–23:00

STAYING IN

Definitely plan to stay in one night and have dinner at the restaurant. Be aware that it is often fully booked, so I highly encourage you to book at least one week in advance. In the spring and summer months, make time to enjoy the terrace. It is the perfect tranquil escape, with an all-encompassing panoramic view of the city.

ALSO WORTH NOTING

Only Deluxe rooms and higher (Grand Deluxe, etc.) offer rooms with a view. In my humble opinion, I see no reason to stay at this hotel unless you get a room with a view, so factor this into your budget. There is a €30 surcharge to request a specific room, but I assure you, this is money well spent.

Leave the stilettos at home. For this hotel, sneakers or comfy walking shoes are the *only* shoes you will desire – trust me.

If you plan to work, this hotel is *not* for you, as in-room desks seem to have been a total afterthought – the one in my room was not even large enough for a netbook!

ACTIVITIES

The hotel can arrange for a masseur / masseuse to visit your room. One hour = €77.

FUN & FABULOUS FEATURES

All rooms include an iPod preloaded with 500 songs (Billie Holiday was playing upon my arrival).

I also loved their slippers, orange for girls and red for boys. Truly original and very comfy – I proceeded to steal mine and brought them on the remainder of my hotel visits.

■ ■ ■ ■ ■ ■ ■ ■ ■ ■ ■

Grand Hotel Bohemia

Králodvorská 4, Prague 1, Staré Město (Map A)
www.grandhotelbohemia.cz
TEL 234 608 111
METRO Náměstí Republiky ●
TRAM 5, 8, 14, 26 to Náměstí Republiky

When it opened in 1927, the Grand Hotel Bohemia was the most modern hotel in Prague. The property enjoys a great location right in the center of downtown Prague, and it also happens to be catty-corner to one of ARTĚL's stores – bonus! What really won me over at the this property were two things: First, I think it is simply excellent value for money – I don't think you will do better anywhere in town. Secondly, their spectacular Neo-Baroque ballroom, Boccaccio, used by Prague's elite for soirées and cabaret shows back in the day, simply must be seen to be believed (be sure to request a visit).

DESIGN

Art Deco building with contemporary interior.

STATS

Rooms: 78 rooms, including two suites.

Rates: Start at €145 Low Season / €185 High Season, including breakfast.

Check-in: 14:00
Checkout: 12:00
Gym: No
Free Internet: Yes
DVD Player: No
Linen Factor: Lovely – almost as nice as my own bed.
Bath Products: Eco Boutique in Superior & Deluxe rooms / Penhaligon in Executive rooms and higher.
Daily Newspaper: Room delivery upon request, wide selection available in Breakfast Room.
Pets: Yes – €15 per day per dog.
Parking: 740 CZK per day.

ROOM RECOMMENDATIONS

Room 711: Although this Executive room is not the biggest room on offer, it would definitely be my first choice, as it features a large fabulous terrace with unobstructed views of the Powder Tower, Týn Church, Old Town and even the Prague Castle; also, since it is located on the seventh floor, you really feel as though you are part of city and its landscape. The view is so good that it gives the Mandarin Oriental's Presidential Suite a run for the money, for a mere fraction of the price. The hotel is able to provide private dining on the terrace, which also happens to feature a swing, a dining table, and even binoculars, providing a whole day or evening of fun. Rates start at €205 Low Season / €245 High Season.

Room 80: This Junior Suite features a to-die-for view, with Týn Church in the foreground and the Prague Castle and Letná Hill behind. If you require a bit more space, this is a great option to consider.

Room: 615: This suite has a fantastic view of the steepled rooftops of Old Town and beyond, and is also one of only two rooms to feature a private balcony.

EATING IN
Breakfast: 06:30–10:30 / 11:30 on weekends. Buffet plus an extensive à la carte menu.
Lunch & Dinner: 12:00–15:00 / 18:00–23:00
The hotel's restaurant, Franc Josef, offers a lunchtime special that's a pretty good deal: 145 CZK for two courses + 50% off all beverages.
Room Service: 24 hours

STAYING IN
Why not request a massage in the privacy of your room? The front desk will be happy to set one up for you.

ALSO WORTH NOTING
Floors 3 and 7 feature large French windows; I would definitely recommend requesting a room on one of these floors, with the 7th being my first choice due to its slightly better view.

FUN & FABULOUS FEATURES
Deluxe rooms come with a very unique bonus: a FREE daily metro ticket. Love it!

■ ■ ■ ■ ■ ■ ■ ■ ■ ■ ■ ■ ■
Hotel Josef
Rybná 20, Prague 1, Staré Město (Map A)
www.hoteljosef.com
TEL 221 700 111
METRO Náměstí Republiky ◉
TRAM 5, 8, 14, 26 to Dlouhá třída

The Josef is a boutique hotel specifically designed for the very hip, and while I would not describe myself as their target audience, I had a great stay that far exceeded my expectations. The service was excellent, and the bed, sheets, heated bathroom floor and amenities were all far more deluxe than I'd expected. Its close proximity to both Old Town Square and Obecní dům (see p. 64) is a definite plus as well. I often book it for visiting clients, as the location is great and rates are less expensive than many of the other hotels I've listed. However, this hotel is definitely *not* for everyone, as the very contemporary décor is simply not neutral enough to agree with everyone's personal aesthetic. Check out their website for yourself before deciding whether it might be for you.

DESIGN
Sleek and modern, inside and out.

STATS
Rooms: 109 rooms.
Rates: Start at €147 Low Season / €164 High Season, including breakfast.
Check-in: 14:00
Checkout: 12:00
Gym: Yes – but it's small. If a gym is important to you, I don't think you will be happy...but they do have a boxing bag!
Free Internet: Yes – plus three computers in Business Center.
DVD Player: Yes
Nightly turndown service: Yes
Linen Factor: Lovely – almost as nice as my own bed.
Bath Products: Aveda
Daily Newspaper: Wide selection available in Breakfast Room.
Pets: Yes – €24 per day.
Parking: €26 per day.

ROOM RECOMMENDATIONS

Rooms 704 & 801: Superior double rooms, each with a glass bathtub and a terrace offering a view of the Prague Castle.

Room 803: Although this Superior double room lacks a glass bathtub, it does have a fine view of the Prague Castle.

Room 802: Standard single room that happens to have a castle view at no extra charge.

NOTE: With a few exceptions (including Room 803 described above), all Superior rooms have glass showers or bathtubs; this is what differentiates them from the Standard rooms, not size.

EATING IN

Breakfast: 06:30–11:30 / 12:30 on weekends
Buffet, plus an extensive à la carte menu.

Table Request: Ask to sit next to the window overlooking the courtyard.

Room Service: 07:00–23:00

STAYING IN

Book the private sauna, located in the gym. Please note it takes one hour for the hotel to prepare, so factor this into your planning.

Borrow a DVD or two, free of charge, from the hotel's extensive collection and enjoy a cozy evening watching a movie in bed. Reception will even prepare microwaved popcorn for you!

ALSO WORTH NOTING

Josef's Choice, a booklet you'll find in your room, offers excellent suggestions for cafés, design shops, dining and entertainment.

FUN & FABULOUS FEATURES

How about a morning run led by a hotel staff member? It is possible every Tuesday and Friday at 07:15. The runs last approximately 35 minutes and the staff is happy to cater it to your interests.

■ ■ ■ ■ ■ ■ ■ ■ ■ ■ ■ ■ ■

ICON Hotel

V Jámě 6, Prague 1,
Nové Město (Map C)
www.iconhotel.eu
TEL 221 634 100
METRO Můstek ● ◉
TRAM 3, 9, 14, 24 to Vodičkova

The ICON opened in March 2007 and is definitely one of the most progressive hotels in town. I'd describe it as a boutique hotel for those in the under-45 set who either are extremely hip or simply love gadgets. The staff is very friendly and the protocol is informal, with reference on a first name basis (if you allow). What really won me over, however, were the beds – I hardly moved from mine during my 18-hour stay, as it was simply too delicious to leave! They are by Hästens (a Swedish company rumored to have the best beds in the world) and have sheets far more luxurious than I'd expected. The hotel's close proximity to Old Town Square (as well as to many metros and trams) is also a definite plus. The daylong breakfast is another great bonus, as there's nothing I hate more then forcing myself out of bed just to avoid missing breakfast! I have opened a corporate account here, as the location – while not exactly picturesque – is very convenient for hopping around downtown, and the rates are less expensive than any of the other hotels I've listed. However, this hotel is definitely *not* for everyone, as the informal protocol and trendy atmosphere simply will not agree with all tastes.

DESIGN

Extremely modern, high-design boutique hotel in an 18th-century building.

STATS

Rooms: 31 rooms, including two suites.

Rates: Start at €80 Low Season / €120 High Season, including breakfast.

Check-in: 15:00

Checkout: 12:00

Gym: No – but there is a small wellness center (see below).

Free Internet: Yes – plus one computer at the bar.

DVD Player: Yes

Nightly turndown service: Yes – but only by request.

Linen Factor: So nice you want to steal the sheets.

Bath Products: Rituals

Daily Newspaper: Wide selection available in Breakfast Room.

Pets: Yes – €18 per day.

Parking: No

ROOM RECOMMENDATIONS

Room 209: This suite feels more like a lovely little apartment than a hotel room. Of the two suites in the hotel, this one is my favorite, as it has more light.

Room 205: This Deluxe room with super-high ceilings is very spacious and bright, and features a surprisingly long and comfy bathtub.

Room 404: This Standard room on the top floor features wood beams, making the space very cozy.

EATING IN

Breakfast: 06:30–24:00
Buffet plus an à la carte menu. Yes, the hours are correct (all-day breakfast), so there's no need to rush out of bed!

Lunch & Dinner: 11:30–23:00
ICON's restaurant offers a limited (but diverse) menu at very affordable prices.

Table Request: Join the communal table if you feel like being social. If not, ask to sit in the back under the big skylight.

Room Service: 06:30–23:00

STAYING IN

Lounge BAR: 09:00–24:00
The bar here is rather chic. Why not stay in for cocktails and lounge on their purple leather bed-sized couches?

Zen Asian Wellness Spa: 10:00–22:00
A peaceful massage studio offering everything from a 15-minute "Backscratch" (290 CZK) to a 90-minute Thai massage (1,290 CZK). I opted for the 60-minute "Foot Joy" treatment (850 CZK) that combines acupressure and reflexology – perfect after a long day of trekking around Prague!

ALSO WORTH NOTING

Avoid rooms on the first floor, especially on Friday and Saturday nights, as rooms can be loud due to noise from the bar.

Biometric safes, as well as iPod and Skype connections, are standard features in all rooms.

■ ■ ■ ■ ■ ■ ■ ■ ■ ■ ■ ■ ■

InterContinental Prague

Pařížská 30, Prague 1, Staré Město (Map A)
www.icprague.com
TEL 296 631 111
METRO Staroměstská ●
TRAM 17 to Právnická fakulta

Opened in 1974, the InterContinental enjoys one of the best riverside locations in town, including phenomenal views of the Prague Castle and the spires of Old Town from its outstanding rooftop restaurant, Zlatá Praha. Located at the end of a beautiful tree-lined street with some of the ritziest shops in town, the hotel is just a five-minute walk from Old Town Square.

DESIGN

A textbook example of the Brutalist style that flourished from the 1950s–70s, the building (surprisingly) is listed as a national architectural monument.

STATS

Rooms: 372 rooms, including 32 suites.
Rates: Start at €129 Low Season / €189 High Season, including breakfast.

INTERCONTINENTAL PRAGUE HOTEL, C. 1975

Check-in: 14:00
Checkout: 12:00
Gym: Yes – large and well equipped, including saltwater pool and sauna.
Free Internet: Yes
DVD Player: No
Linen Factor: Lovely – almost as nice as my own bed.
Bath Products: Ginseng & Macadamia (made in the Czech Republic)
Daily Newspaper: Available upon request.
Pets: Yes – €30 per day per dog.
Parking: €40 per day.

ROOM RECOMMENDATIONS

Room 700: Executive Suite with a brilliant river view.
Rooms 739, 639, 539, 439 & 339 ("Ladies' Rooms"): Though a bit on the small side, these Executive rooms were my favorite. Originally designed for women rooming separately from their husbands, they feature fabulous pink marble bathrooms – need I say more?
Room 500: This Executive room overlooking the Vltava River and Charles University has a wonderfully spacious feel.

EATING IN

Breakfast: 06:30–11:30 / 11:00 on weekends Buffet.
Sunday Brunch: 11:00–15:00
Dinner: 18:00–23:30
Zlatá Praha, the InterContinental's rooftop restaurant, is exceptional in every way – food, service and location.
Table Request: Ask for a table with a view (it would be sinful not to); in the warmer months, terrace dining is a must.
Room Service: 24 hours

STAYING IN

Pack a swimsuit and enjoy the indoor saltwater swimming pool and sauna. In summer there is even a lush green lawn for sunbathing! My father highly recommends the spa; he was so satisfied with his masseur that he booked a visit the following day.

ALSO WORTH NOTING

The Brutalist style of Czech architect Karel Filsak is not for everyone, but look closely and there are brilliant details to be found, many of which were designed exclusively for the hotel by leading Czech artists and craftsmen. My favorites are the original chandeliers in the Congress Hall and Ballroom.

Club InterContinental, a private lounge on the 8th floor, offers refreshments, concierge services, free Wi-Fi, and international newspapers.

Rooms include an ironing board and iron, and even a power converter in the minibar! (Trust me, this is a bonus: converters are hard to come by in this town.)

▪▪▪▪▪▪▪▪▪▪▪▪▪▪
Kempinski Hotel Hybernská

Hybernská 12, Prague 1, Nové Město (Map C)
www.kempinski.com/prague
TEL 226 226 111
METRO Náměstí Republiky ●
TRAM 5, 8, 14, 26 to Náměstí Republiky

More than anything else, what won me over at the Kempinski Hotel was its immense private garden. This garden is truly spectacular; it includes several Baroque sculptures and a fountain from the palace that was originally housed at this address; a great little secret hidden away from the hordes of tourists that may be swarming downtown. It has become a favorite escape of mine during the warmer months, as it is the perfect oasis for lunch in the afternoon or cocktails in the evening. Everything about this hotel is top-notch, and each of its 75 rooms features a different layout.

DESIGN

A Neo-Classical building (originally a Baroque palace) with a classic modern interior.

STATS

Rooms: 75, including 62 suites.
Rates: Start at €300 Low Season / €390 High Season, including breakfast.
Check-in: 14:00
Checkout: 12:00
Gym: Yes – but it's small; if a gym is important to you, they will provide a free voucher to the nearby World Class Gym, which is excellent.
Free Internet: Yes; in-room broadband service available for 795 CZK per day.
DVD Player: Yes – available upon request; concierge has a small selection of movies available free of charge.
Nightly turndown service: Yes
Linen Factor: So nice you want to steal the sheets.
Bath Products: Kempinski / Molton Brown in the Presidential and Bohemian Suites.
Daily Newspaper: Wide selection available in atrium and Breakfast Room.
Pets: Yes – €50 per day ("same as children").
Parking: 950 CZK per day.

ROOM RECOMMENDATIONS

Room 506: This Premium suite is perfect for long-term stays, or if you simply want to feel like you are living in your own fabulous one-bedroom apartment for a few days. The room is very bright, which is true of many of the rooms in this property, and it features a big balcony that runs the length of the room; from there you can see the Powder Tower, as well as the wonderfully detailed Baroque palaces across the way. If I had to choose, this room would be my choice...I can't afford the Presidential Suite!

Room 604: This Superior room, with subtle lilac walls, is a real deal (as it falls in the lowest price category); it is one of only two Superior rooms to feature a balcony with a view – in fact, it has the same view as Room 506 listed above, but at a fraction of the price.

Room 701: The two-bedroom Presidential Suite is equally perfect for rock stars and families. The suite is extremely spacious and features a fabulous rooftop terrace, including a Jacuzzi that overlooks not only the hotel's enclosed garden but also the skyline of Old Town. There is also a working fireplace, a large dining table and, of course, a kitchenette. If you like to dine in every now and then, even when traveling, or prefer room service for breakfast, this room is perfect. The staff will be happy to arrange a catered dinner; just let them know in the morning.

EATING IN
Breakfast: 07:00–11:00

Buffet plus an extensive à la carte menu.

Lunch & Dinner: 12:00–15:00 / 18:00–22:30

The Kempinski's restaurant, Le Grill, serves excellent cuisine at a princely price. The service is very Old World, especially in the main dining room, so if you are looking for casual dining you might not be happy with all the fuss. The service in the garden, thankfully, tends to be more relaxed.

Table Request: Ask to sit in the garden if the weather is good. If inside, ask for a banquette along the far wall – or in the Winter Garden if you prefer a bit of privacy.

Room Service: 24 hours (€8 service charge).

STAYING IN
Take advantage of the hotel's excellent public spaces. In the warmer months, the garden is a must. I love the original Baroque fountain; I'm dying to dip my feet in it one of these days! In the autumn and winter, the bright atrium is perfect for a mid-day break. At night, enjoy a cozy cocktail or two at their sophisticated Two Steps bar, or have dinner at their exceptionally delicious restaurant, Le Grill.

Should you find yourself staying in on a Thursday, you're in luck. During the colder months the restaurant offers an excellent multi-course tasting menu – each dish was honestly better than the last. If plum dumplings with poppy seeds are still on the menu, I must encourage you try this dessert as it is

super-Czech and sublimely delicious. In the summer, they offer an all-you-can-eat barbeque in the garden.

Seeking even more relaxation? Order a massage in the privacy of your room; the options include everything from a sport massage to hot lava stones.

ALSO WORTH NOTING
The kitchenettes in all rooms (except Superiors) are fabulous, so if you like to eat in (or have kids to feed), this could be a very big help. They include a microwave, cooktop and refrigerator.

Avoid rooms with an atrium view, especially the small atrium; I found them to be very dark and the views were less than picturesque.

Although the property views its main competitors as the Four Seasons, Mandarin Oriental and Augustine, I honestly did not find their service to be as polished as these other properties. So, if outstanding service is important to you, you're better off spending a bit more to stay elsewhere.

■ ■ ■ ■ ■ ■ ■ ■ ■ ■ ■ ■ ■
Mandarin Oriental, Prague
Nebovidská 1, Prague 1, Malá Strana (Map B)
www.mandarinoriental.com/prague
TEL 233 088 888
METRO Malostranská ●
TRAM 12, 20, 22 to Hellichova

The Mandarin Oriental opened in 2006 and has become my personal hotel of choice in Prague. No request is too big or too eccentric. I should know – I have stayed here more than a handful of times!

The service is not just impeccable but truly personable, and the staff always makes me feel very much at home (albeit in a *much* nicer home than my own). The rooms in the historic parts of the building are my favorite because they all have parquet floors, which add to the feeling of spending the night in a very stylish home rather than a hotel. The bathrooms throughout the hotel, featuring polished limestone, heated floors, and LCD screen TVs, are quite large and among the chicest in town. Plus, the spa also happens to be the best in Prague, hands-down! Need I say more?

DESIGN
Contemporary Asian interior, housed in a beautiful 14th-century monastery.

STATS
Rooms: 99 rooms, including 20 suites.
Rates: Start at €340 Low Season / €454 High Season, including breakfast.
Check-in: 14:00
Checkout: 12:00
Gym: Yes – Large and well equipped, including two saunas.
Free Internet: No – Wi-Fi service IS available, but fees apply (except in the Business Center).
DVD Player: Yes
Nightly turndown service: Yes
Linen Factor: So nice you want to steal the sheets.
Bath Products: Aromatherapy Associates
Daily Newspaper: *The International Herald Tribune*, *The Daily Telegraph*, *Financial Times*, or whatever you wish, delivered to your room.

PRAGUE CASTLE, C. 1934

Pets: Yes – no charge; small pets only.
Parking: 1,000 CZK per day.

ROOM RECOMMENDATIONS
Presidential Suite: If you've ever imagined having an intimate dinner party – or cocktails for two – on your own private terrace overlooking the Prague Castle and Malá Strana, this is the duplex suite for you. Besides being spacious and beautiful, this room provides what is, quite simply, one of the all-time greatest views of Prague that one can find anywhere. Naturally, such luxury is not inexpensive, but if you happen to be a rock star, royalty, or just lucky enough to have some deep pockets, you'll certainly feel as special as ever in this fabulous suite.
Room 506: This Premier Castle View room is located on a lovely private corridor in the historic Baroque section of the building that housed the monks when it was a monastery. This particular room is great to know about, as it offers a fantastic view of the Prague Castle at a price that is a relative "bargain" (at least for the Mandarin Oriental).

Room 332: Located on top of the Spa building, this room is a little hidden gem. One of the least expensive rooms in the hotel due to its small size, it is nevertheless huge on character and charm thanks to rustic beams, a picture window with a view of Petřín Hill (see p. 74), and a bathroom with a fabulous sunken tub that is certain to make your jaw drop. It is also worth noting that this room can only be accessed via a flight of stairs (as the elevator tops out on the floor below), so keep that in mind if climbing stairs is an issue for you.

EATING IN

Breakfast: 6:30–11:00
Buffet plus an extensive à la carte menu.
Lunch & Dinner: 11:00–23:00
Essensia, the Mandarin Oriental's restaurant, is certain to hit the spot for virtually any palate, day or night, as it features both European and Asian offerings prepared to perfection.
Table Request: Ask to sit in the first room (where one waits to be seated), as I find this to be the prettiest of the five rooms, and it always has wonderful floral arrangements.
Room Service: 24 hours

STAYING IN

Spa: 10:00–20:30
See p. 147 for a complete description.
Barego Bar: 09:00–02:00
Named "Best Bar in the Czech Republic" in the 2011 *Grand Bar Awards*, Barego has fabulous martinis, and is quiet enough that you can actually have a conversation. No stay at the Mandarin would be complete without at least one visit here.

ALSO WORTH NOTING
If visiting the spa is on your agenda (and it should be), make sure to book your treatments well in advance of your arrival – especially if you're planning to visit over a weekend – as it's often fully booked.

I always thought all hotel slippers were created equal, but I was wrong; the Mandarin Oriental's are better than most – so plump and velvety, you will definitely want to take them home.

■ ■ ■ ■ ■ ■ ■ ■ ■ ■ ■ ■ ■
Mosaic House
Odborů 4, Prague 2, Nové Město (Map C)
www.mosaichouse.com
TEL 221 595 350
METRO Karlovo náměstí ●
TRAM 14 to Myslíkova or 3, 4, 6, 10, 16, 18, 22, 24 to Karlovo náměstí

Lodging on a budget has never looked so chic, nor been so luxurious or so conveniently located. Mosaic House, which opened in 2010, offers a new concept in lodging – a fusion of private rooms and hostel-style dormitories all under one roof. I will admit I was a bit leery of the idea of staying in the same place as backpackers, but it turns out that I absolutely enjoyed my stay and it far exceeded my expectations. The private rooms are quiet, very pretty, and their bathrooms are much nicer than what you often find at properties charging double the price. I can simply say that at the prices they are charging here, this is the best deal in town – and

you can feel good about your stay, as the property also happens to be the first hotel in the Czech Republic to utilize 100% renewable-source electricity, as well as numerous other green features.

DESIGN
1930s Functionalist building, with a funky, modern interior.

STATS
Rooms: 27 private rooms, including 10 Deluxe rooms. (I would definitely recommend splurging for a Deluxe room if your budget allows!)
Rates: Start at €52 in Low Season / €60 in High Season, not including breakfast.
Check-in: 15:00
Checkout: 12:00
Gym: No – but they are happy to recommend a local fitness center or yoga studio.
Free Internet: Yes – plus four computers in the lobby.
DVD Player: No – TVs with international channels in private rooms only.
Nightly turndown service: No
Linen Factor: Perfectly adequate
Bath Products: fourelements
Daily Newspaper: *Prague Post* available for purchase at reception.
Pets: Maybe, just ask.
Parking: €20 per day.

ROOM RECOMMENDATIONS
Room 602: This Deluxe room is definitely my first choice, especially in the warmer months. Although it is not the largest in the hotel, the spacious terrace boasts a truly spectacular view of the Prague Castle, as well as the National Museum.

Room 601: This Deluxe room is a brilliant backup if Room 601 is not available or if you prefer a room with a bit more space, as it also features a spacious terrace with a similar – if slightly less perfect – view of the Prague Castle and National Museum.

Room 513: Sun goddesses sign up here, as this Deluxe room features an enormous private terrace that is ideal for sunbathing or even hosting a cocktail hour – need I say more?

EATING IN

Breakfast: 07:00–11:30 À la carte. The food is, frankly, less than extraordinary, so if you have time I recommend that you go to eat at Café Amandine (Na Moráni 17), which is a five-minute walk from the hotel. The breakfast is excellent and the prices are very similar to those at the hotel.

Café Louvre (see p. 167) is another option, although their breakfast is not as good as Café Amandine.

Lunch & Dinner: 12:00–23:00 Belushi's, the Mosaic House bar and restaurant, can be summed up as a basic hamburger joint. The food is perfectly adequate, but nothing to write home about.

Table Request: If you like people watching, sit in the bar area.

Room Service: No – but all private rooms do have minibars that are very reasonably priced.

STAYING IN

Belushi's stays open until 01:00 and offers entertainment (live music / DJs) two or three nights a week. The crowd is a mix of locals and hotel guests.

ALSO WORTH NOTING

Request a room on the highest floor possible and in the front of the building, as these rooms are the quietest and offer the best views.

Request a Mosaic House Map when you check in; it offers lots of excellent budget-sensitive suggestions, which I can confirm are spot-on accurate, as I actually live in the same neighborhood.

Private rooms include TV, iPod docking station, telephone, hair dryer, minibar and safe; Deluxe rooms also include a balcony or terrace, plush terry bathrobes and slippers (rather posh for budget lodging!).

FUN & FABULOUS FEATURE

A 4–5 hour walking tour of Prague, including the Prague Castle and Old Town, is offered daily (400 CZK).

PACHTŮV PALACE COURTYARD (PHOTO COURTESY OF PACHTŮV PALACE)

Pachtův Palace

Karoliny Světlé 34,
Prague 1, Staré Město
(Map A)
www.pachtuvpalace.com
TEL 234 705 111
METRO Staroměstská ●
TRAM 17, 18 to Karlovy lázně

The Pachtův Palace enjoys one of the most exceptional riverside locations in town, including a beautiful view of the Charles Bridge and the Prague Castle. It also happens to be a two-minute walk from the Charles Bridge and a five-minute walk from Old Town Square, so it's also exceptionally convenient for sightseeing. The buildings that make up the hotel have a long and interesting history: the Pachta family acquired this property around 1700, and their houseguests included W.A. Mozart – who, as the story goes, composed six dances for Count Jan Pachta in his music salon before lunch one day, and presented the new works at a ball held onsite that very same evening. The present hotel was created by combining two existing palaces into 60 unique apartments, each with a different layout and décor. The architectural features include antique wooden beams, frescos, vaulted ceilings, and fireplaces.

DESIGN
Lovely Baroque palace setting with Old World interiors to match.

STATS
Rooms: 50, including 43 suites; 20 rooms feature river and castle views.
Rates: Start at €142 Low Season / €182 High Season, including breakfast.

Check-in: 15:00
Checkout: 12:00
Gym: Yes – but it's small; if a gym is important to you, I don't think you will be happy.
Free Internet: Yes
DVD Player: Yes
Nightly turndown service: Yes
Linen Factor: Perfectly adequate.
Bath Products: L'Occitane
Daily Newspaper: Wide selection available in lobby.
Pets: Yes – €30 per day.
Parking: €38 per day.

ROOM RECOMMENDATIONS
Room 209: The Smetana Suite, with its frescoed ceiling, spacious balcony, and large windows overlooking the Vltava River, Charles Bridge and the Prague Castle, is a perfect option for first-time visitors to Prague.
Rooms 305 & 405: These Deluxe one-bedroom corner suites are quite spacious, and they both offer excellent river views.
Room 214: This one-bedroom suite with windows facing the street features fabulous original marble walls and a large dining table. If you like to eat in every now and then – or prefer room service for breakfast – this room is perfect. The staff will be happy to arrange a catered dinner; just let them know in the morning. I'm thinking of having my Thanksgiving dinner party here!

EATING IN
Breakfast: 07:00–10:30 Buffet.
Lunch & Dinner: 12:00–23:00 Amade, the Pachtův Palace restaurant, is independently run and, to be honest, I was not nearly as impressed with it as

I was with the hotel. I recommend you eat elsewhere.
Table Request: Ask to sit in the courtyard if the weather is good; if you're inside, request a table by the window with a castle view.
Room Service: 24 hours (€11 service charge).

STAYING IN
The charming courtyards offer an idyllic retreat from the hordes of tourists swarming around the Charles Bridge just two minutes away; they are simply perfect for a late morning coffee or afternoon tea before heading out to hit the sights and shops.

Why not request a massage in the privacy of your room? The front desk will be happy to set one up for you. It's best to order in advance, but they can often accommodate you with about 30 minutes' notice.

ALSO WORTH NOTING
All rooms feature kitchenettes, so if you have kids or simply like to eat in, this could be a very big help.

Rooms with a view command a €20 surcharge per day – a small price to pay, trust me.

Romantik hotel U raka

Černínská 10, Prague 1, Hradčany (Map D)
www.romantikhotel-uraka.cz
TEL 220 511 100
TRAM 22, 25 to Brusnice

Have you dreamed of visiting the Bohemian countryside, but don't think you will have the time? Fear not, with a bit of luck and advance planning (as reservations are hard to come by), you can stay at an 18th-century Bohemian *chalupa* (country house) located just a ten-minute walk from the Prague Castle. Nestled at the end of Nový Svět, quite possibly the most picturesque cobblestoned street in all of Prague, and just steps from the Loreto Church and Foreign Ministry, this is a romantic and idyllic place to spend a few days. The rustic interior features exposed-beamed ceilings, stone and brick walls, dark furnishings, and even traditional "blue onion" china – all highly representative of what a true Czech country house looks like. The only difference is that here you will also find all the modern conveniences you might wish for, including air conditioning (which surprised me). The proprietor, Mr. Alexander Paul, is a renaissance man who is often on hand not only to assist you but also to share stories and recommendations over a nice glass of brandy in their charming café. Mr. Paul purchased the house in 1987 (two years before the fall of Czech communism), for a sum equivalent to €3,000 – a huge amount of money back then, but I'm sure you'll agree he made a brilliant real estate investment.

DESIGN
18th-century Bohemian *chalupa* (country house), complete with upscale-rustic interior details.

STATS
Rooms: Six total, including five doubles and one triple.

Rates: Range from €135–€175, including breakfast.
Check-in: 15:00
Checkout: 11:00
Gym: No
Free Internet: Yes
DVD Player: Yes
Nightly turndown service: Yes
Linen Factor: Perfectly adequate.
Bath Products: Vega "Touch Nature"
Daily Newspaper: No
Pets: Yes – no charge; small pets only.
Parking: €10 per day – this is a deal, trust me!

ROOM RECOMMENDATIONS
Room 6: If your budget is sufficient I'd *definitely* suggest staying in this room, which is the only suite. It features a wood-burning fireplace, a Japanese-inspired sunroom, and even a small private garden where you can eat breakfast during the warmer months.
Room 3: Another perennial favorite with guests, featuring its own private entrance, this charming small-ish room feels more like your own private apartment than a hotel.
Room 4: This favorite comes recommended by Mr. Paul, as it is where he says he always sleeps the best. It also happens to be the only triple room at the property.

EATING IN
Breakfast: 07:30–10:00
Buffet, plus a limited à la carte menu. Try the scrambled eggs with onions, they were delicious! In the summer, breakfast is served in the garden.
Café: 14:00–19:00
The café, which features a wood burning fireplace, is cozy and delicious.

I recommend trying the Apple Strudel with Vanilla Sauce, which is made daily by the owner's wife.
Table Request: Ask to sit by the window, so you can look up the cobblestone street at the wonderfully colorful medieval stucco homes.
Room Service: 7:30–10:00 / 12:00–18:00

STAYING IN
In the spring and summer months, enjoy the garden. It is a tranquil escape from the city, with a great view of the foreign ministry building from the upper terrace.

If you want to stay in and watch a movie in bed, be prepared to supply your own DVD; they can be purchased at local *tabáks* (newspaper shops) for approximately 79 CZK.

ALSO WORTH NOTING
Rooms do not include robes; if that's a sticking point, you'll need to pack your own.

FUN & FABULOUS FEATURE
How about a ride around Prague in a 1931 Model A Ford (imported from Ohio), with Mr. Paul as your driver and guide? From April through October, this can be arranged for 2,000 CZK per hour.

You can also arrange a barbeque in the garden for up to eight people (one day advance notice required). I cannot think of a more fabulous place in Prague to enjoy a traditional Czech barbeque, including such classics as sausages, *krkovička* (marinated grilled pork), toasted bread and, of course, beer.

SHORT-TERM APARTMENT RENTALS

■ ■ ■ ■ ■ ■ ■ ■ ■ ■ ■ ■ ■ ■

Prague Stay
Prague 1
www.prague-stay.com
TEL 222 311 084

If, like my brother, you prefer to stay in apartments instead of hotels, Prague Stay is the go-to choice. He used their service in summer of 2010 and was more than delighted with the results. Their apartments are all located in Prague 1, so it is *impossible* not to have a good location, and they include kitchens that are fully equipped (down to the detergent tablets for the dishwasher), washing machines (80% have dryers – trust me, this is a novelty), towels, bed linens, TVs and even a DVD player. It seems they've thought of everything – and as an added bonus, they're even happy to deliver breakfast or groceries!

DESIGN
It depends – apartment styles vary, so you will need to check the website to find the ideal property for you.

STATS
Apartments: 50, ranging from studios up to 3-bedroom flats that can sleep up to eight people.
Rates: Starts at €45 Low Season / €70 High Season, not including breakfast.
Check-in: 14:00
Checkout: 10:00
Gym: No
Free Internet: Yes – in all apartments.
DVD Player: Yes – in all apartments.
Nightly turndown service: No
Linen Factor: Perfectly adequate.
Bath Products: You will need to bring your own.
Daily Newspaper: No
Pets: Maybe, just ask.
Parking: Available upon request.

APARTMENT RECOMMENDATIONS
ID 158: *The Kampa Apartment* is a rustic attic apartment with exposed beams and a very cozy feeling. It also happens to feature a view of the Prague Castle! Located on Kampa Island, one of the most picturesque locations in Prague, it features a working fireplace as well as a piano (although they cannot promise that it will be in tune), and can sleep up to six people. Should you stay here, definitely put the Bella Vida Café (Malostranské nábřeží 3, p. 167) on your agenda – they make excellent lattes, as well as great ham and cheese omelets, and their prices are more than reasonable.

ID 102: *The Glass Suite Apartment* is on the 4th floor of a modern building in the heart of downtown and overlooks the Franciscan Garden (see p. 74). It is extremely spacious with 130 square meters of living space, offers great light and views, has a small terrace, and can sleep up to five people. The building offers 24-hour security.

ID 133: *The Elegant Apartment* overlooks the picturesque square of Malé náměstí, which is a stone's throw from Old Town Square. The beautiful Baroque building is under UNESCO protection due to its architectural significance, and the third-floor apartment features very thoughtful interior design and can sleep up to four people. The building offers a 24-hour reception service.

EATING IN
Breakfast: 07:00–11:00
They will deliver! There are five options to choose from and the price is 12 Euros.
Lunch & Dinner: No
Room Service: No

STAYING IN
Why not buy a DVD at the local *tabák* (newspaper shop) for 79 CZK and enjoy a movie night?

ALSO WORTH NOTING
They offer a transfer service from the airport and train station, and the price is absolutely fair. I highly recommend you take advantage of this service.

They are also able to arrange private tour guides, masseurs to come to your apartment, and car rentals. A 24/7 helpline is available to all guests (222 310 117).

FUN & FABULOUS FEATURE
Their website features a section called Prague Lifestyle, which offers excellent reviews for just about anything you will be interested in knowing about during your visit – even which tourist traps to avoid. I encourage you to take advantage of this excellent tool.

Slightly Further Afield

■ ■ ■ ■ ■ ■ ■ ■ ■ ■ ■

Sir Toby's Hostel

Dělnická 24, Prague 7,
Holešovice (Map F)
www.sirtobys.com
TEL 246 032 611
METRO Vltavská ●
TRAM 1, 3, 5, 12, 25 to
Dělnická
TRAVEL TIME 20–25 min.

Yes, I know you are probably shocked that I'm recommending a hostel – especially one in such an off-the-beaten track location – but I can assure you that Sir Toby's is no ordinary hostel. Not only does it offer private rooms, but it also boasts a remarkably fabulous interior design scheme. The rooms are simple, cozy and thoughtfully decorated with vintage furniture and artwork from the early 19th-century (very ARTĚL style). If you are a design lover on a budget – or simply prefer a small, laid-back, and extremely friendly place with a brilliant atmosphere – you will not be disappointed here.

DESIGN
Quirky, cute, clean, and Art Nouveau – on a budget.

STATS
Rooms: Nine ensuite private rooms.
Rates: Start at €28 Low Season / €28 High Season, not including breakfast.
Check-in: 15:00
Checkout: 11:00
Gym: No
Free Internet: Yes – plus five computers in the lobby.
DVD Player: No – and no TVs either.
Nightly turndown service: No
Linen Factor: Perfectly adequate.

Bath Products: You'll need to bring your own or purchase at reception...if they have any.
Bath Towels: A 200 CZK deposit is required, but the towel is actually very nice – trust me, you will probably want to steal it as a memento of your visit to Prague.
Daily Newspaper: No
Pets: Maybe, just ask.
Parking: 250 CZK per day.

ROOM RECOMMENDATIONS
Morning Dew Room: This was definitely my favorite room at this property. It's very cozy and also happens to have the nicest shower.
Le Petite Room: This would be my second choice, as it is a bit smaller than *Morning Dew*, but it also offers an excellent shower and a charming atmosphere.

EATING IN
Breakfast: 08:00–12:00 Buffet (120 CZK).
Table Request: Ask to sit downstairs, as it is a much more pleasant atmosphere than the reception area, where breakfast is also served.
Room Service: No

STAYING IN
There is always something going on in the evening at this very laid-back and social hostel, so don't be shy – join in! Activities range from beer tastings to trivia and game nights.

ALSO WORTH NOTING
Request a Sir Toby's Map when you check in, as it offers lots of excellent, budget-sensitive suggestions in the neighborhood.

The Summer Garden is open from April through September and features

Friday evening barbecues; most guests absolutely take advantage of this great bonus.

WARNING: Avoid the *Balcony Room*! Although this room does feature the only balcony, it also happens to feature the second-worst bathroom I have ever experienced at a hotel: not only is it extremely small, but the shower (with no curtain) is located directly opposite the toilet, resulting in an unavoidably wet bathroom experience.

FUN & FABULOUS FEATURE
There is a communal kitchen available for all guests to use. This seems to be a real bonus for many guests – visitors were definitely taking advantage of this unusual feature during my stay.

Walking tours of Prague with Richard, who is a real character, are offered on Tuesdays and Fridays; the 4-5 hour tour includes the Prague Castle and Old Town (200 CZK per person).

Further Afield

■ ■ ■ ■ ■ ■ ■ ■ ■ ■ ■

Chateau Mcely

Mcely 61, Mcely
www.chateaumcely.com
TEL 325 600 000
TRAVEL TIME 1 hour

You don't have to sacrifice deluxe accommodations during your dream trip to the Bohemian countryside. Chateau Mcely, just one hour from Prague, is a member of the *Leading Small Hotels of the World* and a truly idyllic place to unwind. Originally built in 1650 and recently renovated, the chateau is elegant and comfortable, featuring

CHATEAU MCELY (PHOTO COURTESY OF CHATEAU MCELY)

grand public rooms on the ground floor, a library in the attic, and a rooftop observatory (complete with telescope, of course). If your budget is sufficient I'd *definitely* choose to stay in one of the suites, as it is here that the hotel really shines. The interior designer, Oto Bláha, chose to use Czech talent and materials as much as possible during the renovation; charmingly, eighty percent of what you find in the chateau is Czech-made.

DESIGN
A 17th-century Baroque chateau with individually-themed guestrooms, nestled in a pristine forest setting.

STATS
Rooms: 24, including 8 suites, 6 doubles and 10 singles.
Rates: Start at €172 Low Season / €181 High Season, including breakfast.
Check-in: 14:00
Checkout: 12:00
Gym: No – but there's an outdoor fitness circuit around the property, a tennis court, and even an outdoor swimming pool that's open at night – stargazing has never been so good!
Free Internet: Yes – plus one computer in the library.
DVD Player: A selection of 200 DVDs is available to borrow, free of charge, from reception.
Nightly turndown service: Yes
Linen Factor: Perfectly adequate.
Bath Products: L'Occitane (from wall dispensers – yuck! I felt like I was at the gym.)
Daily Newspaper: Daily selection at reception.
Pets: Yes – €12 per day (small); €30 per day (large). A special dog menu is available, offering healthy and delicious treats for your furry friends! My puppy chose the chicken with fresh vegetables and he loved it.
Parking: Yes

ROOM RECOMMENDATIONS
Room 116 (Mark Twain): Named for the author who spent time here in 1899, this is one of the Chateau's most popular rooms. With its handsome color scheme of chocolate brown and sage green, and a lovely Ridinger print over the desk, it's not hard to see why. There is no better room at the Chateau to view the blossoming of spring or the changing leaves in autumn, as it's located high up on the third floor, providing an ideal view of the garden and valley beyond.

Room 118 (America): Another perennial guest favorite, it also has a lovely view of the valley. With subdued hues of red and cream and a wonderful display of antique china on the wall, it's certain to set an appropriate tone for your visit to the Bohemian countryside, regardless of its name.

If you're on a budget and can only afford a single room that can easily sleep two, **Room 103 (March)** is my favorite, with its fresh, spring-like colors.

MUSHROOM PICKING
GUIDEBOOK, 1938

Room 105 (May) is also a nice choice, with warm lavender colors and slightly more space.

The best bathrooms are in **Room 124 (Orient)** and **Room 125 (Legend)**; the latter includes a balcony overlooking the valley.

EATING IN
Breakfast: 08:00–10:00 (but if you sleep late, as I did, breakfast will still be waiting for you).
Buffet plus a limited à la carte menu.
Tea: 17:00
Lunch & Dinner: 12:00–24:00 The Piano Nobile restaurant specializes in international cuisine and has a Czech chef at the helm, so don't be shy if you want to request Czech specialties – it's clear they are here to please. The menu changes daily and they are happy to meet all dietary requests.
Table Request: Ask to sit by the window overlooking the garden.
Room Service: 24 hours – the menu is limited to sandwiches; however, just ask for anything you want, sandwich-wise, and you shall receive it.

STAYING IN
The **Mcely Spa** is an absolute must for any visitor – trust me! See p. 149 for a complete description.
Alchemist Bar: Located in the cellar, this boozy retreat offers "rejuvenating elixirs" created by the proprietor, as well as a fabulous Wurlitzer jukebox featuring the tunes of Aretha Franklin, the Beach Boys, the Doors, etc.
The Theatre Hall (located among the public rooms on the ground floor): If you want to watch a movie and the plasma TV in your room just won't do, the staff will be happy to set this room up for you.

ALSO WORTH NOTING
Wondering how to get to the Chateau? No worries; for prices starting from €40, they will send a car to Prague to pick you up. And if you book a suite for two nights or more, you will receive complimentary roundtrip limousine service.

If you want to visit the forest or stroll around the garden during wet weather, complimentary raincoats and boots are available at reception.

ACTIVITIES
Pondering what one might do during the day? Here are a few suggestions:
Bike Rental: €8 for a half day, €14 for a full day.
Golf Courses: Benátky nad Jizerou (18 holes) is 15 minutes away; Poděbrady (18 holes) is 25 minutes away.
Horseback Riding: 690 CZK per hour.
Mushroom Picking in St. George Forest: The hotel can make arrangements (including a guide and basket), and your forest finds can be cooked for dinner by the chef. Inquire at the front desk.
Skeet shooting: 600 CZK per hour.

STALKING DEER IN ST. GEORGE FOREST, C. 1919
(PHOTO COURTESY OF CHATEAU MCELY)

(opposite page) BAROQUE ARCHES BY TÝN, C. 1940

Sights

As mentioned previously, the purpose of this book is *not* to offer a comprehensive guide to all the sights in Prague, since every other guidebook to the city includes information about the main tourist attractions (Prague Castle, Charles Bridge, the Jewish Quarter, Old Town, Wenceslas Square, etc.). Rather than listing these standard (and, of course, essential!) destination points, I've simply opted to describe a few of my own favorite sights, focusing in particular on those that I feel are usually overlooked.

CASTLES & PALACES

■ ■ ■ ■ ■ ■ ■ ■ ■ ■ ■ ■ ■

Lobkowicz Palace
Jiřská 3, Prague 1, Hradčany
(Map D)
www.lobkowicz.cz
TEL 233 312 925
HOURS Daily: 10:00–18:00
ENTRANCE FEE 275 CZK
Adults; 200 CZK Children &
Seniors; 6 and under Free
METRO Malostranská ●
TRAM 22 to Pražský hrad

Located within the Prague Castle complex, the Lobkowicz Palace houses a significant portion of what is one of the most important private collections of historically important art and artifacts in all of Central Europe. The paintings on view here rival those found in the world's top-tier museums and include Pieter Brueghel the Elder's *Haymaking*, arguably the single most important painting in the Czech Republic. My favorite part of the exhibition, however, is the series of landscape paintings by Carl Robert Croll, which document the Lobkowicz family's many estates and the stunning Bohemian countryside of the 1840s. The family's sheet music archive is also quite impressive and features more than 4,000 scores, including original copies of Beethoven's Fourth and Fifth Symphonies (complete with his own corrections), and a manuscript of Handel's *Messiah* that was later revised and re-orchestrated by Mozart in a torrent of briskly inked annotations.

At least as impressive is the palace itself. Built in the mid-16th century and occupied by the family since

---

Getting Oriented...In A Vintage Automobile

Even though Prague is a relatively small city, its maze-like streets can make it difficult for first-time visitors to get a clear sense of where various landmarks are in relation to others. One of the best ways to get a visual overview of the city – and do so in style – is in a chauffeur-driven vintage convertible. While there are several tour companies offering this service, my recommendation is that you contact "Walter" (see contact info below), who can arrange to have an English-speaking driver pick you up at your hotel in a classic 1920s-era Czech-made open-top car. There are two different tours to choose from; I recommend you opt for the fun and informative "big" tour (1,500 CZK), which lasts approximately one hour and includes all the major tourist sites, including Wenceslas Square, Old Town, and the Prague Castle. It's best to do the tour on the first day of your trip to Prague, and if possible I would arrange the tour on a weekend morning or evening when the streets are emptier. Even as a long-term resident, I loved it and even learned a few new things! Next time, I'm going for two hours...

■ ■

To arrange a pickup at your hotel, contact Walter:
TEL 603 720 290
DATES April–October (depending on weather)

MANUSCRIPT OF HANDEL'S *MESSIAH*, WITH ANNOTATIONS BY W. A. MOZART (detail) (PHOTO BY EDWARD OWEN, COURTESY OF THE LOBKOWICZ COLLECTION, LOBKOWICZ PALACE)

that time, it was confiscated by the government in the 1940s, when the exiled family relocated to Boston, Massachusetts. The fall of communism in 1989 led to the passing of restitution laws in the early 1990s, which, in turn, led to the Lobkowicz family finally regaining ownership of their many holdings throughout the Czech Republic, including the palace itself in 2002. The museum was opened to the public in April of 2007.

ASSORTED HUNTING RIFLES FROM SILESIA AND BOHEMIA, 17–18TH CENTURY (detail) (PHOTO BY EDWARD OWEN, COURTESY OF THE LOBKOWICZ COLLECTION, LOBKOWICZ PALACE)

The palace features an excellent gift shop, as well as a café that offers breathtaking views of the entire city (see p. 171). So ditch the hordes trampling the cobblestones of Prague castle, sneak beneath the archway of Jiřská 3, and spend some time absorbing Bohemian history in this unique setting. Don't miss it.

HAYMAKING (1565), BY PIETER BRUEGHEL THE ELDER (PHOTO BY EDWARD OWEN, COURTESY OF THE LOBKOWICZ COLLECTION, LOBKOWICZ PALACE)

Vyšehrad

V Pevnosti 5b, Prague 2,
Vyšehrad (Map C)
www.praha-vysehrad.cz
TEL 241 410 348
METRO Vyšehrad ● then a
10-minute walk; there will be
signs to follow.
TRAM 3, 7, 17, 21 to Výtoň
or 7, 18, 24 to Albertov, then
a 10-minute walk uphill.
(I recommend the Metro
option).

If you fancy a visit to a
castle with more history
than tourist crowds,
Vyšehrad is just what
you're looking for. Perched
on a rocky hilltop above the
Vltava River, Vyšehrad
dates back to the 10th
century and was the long-
time home of Prague's
early Přemyslid princes.
More ancient ruin than
functioning castle,
Vyšehrad is still very much
worth your time, especially
if the weather is nice.
While the winding paths
and sweeping views attract
many locals seeking
picturesque strolls, the site
is virtually ignored by
tourists. When you visit,
take the time to walk
through the leafy and
serene National Cemetery,
the final resting place of
many famous Czechs, from
the composers Antonín

VYŠEHRAD, PRAGUE'S 'OTHER' CASTLE, C. 1920

Dvořák and Bedřich
Smetana to the painter
Alfons Mucha. Additionally,
many of the sculpted
memorials are simply
fabulous. Although there
has been a church at this
site since the 14th century,
the present one, called the
Church of St. Peter and
Paul, dates from the
beginning of the 20th
century and you'll
immediately recognize the
Art Nouveau influence

throughout the Neo-Gothic
design of the church's
interior. Also, if you've
fallen in love with Czech
Cubist architecture, be
sure to follow the steep
path down to the river and
stop at the following
destinations to see several
fabulous examples of this
unique architectural style
that were designed by Josef
Chochol:

Neklanova 2 & 30: Two
apartment blocks
Rašínovo nábřeží 6–10: Family
houses
Libušina 3: Kovařovic Villa

CZECH CUBIST BUILDING,
C. 1914

Further Afield

▪ ▪ ▪ ▪ ▪ ▪ ▪ ▪ ▪ ▪ ▪ ▪

Konopiště Castle
Benešov
www.zamek-konopiste.cz
TEL 317 721 366
HOURS Tue–Sun: 10:00–
12:00 & 13:00–16:00 (April–
November)
TRAVEL TIME 45 min.
You can get there by train
(the castle is 2.5km from the
Benešov train station), but I
recommend either renting a
car or hiring a driver for the
day (see p. 219).

Konopiště, a Renaissance-
style castle that dates back
to the Gothic era, was
erected at the end of the
13th century on 14,600
acres. In subsequent
centuries, it went through
several renovations, the
most recent of these being
ordered by Archduke Franz
Ferdinand d'Este (the
successor to the Austro-
Hungarian Empire's last
emperor, Franz Josef), who
was famously assassinated
during a state visit to
Sarajevo in 1914, triggering
World War I. Right up
until the day he himself
was shot, Franz Ferdinand
had been obsessed with
hunting, and his entire
castle is at once gloriously
and ghoulishly decorated
with his trophies. He
recorded some 300,000
animals shot, including
fox, deer, wild boar, bear,
and even tigers! The castle
itself has 100,000 of his
triumphs on display.

NOTE: Three different tours
are offered daily, with
entrance fees ranging from
210 CZK to 310 CZK (130 to
210 CZK for children &
seniors). Tours are limited
in November; check their
website for availability.

FRUITWOOD GAME BOARD, C. LATE 1600S
(PHOTO BY EDWARD OWEN, COURTESY OF THE LOBKOWICZ
COLLECTION, NELAHOZEVES)

▪ ▪ ▪ ▪ ▪ ▪ ▪ ▪ ▪ ▪ ▪ ▪

Nelahozeves Castle
www.lobkowicz.cz
TEL 315 709 121
HOURS Tue–Sun:
09:00–17:00; Mondays by
appointment only (April–
October)
ENTRANCE FEE 250 CZK
Adults; 170 CZK Children
TRAVEL TIME 30–40 min.
You can get there by train,
but I recommend either
renting a car or hiring a driver
for the day (see p. 219).

Following the Velvet
Revolution of 1989 and the
passing of restitution laws
in the early 1990s, the
Lobkowicz family received
back from the state 13
castles and innumerable
other properties, including
vineyards and a brewery
that's been in operation
since 1466. Nelahozeves, a

spectacular Renaissance
palace perched above the
Vltava River, is just one of
these. It has been open to
the public since 1997, and
the family's impressive art
collections are now divided
between this location and
the Lobkowicz Palace in the
Prague Castle complex (see
p. 52). The castle's
permanent art collection
includes important works
by Veronese and Rubens,
and a permanent exhibi-
tion focuses on the more
personal side of the family's
life and history. Spanning
25 rooms, the exhibition
features furniture and
major decorative arts from
the Middle Ages through
the 1930s, as well as
thousands of objects used
in daily life over the years.
The family played an

A Few Tips for Visiting Prague Castle

My favorite way to visit the castle is by starting at the top – taking the #22 tram to the Pohořelec stop – and dropping by the often-overlooked Strahov Monestary Library (Strahovské nádvoří 1 | www.strahovskyklaster.cz), which dates back to the 12th century, to view the incredible frescoed ceilings.

From there, it's just a short downhill stroll to the main castle entrance. Along the way, two worthy stops: Toy lovers will want to check out Hračky (see p. 136) and beer lovers – or anyone seeking a "real" Czech pub experience – should seek out U Černého vola (see p. 177), which opens at 10:00 if you happen to be an early bird!

Right across the street from the pub is the impressive Loreto Church (Loretánské nám. 7), which was built in 1720 in the Baroque style – if you're in the area near the top of any hour, stick around to hear the 27-bell tower ring out.

At the castle itself, as in so much of this city, what I find most gratifying is to walk through all the nooks and crannies to see the mesmerizing architecture, as opposed to going inside to see every sight listed in the tourist guides. You don't need to pay to enter the castle grounds, but you'll need tickets to see the main sights – St. Vitus Cathedral (completed on its 1,000th anniversary in 1929) and the Royal Gardens being the two I'd most strongly encourage you to visit.

Before leaving the castle grounds, I highly recommend a visit to the Lobkowicz Palace (see p. 52); even though it requires a separate admission fee, it's well worth the investment.

(left) STRAHOV MONASTERY LIBRARY, 1953

(right) THE GOLDEN LANE, HRADČANY, 1949

▪ ▪ ▪ ▪ ▪ ▪ ▪ ▪ ▪ ▪ ▪ ▪ ▪ ▪

Prague Castle

Hradčanské náměstí, Prague 1, Hradčany (Map D)
www.hrad.cz/en
TEL 224 373 368
HOURS Apr–Oct: 09:00–18:00; Nov–Mar: 09:00–16:00
ENTRANCE FEE 250–350 CZK Adults; 125–175 CZK Children & Seniors

LORETO CHURCH, 1958

integral role in European politics – starting in the early 17th century as Chancellors of Bohemia under Emperor Rudolph II, and continuing through the dark days of the German Occupation in the 1940s, when the last Duke served the Czechoslovak government-in-exile in England – and the exhibition clearly reflects their intriguing history. Don't miss the giant lobster shell!

Tours are offered every half hour daily during high season (April–October).

MUSEUMS & MONUMENTS

■ ■ ■ ■ ■ ■ ■ ■ ■ ■ ■ ■

Folk Art Museum
Národopisné muzeum
Kinský Summer Palace at Petřín Hill (Letohrádek Kinských)
Kinského zahrada 98, Prague 5, Smíchov (Map B)
TEL 257 214 806
HOURS Tue–Sun: 10:00–18:00
ENTRANCE FEE 70 CZK Adults; 40 CZK Children; 6 and under Free
TRAM 6, 9, 12, 20 to Švandovo divadlo

Beyond a few very general introductions, this museum is not exactly English-friendly; however, it's definitely high on my recommendation list. It reopened in 2005 after what was clearly a very loving restoration, and has been curated to perfection. The museum is filled with exquisite folk costumes, everyday wear and artifacts such as ceramics, farming tools and furniture. Anyone who is interested in textiles will have a special

MORAVIAN MAIDENS PAINTING THE FAÇADE OF A HOUSE, 1941

VILLAGE PEOPLE, 1940

appreciation of the collection, as it shows off the intricate handiwork of sewing, embroidery and weaving that only the deftest of hands could have executed; additionally, you'll see very interesting use of sequins and metallic threads. The exhibit with the baby clothing gets me every time, but I also love the dioramas that provide insight into how Czechs experienced everyday life.

Sadly, the gift shop has not embraced the glorious potential of modern consumerism, but there are a few items inspired by pieces in the museum collection that I feel are worth noting: the wooden toys, painted ceramic

BOHEMIAN FOLK COSTUME,
C. 1941

bowls, and traditional gingerbread in various forms (including Christmas ornaments) are especially nice; my personal favorites are wood pendant necklaces on leather twine, many of them hand-painted with religious icons. On my last visit, I bought a lamb pendant that I love for 150 CZK.

Kampa Museum
Muzeum Kampa
U Sovových mlýnů 2, Prague 1, Malá Strana (Map B)
www.museumkampa.cz
TEL 257 286 147
HOURS Daily: 10:00–18:00
ENTRANCE FEE 260 CZK Adults; 130 CZK Children; 6 and under Free
METRO Malostranská ●
TRAM 12, 20, 22 to Hellichova

This museum houses the private art collection of Jan and Meda Mládek, who collected work by a wide range of Eastern European and Czech artists while living abroad in the US during the 1950s and 60s. The collection includes works by such heavy-hitters as František Kupka, often thought of as the

father of abstract painting; Otto Gutfreund, one of the outstanding 20th-century Czech sculptors; and Jiří Kolář, a postwar surrealist known for his work in collage. Before or after your visit, be sure to stop for a coffee at the museum's lovely café overlooking the river.

Museum of Czech Cubism at the House of the Black Madonna
Muzeum českého kubismu, Dům U Černé Matky boží
Ovocný trh 19, Prague 1, Staré Město (Map A)
www.ngprague.cz
TEL 224 211 746
HOURS Tue–Sun: 10:00–18:00
ENTRANCE FEE 100 CZK Adults; 50 CZK Children; 6 and under Free
METRO Náměstí Republiky ●
TRAM 5, 8, 14, 26 to Náměstí Republiky

Now the site of the Museum of Czech Cubism, The House of the Black Madonna was originally a department store with a famous coffee house, the Grand Café Orient, on the first floor (see p. 169). Itself

a masterpiece of Czech Cubist architecture, the building was designed by the godfather of Czech Cubism, Josef Gočár, and built in 1911. If you're at all interested in modern art history, a visit to this small museum focusing on Czech Cubism in paintings, sculpture, furniture and ceramics is a must.

The National Museum
Národní muzeum
Václavské náměstí 68, Prague 1, Nové Město (Map C)
www.nm.cz
TEL 222 497 111
HOURS Daily: 10:00–18:00 (May–Sept); 09:00–17:00 (Oct–Apr)
Closed the first Tuesday of each month.
ENTRANCE FEE 110 CZK Adult, 50 CZK Children, 6 and under Free
METRO Muzeum ● ●
TRAM 11 to Muzeum
NOTE: Closed due to reconstruction; reopening planned for July 2015.

The 1891 Neo-Renaissance building housing the National Museum is more than striking enough to steal the show – especially the lobby and grand staircase – but its zoological

CUBIST FURNITURE DESIGNS, 1913
(SOURCE: NTM COLLECTION NO. 14)

ST. WENCESLAS MONUMENT, WITH NATIONAL MUSEUM IN BACKGROUND, 1953

collection runs a close second if you have any interest in taxidermy. So, if Deyrolle happens to be your favorite shop in Paris, you might have just found heaven…except for the fact that you can't charge the polar bear to your AMEX and send it home. Highlights include an elephant head, an entire giraffe, various bats, squirrels, rats, and a very cute little baby penguin. The display vitrines are the original furnishings from 1891, giving the museum a wonderfully Victorian feel. The building also affords a great view of Václavské náměstí (Wenceslas Square) from the entry stairs.

National Technical Museum
Národní technické muzeum
Kostelní 42, Prague 7, Holešovice (Map F)
www.ntm.cz
TEL 220 399 111
HOURS Tue–Fri: 09:00–17:30; Sat & Sun: 10:00–18:00
ENTRANCE FEE 170 CZK Adults; 90 CZK Children; 6 and under Free
METRO Hradčanská ● or Vltavská ●
TRAM 1, 8, 15, 25, 26 to Letenské náměstí

This museum is just really, really fun. The Transport Hall, a great Functionalist space filled to the brim with Czech-made vehicles, including vintage steam engines, cars, trucks, motorcycles (many with the mud still on the tires), and bicycles, as well as airplanes suspended from the ceiling, is by far my favorite room. I also love the photography exhibit, which houses a very

TRANSPORT HALL, NATIONAL TECHNICAL MUSEUM (PHOTO COURTESY OF NTM)

extensive collection of vintage cameras, including lots of Kodaks.

Church of Our Lady of Victory – Infant Jesus
kostel Panny Marie Vítězné – Pražské Jezulátko

Karmelitská 9, Prague 1, Malá Strana (Map B)
www.pragjesu.info/en/
TEL 257 533 646
HOURS Mon–Sat: 09:30–17:30; Sun: 13:00–18:00
ENTRANCE FEE FREE
METRO Malostranská ●
TRAM 12, 20, 22 to Hellichova

Although the Renaissance and early Baroque church from 1613 is lovely, what I really fancy about this site is the 45cm-tall Infant Jesus statue made of wax (yes, wax!), which originally came from Spain and was bequeathed to the church in 1628 by Polyxena Lobkowicz (see p. 53 for further information on the Lobkowicz family) and has now become a pilgrimage destination for devout Christians from around the world. The church also has a very curious museum paying homage to the Infant Jesus, which shows off several of

INFANT JESUS POSTCARD, C. 1919

the most interesting and intriguing robes that the statue has received as offerings over the years. My personal favorite is a beautifully hand-embroidered robe from China. While it is possible to buy your own Infant Jesus in the gift shop, prices range from 2,650 to 48,900 CZK, which seems a bit steep – I recommend that you forgo personal ownership and simply enjoy the oddity of it all.

Public Transport Museum
Muzeum městské hromadné dopravy

Patočkova 4, Prague 6, Střešovice (Map D)
www.dpp.cz/muzeum-mhd
TEL 296 128 900
HOURS Sat–Sun: 09:00–17:00; other times by appointment (Mar 31–Nov 18)
ENTRANCE FEE 35 CZK Adults; 20 CZK Children; 6 and under Free
METRO Hradčanská ●
TRAM 1, 2, 18 to Vozovna Střešovice

This museum is a wonderful hands-on experience for young and old alike, featuring a wide selection of historic trams and buses, several of which you can even climb into and explore. The oldest is a horse-drawn tram that dates back to 1886. Located in an historic Prague tram depot built in 1909, the facility was used up until 1992. The museum provides a delightful window into Prague's past. A number of unusual items are for sale by the ticket booth; my favorite find is a puzzle of the Prague metro system.
CASH ONLY

Toy Museum
Muzeum hraček

Prague Castle, Jiřská 6, Prague 1, Hradčany (Map D)
TEL 224 372 294
HOURS Daily: 09:30–17:30
ENTRANCE FEE 70 CZK Adults; 30 CZK Children
METRO Malostranská ●
TRAM 22 to Pražský hrad

If, like me, you love toys, definitely add this museum to your to-do list. The collection dates back over 150 years, and runs the gamut from Markin toy trains and stations to turn-of-the-20th-century kitchen dioramas, teddy bears, dolls, tin toys, and even Barbie (who gets an entire floor all to herself, even though the only thing remotely Czech about her is her rather impossible measurements!).
CASH ONLY

Slightly Further Afield

National Gallery
Veletržní palác

Dukelských hrdinů 47, Prague 7, Holešovice (Map F)
www.ngprague.cz
TEL 224 301 111
HOURS Tue–Sun: 10:00–18:00
ENTRANCE FEE 180 CZK Adults; 90 CZK Children; 6 and under Free
METRO Vltavská ●
TRAM 12, 14, 15, 17 to Veletržní
TRAVEL TIME 15–20 min.

Housed in a Functionalist masterpiece built in 1928, the interior space of this museum is in many ways just as worthy of a visit as the artwork on display. The museum is bewilderingly large, and taking it all in is probably not realistic, so it's a good idea to plan what to focus on in advance. One major attraction is Alfons Mucha's *Slav Epic* – a series of 20 huge murals depicting a grand (and somewhat idealized) vision of Slavic history that was bestowed to the city of Prague in 1928; this is definitely worth seeing, but requires a fair amount of time if you read the detailed brochure information about each piece. The museum offers separate entry prices for viewing only the *Slav Epic* or the entire collection; even if you only have time to see the Mucha murals, I still recommend that you pay the full entry fee and visit the fourth floor, as this allows you to fully appreciate the building's structure. The permanent collection predominately consists of paintings and sculptures, but you'll also find some furniture, applied arts and even a few classic Czech motorcars. French masters including Cezanne, Degas and Matisse are also well represented here, but you'll probably find it more rewarding to visit the sections focused specifically on Czech art, such as the second floor's Socialist Realism section, which is a real favorite of mine. The bookstore is also worthy of a stop.

■ ■ ■ ■ ■ ■ ■ ■ ■ ■ ■ ■ ■

Police Museum
Muzeum policie ČR
Ke Karlovu 1, Prague 2,
Nové Město (Map E)
www.muzeumpolicie.cz
TEL 974 824 855
HOURS Tue–Sun: 10:00–17:00
ENTRANCE FEE 30 CZK Adults; 10 CZK Children; 6 and under Free
METRO I. P. Pavlova ●
TRAM 6, 11 to Pod Karlovem
TRAVEL TIME 15–20 min.

Located in a former convent (of all places), the Police Museum has always been one of my favorite off-the-beaten-track and not-for-everyone museums. It's ghoulishly fun and surprisingly interesting, featuring

POLICE MUSEUM HIGHLIGHTS, C. 1996

wonderfully creepy crime scene mock-ups and photographs, including depictions of captured dissidents who did not succeed in their attempts to flee. All of which seems particularly inappropriate for a museum where school groups often visit, and, needless to say, the kids seem to love it. There's also a vast arsenal of weaponry on display. The text is in Czech, but with this much visual delight, it's hardly necessary to know exactly what is going on.

■■■■■■■■■■■■■■
Vítkov National Monument

U Památníku 1900, Prague 3, Žižkov
www.nm.cz
TEL 222 781 676
HOURS Wed–Sun: 10:00–18:00
ENTRANCE FEE 110 CZK Adults; 60 CZK Children & Seniors
TRAM 1, 9, 16 to Ohrada
TRAVEL TIME 10 min. Take a taxi! Advise the driver to go to Koněvova Street and then turn on Pražačka; this will take you right to the monument.

Capped with the world's largest equestrian statue, the Vítkov National Monument is already plenty noteworthy, but there's much more to it than that. Far behind the massive metal doors is a huge mausoleum that was built between the World Wars as a memorial to members of the Czechoslovak Legion, who fought against the Austro-Hungarian forces in World War I. Don't worry, there are no longer dead bodies stored here – these were

VÍTKOV MONUMENT, 1950
(SOURCE: ČTK / CZECH NEWS AGENCY)

JOSEPH STALIN, KLEMENT GOTTWALD, AND FRIENDS, C. 1946

removed in 1990 (which, come to think of it, might be at least as creepy). In any case, the interior space is of true architectural merit, incorporating 29 different types of marble and granite, all from local quarries. There are also fabulous Art Deco furnishings in the Presidential Suite. During World War II, the Germans used the monument for weapons storage; later, the

Communists used it once again as a mausoleum, adding to the structure. The highlight during their occupation must have been the Lenin-style state viewing of the embalmed body of Klement Gottwald, the first and most famous communist leader in Czechoslovakia. After the fall of communism in 1989, the government sold the building for 1 CZK – yes, you read right, 1 CZK – to a clearly very well connected former comrade. Thankfully, he went bankrupt, and the government was later able to reclaim the building. In addition to the permanent exhibition, which covers milestones in the history of the Czechoslovak statehood, be certain not to miss the underground "Basement of Gottwald's Mausoleum," which contains the technical equipment used for the embalming and upkeep of Klement Gottwald's corpse – it's creeptastic! Additionally, try to visit on day where the weather is good, so you can visit the 360-degree rooftop viewpoint, which is among the best in the city, offering a wholly unique vantage that clearly outlines the neighborhoods

ŠKODA POSTCARD, C. 1975

of Prague. The café also offers a great view, but it's not nearly as spectacular as the one from the roof. Although difficult to get to, this unique monument is definitely worth the effort. Sadly, there's virtually nothing to buy with which

to commemorate your visit, but you certainly won't forget it.

NOTE: The monument is open year round, but be forewarned: there is limited heating in winter, and it can get rather chilly inside.

What's the Best Way to See the Jewish Cemetery?

If you have neither the time nor the inclination to take a proper tour, your best bet – believe it or not – is to view it from the bathroom at the Decorative Arts Museum (17. listopadu 2, Staré Město, Prague 1 [Map A], *www.upm.cz*), which happens to border the cemetery and offers an excellent vantage point.

OLD-NEW SYNAGOGUE ON PAŘÍŽSKÁ STREET, C. 1900

Further Afield

▪ ▪ ▪ ▪ ▪ ▪ ▪ ▪ ▪ ▪ ▪ ▪ ▪
ŠKODA Auto Museum
Třída Václava Klementa 294, Mladá Boleslav
http://new.skoda-auto.com/en/experience/museum
TEL 326 831 134
HOURS Daily: 09:00–17:00
ENTRANCE FEE 25 CZK Adults; 13 CZK Children & Seniors
TRAVEL TIME 50 min.
You can get there by train, which takes about 1 hour, but I highly recommend either driving or being driven (see p. 219).

The exhibition here incorporates over 25 old Škodas (see p. 138), including a rather heroic fire engine from 1917. The bulk of the collection is from the 1920s and 1930s.

Tatra Technical Museum

Záhumenní 367, Kopřivnice (look for the red locomotive outside)
www.tatramuseum.cz
TEL 556 808 421
HOURS Tue–Sun: 09:00–17:00
WINTER HOURS Tue–Sun 09:00–16:00
ENTRANCE FEE 110 CZK Adults; 70 CZK Children & Seniors; 6 and under Free
TRAVEL TIME 4 hours
The only way to get to this museum is by driving or being driven (see p. 219).

Old cars, trucks and trains are housed at this very off-the-beaten-track museum in Moravia. I brought my parents and we all loved it. Our only regret is that we did not actually purchase the Tatra 77 (see p. 138) that was for sale at that time. Don't make our mistake!

ARCHITECTURE

Municipal House
Obecní dům

Náměstí Republiky 5, Prague 1, Staré Město (Map A)
www.obecnidum.cz
TEL 222 002 101
ENTRANCE FEE 290 CZK Adults; 240 CZK Children
METRO Náměstí Republiky ●
TRAM 5, 8, 14, 26 to Náměstí Republiky

Obecní dům is the Art Nouveau architectural gem of the Czech Republic, and a visit to this exquisite building should be included in every person's visit to Prague. The building officially opened in 1912, with interior decoration by the most prominent Czech artists of the day. Most of the building is open to the public, and you should definitely check out the café (Kavárna Obecní dům – see p. 170), French restaurant, and glass elevator on the ground floor, as well as the Pilsner pub and the American Bar in the basement. It's also possible to take a tour of the upstairs rooms, including Smetana Hall, the concert hall where the Prague Symphony performs, and the Mayor's Hall, which

OBECNÍ DŮM
(MUNICIPAL HOUSE), C. 1912

THE ČERNÍNSKÝ PALACE, SEAT OF THE MINISTRY OF FOREIGN AFFAIRS, C. 1940.

JAN MASARYK (MINISTER OF FOREIGN AFFAIRS FOLLOWING WWII) LIVED IN THIS BUILDING. IN 1948, HE WAS FOUND DEAD AFTER APPARENTLY FALLING FROM HIS BATHROOM WINDOW. IT REMAINS A MYSTERY, TO THIS DAY, WHETHER THIS WAS AN ASSASSINATION OR SUICIDE. THE BUILDING IS OPEN TO THE PUBLIC ONLY A FEW TIMES PER YEAR, BUT ON THESE OCCASIONS YOU CAN VISIT JAN MASARYK'S PRIVATE APARTMENT AND SEE THE NOW-FAMOUS BATHROOM. IT'S ALSO WORTH NOTING THAT IN 1991, THE WARSAW PACT WAS OFFICIALLY TERMINATED AT THIS BUILDING.

CHURCH OF THE MOST SACRED HEART OF OUR LORD, C. 1936

DIETZENHOFER'S SUMMER VILLA
(NOW THE DVOŘÁK MUSEUM),
C. 1940

features murals by Alfons Mucha. The building was completely renovated from 1994–1997, drawing on the talents of the country's best craftsmen to restore it back to its original glory. Mission most certainly accomplished.

The information center at Obecní dům happens to have a very nice gift store that features a limited selection of items from the Art Deco Galerie (see p. 81). They carry reproductions of Art Nouveau tiles used in the Obecní dům building that would make a stylish hot plate, as well as silk scarves inspired by the design of the building, and they often have a very interesting display of antique buttons for sale. In addition, their Prague city map is the most useful and practical map I've found – it's the one I always loan to visitors and I highly recommend that you pick one up for yourself. The sales staff is anything but helpful; nevertheless you're sure to find some unique items here.

Slightly Further Afield

■ ■ ■ ■ ■ ■ ■ ■ ■ ■ ■ ■ ■

Church of the Most Sacred Heart of our Lord
kostel Nejsvětějšího srdce Páně
náměstí Jiřího z Poděbrad, Prague 3, Vinohrady (Map E)
www.srdcepane.cz
TEL 222 727 713
HOURS Mon, Wed, Fri: 11:00–14:00; Tue & Thurs: 14:00–17:00 (or by appointment)
METRO Jiřího z Poděbrad ●
TRAM 11 to Jiřího z Poděbrad
TRAVEL TIME 10 min.

Completed in 1932, this Modernist church is a masterpiece by the Slovenian architect Josip Plečnik, who also did extensive renovations at the Prague Castle. Sadly, most Czechs view it simply as an eyesore, when it is, in fact, one of the country's true architectural treasures. The interior is every bit as unique as the exterior, so try to time your visit so you can take in both. The building is open 30 minutes before morning services and one hour before other services, as well as one hour following all services.

■ ■ ■ ■ ■ ■ ■ ■ ■ ■ ■ ■ ■

Dvořák Museum / Villa Amerika
Dvořák Muzeum / Vila Amerika
Ke Karlovu 20, Prague 2, Nové Město (Map E)
www.nm.cz
TEL 224 918 013
HOURS Tue, Wed, Fri, Sat & Sun: 10:00–13:30 &14:00–17:00; Thurs: 11:00–13:30 & 14:00–19:00 (Apr–Sept) | Tue–Sun: 10:00–13:30 & 14:00–17:00 (Oct–Mar)
ENTRANCE FEE 50 CZK Adults; 10 CZK Children; 6 and under Free
METRO I. P. Pavlova ●
TRAM 4, 6, 11, 10, 16, 22 to I. P. Pavlova
TRAVEL TIME 10 min.

Truth be told, the building housing the museum devoted to the great composer, a miniature Baroque summer palace built by Kilian Ignaz Dientzenhofer in 1720, is the true gem in the collection. Nestled behind wrought iron gates virtually in the center of Prague, it's a tidy architectural masterpiece. Were you curious to know what piece of real estate I dream of owning? Well, now you know, and if you visit, I expect you will start dreaming as well. Definitely worth a stop.

Weekend Getaway for Architecture Buffs

Along with Vlastislav Hofman, Josef Chochol and Pavel Janák, Josef Gočár is renowned for promoting the concept of architectural cubism. The Gočár-designed Bauerova Vila (c. 1912), one hour east of Prague, is a masterpiece of this style. The only cubist house outside of Prague by this famous architect, the villa is noteworthy not only for its thoughtful recent renovation, but also for its spectacular collections of cubist furniture, ceramics and glass – all of which are far more extensive, noteworthy and interesting then what you will find at the Museum of Czech Cubism in Prague (see p. 58). Although Bauerova Vila is somewhat difficult to get to, it's definitely worth the effort if you're a fan of cubism, furniture design or architecture.

The trip can also be combined with a visit to Kutná Hora, a town renowned for its Gothic Church dating back to 1388, as well as a wholly unique 'bone church' called the Sedlec Ossuary (for more info on this creepy-yet-fascinating sight, visit *www.ossuary.eu*).

NOTE: If you have time for lunch or an overnight stay, I highly recommend Chateau Kotěra, formerly a private residence but now a hotel and restaurant, designed by the famous Czech architect Jan Kotěra in 1911–1913 (Josef Gočár was a student of Jan Kotěra). The property retains many of its original details, the bedrooms are all appointed with period furnishings, and the food is scrumptious (*www.hotelkotera.cz*).

BAUEROVA VILA, C. 1914 (SOURCE: NCK)

Bauerova Vila Museum & Galerie

Libodřice 111, 280 02 Kolín
www.nck.cz/bauerova-vila
TEL 602 188 419,
777 250 040
HOURS Tours by appointment only: May–Sept: Tue–Fri 10:00–14:00; Sat & Sun: 10:00–16:00

Oct–Apr: Tue–Sun (reserve at least 1 day in advance)
ENTRANCE FEE 400 CZK Adults; 200 CZK Children (maximum 8 people)
TRAVEL TIME 1 hour
I recommend either renting a car or hiring a driver for the day (see p. 219).

Müller Villa

Nad Hradním vodojemem 14, Prague 6, Střešovice
www.mullerovavila.cz
TEL 224 312 012
HOURS Tours by appointment only: Apr–Oct: Tue, Thurs, Sat & Sun: 09:00, 11:00, 13:00, 15:00 &17:00
Nov–Mar: Tue, Thurs, Sat & Sun: 10:00; 12:00; 14:00 & 16:00
ENTRANCE FEE 450 CZK Adults; 350 CZK Children; 6 and under Free
METRO Hradčanská ●
TRAM 1, 2, 18 to Ořechovka
TRAVEL TIME 15–20 min.

Along with Le Corbusier, Walter Gropius and Mies van der Rohe, Adolf Loos was one of the fathers of Classical Modern architecture (known in America as the International Style). The Müller Villa, Loos's masterpiece, is perched in a hilly suburb high above Prague and should not be missed if you're an architectural buff or simply interested in how the upper class lived in late 1920s Prague. The architect not only oversaw the design of the building, but also the entire interior, including furniture, lighting, wallpaper and even door handles. While the exterior certainly bears out his famous pronouncement, "Ornament is Crime," the interior is surprisingly rich and luxurious in its use of materials and furnishings, including extensive marble work and even the deployment of oriental rugs. Each time I visit, I learn something new or notice a small detail I

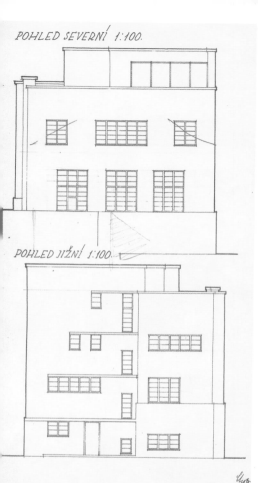

POHLED SEVERNÍ 1:100.

POHLED JIŽNÍ 1:100.

hadn't seen before, and I'm always blown away by Loos's forward-thinking and resourceful use of materials – especially the wonderful wood veneers and marble throughout.

NOTE: I find it easier to take a taxi to the house and then public transport on the way back, as the tram stop is right below the house.

MÜLLER VILLA, PLAN OF NORTHEAST FAÇADE AND SOUTHEAST FAÇADE (1928) (SOURCE: UPM IN PRAGUE ARCHIVE, MM ESTATE INV. NO. B1/167A, P. 3)

Prague Architecture Resources

Prague is an architecture-lover's dream city, with incredible buildings representing a wide range of historical styles from the medieval Romanesque and Gothic to the renaissance-era Baroque to the 20th century Art Deco, Art Nouveau, and (the very unique) Czech Cubism. For complete descriptions of all of the architectural styles that can be seen in and around Prague, complete with photos of noteworthy examples of each, visit www.prague-stay.com/lifestyle/category/36-prague-architecture.

You can also obtain several great local architecture maps with various themes (Art Deco, Art Nouveau, Czech Cubism, and the Prague Metro) at Futurista Universum (see p. 104) and Kubista (see p. 105), as well as online at www.futurista.cz.

(left) CUBIST ARCHITECTURE IN PRAGUE MAP, 2006

(right) PRAGUE METRO MAP, 2010

SIGHTS

Modern Architecture In Prague

Because I'm not an expert on modern architecture, I thought it would be useful to talk to someone who is – so I sat down with Janek Jaros, the former owner of Modernista (a shop that focuses primarily on household objects and furniture from the 1920s–60s – see p. 98), for a brief discussion about Prague architecture...

NATIONAL ASSEMBLY BUILDING, 1973
(SOURCE: ČTK / CZECH NEWS AGENCY)

Karen: Can you give me a quick overview of modern architecture in the Czech Republic?

Janek: The first seeds of Modern architecture in Bohemia were sown by Jan Kotěra and a handful of other young architects who studied in Vienna under the legendary professor Otto Wagner. While Kotěra mostly worked in the style of Wagner and contemporaries such as Josef Hoffmann, the slightly younger group of his assistants and pupils created the radical and internationally unique style of Czech Cubism around 1910. Nowhere else in the world was the Cubist style applied to such an extent. Indeed, for a time, the well-heeled of Prague could live in Cubist houses, furnished with Cubist furniture, drink coffee from Cubist cups and follow time on Cubist clocks. The movement was extremely short-lived, however, and came to a halt at the outset of WWI. Following the war, it briefly evolved into the so-called Rondo-Cubist style, which came to be called the 'Czech National Style,' but this later stage is less distinguishable from what is more generally known as Art Deco. Towards the end of the 1920s, most progressive architects jumped on the Functionalist bandwagon, arriving via the Bauhaus. Some of the Modernist apartment blocks built in the 1930s still count among the best places to live in Prague. It's not too much of an exaggeration to say that Functionalism remained the dominant architectural style in the country until the Velvet Revolution – particularly in the area of public commissions.

Karen: What are your favorite examples of the various modern styles of architecture in Prague?

Janek: For Cubist architecture, I'd say the Kovařovic Villa, just below Vyšehrad Castle (see p. 54). And for Functionalist or Modernist architecture, the Müller Villa beats everything else, hands down. As far as the Communist architecture of the 1950s and 1960s goes, the National Assembly building near the National Museum, I would have to say, is notable for its utter monstrosity and sheer ignorance of its surroundings.

Karen: What are your thoughts on the Crowne Plaza Hotel (formerly the Hotel International) in Prague 6, which is a striking example of the Stalinist style? Wasn't it was recently declared a national monument?

Janek: Well, now that we're stuck with it, it may as well be listed in your book, though I wonder what it symbolizes — either the Russians trying to impose something on us, or some zealous Czech trying to please the Russians out of their own initiative. Perhaps a combination of both. Certainly it is one of the most shocking examples of how brutal architecture can be when it ignores what surrounds it.

Addresses for buildings Janek has noted:

▪ ▪ ▪ ▪ ▪ ▪ ▪ ▪ ▪ ▪ ▪ ▪ ▪

FUNCTIONALIST
Müller Villa
(see p. 66)

COMMUNIST
National Assembly Building
(Map C)
Legerova 75, Prague 1, Vinohrady
METRO Muzeum ● ●
TRAM 11 to Muzeum
(You can't miss it, it's the rectilinear building nestled between the National Museum and the State Opera House).

STALINIST
Crowne Plaza Hotel
(formerly the Hotel International)
Koulova 15, Prague 6, Dejvice
METRO Dejvická ● then tram 2 or 8 to Podbaba
TRAVEL TIME 15–20 min.

CUBIST
Kovařovic Villa
(Map C)
Libušina 3, Prague 2, Vyšehrad
METRO Vyšehrad ●
TRAM 3, 7, 17, 21 to Výtoň

▪ ▪ ▪ ▪ ▪ ▪ ▪ ▪ ▪ ▪ ▪ ▪ ▪

Other notable examples of Czech Cubism near Kovařovic Villa:

Neklanova 2 & 30
Two apartment blocks

Rašínovo nábřeží 6–10
Family houses

KOVAŘOVIC VILLA, C. 1913

Sneak-A-Peek: A Few Arcades and Buildings To Visit Before You Leave...

▪ ▪ ▪ ▪ ▪ ▪ ▪ ▪ ▪ ▪ ▪ ▪ ▪

Adamova lékárna
Václavské náměstí 8, Prague 1, Nové Město (Map C)
TEL 224 227 532
HOURS Mon–Fri: 08:00–18:00
METRO Můstek ● ●
TRAM 3, 9, 14, 24 to Václavské náměstí

Adamova lékárna has been in operation as a business since 1520 (a fact that this American, for one, found most remarkable). The current building housing this pharmacy was built in 1911–1913, and the interior was installed in 1920. It's not an essential stop, but if you do happen to walk by, pop in to admire the wonderful original cabinetry with intricate wood inlay work.

▪ ▪ ▪ ▪ ▪ ▪ ▪ ▪ ▪ ▪ ▪ ▪ ▪

Bank of the Czechoslovak Legions (now ČSOB)
Na poříčí 24, Prague 1, Nové Město (Map C)
HOURS Mon–Fri: 09:00–17:00
METRO Náměstí Republiky ●
trams 3, 5, 14, 24, 26 to Masarykovo nádraží or 3, 8, 24 to Bílá Labuť

This Rondo-Cubist master-piece by Josef Gočár was built from 1923–1925. While the facade, featuring relief sculptures of Czech and Slovak legionnaires during World War I, is certainly worth noting, the real treasures lie inside. First you will note the fabulous – indeed, fairytale-like – metalwork of the stairwell banister and elevator gate.

Then, at the end of the passageway, you'll enter the main banking hall with its massive glass ceiling, undoubtedly the building's crowning jewel.

- - - - - - - - - - - - - - -
Koruna Palace

Václavské náměstí 1, Prague 1, Nové Město (Map C)
METRO Můstek ● ●
TRAM 3, 9, 14, 24 to Václavské náměstí

Designed by Antonín Pfeiffer and built between 1911 and 1914, this Art Nouveau building and arcade is one of the oldest in Prague. In addition to the many impressive examples of heroic sculptural decoration, you'll want to take full appreciation of the building's magnificent dome, which is bejeweled with clear and amber glass. Have a cup of coffee in the café right under the dome and be mesmerized by all the details. It's an experience not to be missed.

- - - - - - - - - - - - - - -
Lucerna Palace

Vodičkova 36, Prague 1, Nové Město (Map C)
METRO Můstek ● ●
TRAM 3, 9, 14, 24 to Václavské náměstí

The Lucerna Palace – by far the most famous shopping arcade in Prague – was erected from 1907–1910 by Václav Havel, grandfather of the former Czech president. As with the Koruna Palace (described above), the highlight here is definitely the stained-glass dome. Be sure to climb the grand marble staircase to check out the bar on the second floor (where the entrance to the cinema is located – see p. 197), and notice the original metalwork and marble, much of which is original. The statue of St. Wenceslas on his upside-down horse is the work of David Černý, the artist behind the crawling babies on the Žižkov TV tower (see box on the next page), as well as several other sculptures around town (*www. davidcerny.cz*).

BANK OF THE CZECHOSLOVAK LEGIONS (MAIN HALL), C. 1930

BANK OF THE CZECHOSLOVAK LEGIONS, C. 1931
(SOURCE: JAROSLAV ŠETELÍK)

- - - - - - - - - - - - - - -
Main Post Office
Hlavní pošta

Jindřišská 14, Prague 1, Nové Město (Map C)
TEL 221 131 111
HOURS Daily: 02:00–24:00
METRO Můstek ● ●
TRAM 3, 9, 14, 24 to Václavské náměstí

This Neo-Classical structure dating from 1871-1874 boasts a wonderful and extra-ordinarily large atrium in

What Is That Needle-like Structure Sticking Up in the Sky Above Prague?

Among locals, the Žižkov TV Tower (Map E) is the city's most hated structure and was recently named the "second ugliest building in the world." Though not put into use until after the Velvet Revolution, it was intended, according to local lore, to jam foreign radio and television signals. At 216 meters (709 ft.) it's the tallest building in Prague. The Communist regime unabashedly cleared away an old Jewish cemetery to make room for the structure, but was kind enough to leave a little swatch as a reminder of what used to be there. Perhaps this has something to do with the bronze statues of babies crawling up the tower. These were made by local artist David Černý, the same artist who created the upside-down horse in the Lucerna Palace (see facing page).

THE PRIDE OF ŽIŽKOV — COMPLETE WITH CLIMBING FACELESS BABIES

the main lobby that I encourage you to check out, regardless of your interest in sending postcards or collecting stamps. Also of interest are the wall paintings by Karel Vítězslav Mašek, which depict activities connected to the postal service and transport. If you're interested in

KORUNA PALACE, UNDER CONSTRUCTION, 1913 (SOURCE: SVĚTOZOR MAGAZINE)

stamp collecting and first-day covers, go to booth #29, which is where they offer all available stock.

The National Museum
Národní muzeum
(see p. 58)

The lobby and grand staircase of the 1891 Neo-Renaissance building housing the National Museum is absolutely worth a view, and you can explore both of these without paying admission.

NOTE: **Closed for reconstruction; due to reopen June 2015.**

Světozor pasáž
Vodičkova 41, Prague 1, Nové Město (Map C)
METRO Můstek ● ●
TRAM 3, 9, 14, 24 to Václavské náměstí

Built in the late 1940s, this Functionalist shopping arcade culminates at the north end with a spectacular stained glass window made by Tesla, an electronics company named after Nikola Tesla and founded in 1921. As a bonus, this window looks onto the Franciscan Garden (see p. 74).

Unicredit Bank
Na Příkopě 20, Prague 1, Nové Město (Map A)
TEL 221 112 111
HOURS Mon–Fri: 08:30–16:00
METRO Můstek ● ●

Formerly Živnostenská banka, the Provincial Bank of the Bohemian Kingdom, this most impressive building was intended to provide an environment appropriate for high-level finance, and I do believe they succeeded! Walk up the main staircase with confidence and behold the main attraction on the second floor. Note the magnificent glass ceiling and the allegorical figures depicting various Bohemian regions looking down upon you. And then let the high finance begin…

VIEW INCLUDING CLOCK AT THE CHURCH OF ST. NICHOLAS, C. 1940

VIEWS & PANORAMAS

▪ ▪ ▪ ▪ ▪ ▪ ▪ ▪ ▪ ▪ ▪ ▪ ▪ ▪

Astronomical Tower in the Klementinum

Mariánské náměstí 5, Prague 1, Staré Město (Map A)
www.klementinum.com
TEL 222 220 879
HOURS Daily: 10:00–16:00
ENTRANCE FEE 220 CZK Adults; 140 CZK Children; 6 and under Free
METRO Staroměstská ●
TRAM 17, 18 to Karlovy lázně or Staroměstská

Housed in the Czech Republic's massive national library, this is my absolute favorite panoramic view in Prague, as it allows you to take in the whole city, including the Charles Bridge, and I'm confident

that, upon leaving, you'll understand why Prague is known as one of the most beautiful cities in the world. Sound too good to be true? OK, there is a catch: About 120 narrow spiral stairs, to be exact. But if you're up for the climb, the reward is well worth it. Until the 1920s, the tower was used to calculate high noon, at which time a flag was raised for the castle to see, whereupon a cannon was fired to mark the hour. To get to the tower, you need to take the tour, which leaves hourly. On the way, you'll see the absolutely amazing library built by Jesuits, decorated

with fantastic frescoes depicting knowledge, learning and wisdom.

▪ ▪ ▪ ▪ ▪ ▪ ▪ ▪ ▪ ▪ ▪ ▪ ▪ ▪

Clock Tower in Old Town Hall

Old Town Square (enter in rose-colored building marked "Turistické informace" to the left of the clock) (Map A)
www.orloj.eu |
www.prazskeveze.cz
HOURS Tue–Sun: 09:00–22:00; Mon: 11:00–22:00
ENTRANCE FEE 105 CZK Adults; 55 CZK Children; 6 and under 25 CZK
METRO Můstek ● ● or Staroměstská ●

Rising above the very core of Prague, this clock tower affords an unbelievable view you won't find anywhere else. While many other observation points offer views overlooking the Old Town, this is the only one that is located in the Old Town itself. To enter the tower, take the glass elevator to the third floor. Take the stairs on the way down and be sure to note the fabulous wood-inlayed doors. At the bottom of the stairs, walk straight into the foyer with vaulted

---

Recommended Czech Architecture Books in English

Czech Cubism 1909–1925: Art / Architecture / Design
By Tomáš Vlček, Pavel Liška, and Jiří Švestka – Modernista & i3 CZ 2006; 2,450 CZK

Famous Prague Villas
By Přemysl Veverka, Dita Dvořáková, Petr Koudelka, Petr Krajči, Zdeněk Lukeš – Foibos Art Agency, National Technical Museum in Prague 1999; 369 CZK

Prague 20th Century Architecture
By Stefan Templ – Springer Verlag Wien 1999; 550 CZK

Sneak-A-Peek Oddity: The Paternoster

A "paternoster" is a dying breed of elevators that consists of a chain of open compartments that moves slowly up and down in a loop without stopping, so that passengers simply hop on or off as required. The name Paternoster ("Our Father," the first two words of the Lord's Prayer) was originally applied to the lift because it's in the form of a loop of rosary beads, which are used as an aid in reciting the paternoster (thank you, Wikipedia!). These oddities were first built in 1884, and the first one was installed in Prague in 1914. They were popular through the first half of the 20th century, because they could carry more passengers than an ordinary elevator. The construction of new paternosters, however, is no longer allowed, due to the high risk of accidents (mostly people tripping or falling while entering and exiting). So, as the number of working paternosters continually decreases, they have achieved something of a cult status – especially among nostalgic types like me. Be sure to seek one out during your visit, as they are truly a sight to behold, and if you find yourself suitably brave and agile, take a leap of faith and enjoy the ride.

One Good Place Where You Can Brave a Working Paternoster:

■ ■ ■ ■ ■ ■ ■ ■ ■ ■ ■

Palác YMCA
Na Poříčí 12, Prague 1, Nové Město (Map C)
TEL 224 875 811
METRO Náměstí Republiky ●
TRAM 5, 8, 26, 14 to Náměstí Republiky

The paternoster is on the left, directly beyond the reception desk. Walk in like you belong there, hop on, hop off, and exit....

PATERNOSTER

LETNÁ PARK, 1940

ceilings; the entire room is a wonderful turn-of-the-20th-century mosaic celebrating Prague.

■ ■ ■ ■ ■ ■ ■ ■ ■ ■ ■ ■

Letná Park
Letenské sady
Prague 7, Bubeneč (Map F)
METRO Hradčanská ●
TRAM 1, 8, 15, 25, 26 to Letenské náměstí or Sparta

A vast and wonderful series of parks and gardens perched high above the Vltava River, Letná Park allows for some striking city vistas; it also features a lovely beer garden (see p. 182), and a several fun playgrounds – perfect for a sunny day. Under communism it was used for May Day parades, which still take place, though not with the same terrifying flair. It was also home to the largest statue of Stalin in the world, at 30 meters (100 ft.).

Completed in 1955, even as his cult status was failing, the statue was destroyed in 1962; in its place you now find the huge – and very random – red metronome sculpture built in 1991.

- - - - - - - - - - - - - -
Petřín Hill
Petřínské sady
Prague 1, Malá Strana
(Map B)
TRAM 12, 20, 22 to Újezd, then take the funicular railway

Wonderfully free of tourists, the top of Petřín Hill can be reached by taking a funicular (cable car) using standard tram tickets, and the view is excellent. The entire park area is very peaceful in general, making it a wonderful place to spend a few hours or have a picnic.

SECRET GARDENS

- - - - - - - - - - - - - -
Franciscan Garden
Františkánská zahrada
Jungmannovo náměstí,
Prague 1, Nové Město (Map A)
Vodičkova 41 (if entering from Světozor *pasáž*)
HOURS Daily: 07:00–22:00
(May–Sept); 08:00–19:00
(Oct–Apr)
ENTRANCE FREE
METRO Můstek ● ●
TRAM 3, 9, 14, 24 to Václavské náměstí

MY JSME CHLOUBA PRAHY ("WE ARE THE PRIDE OF PRAGUE"), 1910

MARCHERS BELOW LETNÁ PARK, WITH STALIN STATUE
IN BACKGROUND, 1955

The Franciscan Garden dates back to the beginning of the 17th century, but was closed to the public until 1950, when the Communists decided it was worth sharing with the public. Today the park is a secret retreat in the center of town, filled with hedges and lots of benches – a perfect spot to relax with a book or newspaper. If you enter from Vodičkova through the Světozor *pasáž* (shopping arcade, see p. 71), be sure to stop and get an ice cream at Hájek (see p. 169), which was the most famous ice cream shop in town under communism. Hájek remains a favorite among locals, particularly for their cakes with fruit and gelatin.

- - - - - - - - - - - - - -
Gardens Beneath the Prague Castle
Zahrady pod Pražským hradem
Valdštejnské náměstí 3,
Prague 1, Malá Strana
(Map B)
www.palacove-zahrady.cz
TEL 257 214 817
HOURS Daily: Apr: 10:00–
18:00; May & Sept: 10:00–
19:00; June & July: 10:00–
21:00; Aug: 10:00–20:00;
Oct: 10:00–18:00
ENTRANCE 80 CZK Adults;
50 CZK Children; 6 and under
Free
METRO Malostranská ●
TRAM 12, 20, 22 to
Malostranské náměstí

This magical group of terraced Baroque gardens that practically spill down from the castle grounds was originally laid out in the 16th century and then remodeled in the 18th. Exquisite stairways, statues, gazebos and other garden buildings punctuate the space. Again, although the Communists were kind enough to open these gardens to the public, preservation was never their first priority; after years of decay, they were eventually closed for extensive restoration, which was completed in the late 1990s. Thankfully, they have now been fully restored and reopened once again for everyone to enjoy. Definitely not to be missed; these gardens are simply breathtaking!

WALLENSTEIN GARDEN
(SOURCE: ČTK / CZECH NEWS AGENCY)

Vrtbovská Garden

Karmelitská 25, Prague 1, Malá Strana (Map B)
www.vrtbovska.cz
TEL 272 088 350
HOURS Daily: Apr–Oct 10:00–19:00
ENTRANCE FEE 60 CZK Adults; 40 CZK Children
METRO Malostranská ●
TRAM 12, 20, 22 to Malostranské náměstí

The Vrtbovská Garden is another gem that should not be missed if you enjoy formal Baroque gardens. One could easily walk right by, as it is marked only by a rather modest doorway on Malá Strana's Karmelitská Street. Influenced by Italian terrace-style gardens, it was built in the 1720s for the Count Jan Joseph Vrtba and represents the collective work of several prominent Czech artists. The garden itself was designed by Prague native František Maxmilián Kaňka, the sculptures were created by Matyáš Bernard Braun, and the painter Václav Vavřinec Reiner completed the frescoes. Walking all the way to the top, you'll be treated to an incredibly charming rooftop view of Malá Strana. See p. 26 to view a photograph of the Vrtbovská Garden.

NOTE: If you're staying at the Aria hotel (see p. 25), you may even get a room overlooking these gardens, in which case you're very lucky (and I'm most envious!).

Wallenstein Garden
Valdštejnská zahrada

Valdštejnské náměstí 4, Prague 1, Malá Strana (Map B)
TEL 257 075 707
HOURS Apr–Oct: Mon–Fri: 7:30–18:00; Sat & Sun: 10:00–18:00
ENTRANCE FREE
METRO Malostranská ●
TRAM 12, 20, 22 to Malostranské náměstí

This exquisite Baroque garden was designed by the Milanese architect Andrea Spezza between 1624–1630, at the same time that the adjacent palace was being built for General Wallenstein (of Thirty Years War fame), who razed some two dozen houses to make way for his own jaw-droppingly ostentatious vision. Fortunately he had the luck of finding and marrying not one but two rich widows to foot the bill. The garden is geometric in design, and several peacocks are in residence. Open to the public since 2002, it provides an excellent venue for outdoor summer concerts. The palace itself briefly housed the Czech Senate, and now serves as the base for the Ministry of Culture.

Shopping

It always surprises me to hear the common refrain that "there's nothing to buy in Prague," because I can assure you, based on personal experience (and the often sadly precarious balance of my checking account), this statement is simply *not* true.

Look, everyone has a certain skill set, and mine includes locating – and purchasing – fabulous items around the globe. Few things give me more pleasure than finding the perfect special something – be it a small trinket that I know a friend will absolutely love, or a vintage design item that has been on my own 'must find' list for months – and I'm pleased to report that Prague has been the source of some of my most unique acquisitions. It can *absolutely* be a shopper's heaven here, IF you know where to look.

One of the primary purposes of this book, then, is to help you benefit from my vast experience by showing you how to spend your money shopping in Prague.

PRAGUE HARDWARE STORE, C. 1910

A Few Pieces of Basic Advice

TO BUY OR NOT TO BUY…?
All the big brands are available in Prague and are clustered primarily on two streets – Pařížská (where you'll find Christian Dior, Louis Vuitton, and Hermés) and Na Příkopě (where you'll find H&M, Zara, and Mango) – but you can buy these brands in any major city, so there's really no point in mentioning them here.

Also, while some things in Prague – beer, for instance – are quite inexpensive compared to America and western Europe, many consumer goods with international brand recognition (such as clothes, cosmetics, and electronics) actually cost much *more* than if you were to buy them back home, so I definitely recommend you remove such brands as Levi's, Nike, or Apple from your Prague shopping agenda.

Instead, in the listings below, I've featured stores that sell only (or at least primarily) Czech-made merchandise, as I'm sure you will find them much more interesting.

Although there are probably lots of Czech-made items in the tacky souvenir shops scattered across the tourist centers of town, this is not the kind of merchandise I'm talking about. If you're looking for something a little more authentic, whether for yourself or as a gift for the folks back home, read on – you'll find some great suggestions on the pages that follow.

THE SHOPPING EXPERIENCE

When shopping in Prague, you must keep in mind that the merchandising in many stores is disastrous, with customer service that leaves much to be desired – both holdovers from the Communist era. That leaves much of the work of finding what you're after up to you, so it's good to think of shopping here as a kind of sports event, with a "win" being a bag of goodies in your hand upon exiting a store. So maintain a sharp eye and ironclad determination, and I guarantee you'll be rewarded with many fabulous finds that are *not* available everywhere else.

HOW TO PAY

Unless noted otherwise, all of the shops listed below accept credit cards. That being said, for some items – most notably antiques, for which it is possible to engage in some price negotiation – one is always in a better position to receive a discount when offering to pay in cash....

General Gift and Souvenir Ideas

1. **Czech Liquor & Wine** (see p. 142 & 184)

2. **Glass & Crystal** (see p. 116–119)

3. **Czech Handicrafts** (see p. 101–103)

4. **Jewelry** (see p. 119–123)

5. **Antiques** (see p. 80–87)

6. **Vintage Books, Prints or Stamps** (see p. 87–89)

7. **Local Sports Team** Paraphernalia (see p. 135–136)

8. **Books** (see p. 92–95)

9. **Czech Music** (see p. 124–125)

10. **Czech Delicacies**
Czech Wafer Cookies: My favorite brand is Kolonáda.

Švestková povidla: A plum spread that is thicker than jam and simply delicious. (For more foods to try in Prague, see p. 156–157)

Top 10 List of Children's Gift Ideas

1. **Wooden Toys** (see Hračky, p. 136)

2. **Marionettes** (see p. 123-124)

3. **Ballerina Tutus** (see Grishko, p. 131)

4. **Stuffed Animals or Other Accessories of Uniquely Czech Characters** (see Sparkys, p. 140)

5. **Play Figures of Local Hockey Teams** (see Sparkys, p. 140)

6. **Igráček figures** The Czech equivalent of Playmobil (see Old Toys, p. 137, or Sparkys, p. 140)

CZECH'S ANSWER TO PLAYMOBIL – IGRÁČEK TOYS: CEMENT WORKER AND BRICK-LAYER, C. 1977 (SOURCE: WWW.IGRA.CZ)

7. **Books** (see p. 92–95)

8. **Tin Toys** (see ARTĚL, p. 116)

9. **Policeman, Postman and Trainman Uniforms and Play Sets** (see Sparkys, p. 140)

10. **1970s-era Inflatable Buffalo** This fun item, designed by Libuše Niklová, is one of the *100 Czech Design Icons* (see p. 106) and available for 650 CZK at either of the two ARTĚL shops in town (see p. 116).

1970S-ERA INFLATABLE BUFFALO

ANTIQUE STORES

If you love antiquing, Prague will be right up your alley. The city is filled with an endless supply of antique stores and bazaars, and prices are always negotiable, especially if you pay with cash. Utilizing several of the resources below, I've managed to fully furnish my apartment, country house, and office, to say nothing of bestowing friends and family with many fabulous finds. Have fun, but be sure to leave a few items for me...

AAA Antiques Art Auctions
LOOK FOR: Art, Ceramics, Glassware & Jewelry
Vinohradská 38, Prague 2, Vinohrady (Map E)
www.aukcnidum.cz
TEL 224 322 418, 224 323 218
HOURS Mon–Fri: 09:30–13:00 & 14:00–18:00
METRO Náměstí míru ●
TRAM 4, 10, 16, 22 to Náměstí míru or 11 to Italská

This shop leans toward the higher end, pricewise, although they do have some very affordable items as well, and I've purchased interesting jewelry here (both fine and costume) over the years. If you like costume jewelry, I definitely encourage you to take some time to look through the stack of thin black drawers to the right of the checkout counter – without fail, I always find something I need! They also happen to have the best collection of clip earrings in town.

Alma Mahler
LOOK FOR: Linens & Costumes
Valentinská 7, Prague 1, Staré Město (Map A)
TEL 224 813 991
HOURS Mon–Sat: 10:00–18:00
METRO Staroměstská ●
TRAM 17, 18 to Staroměstská

At this store you will find everything from china and crystal to toys and clothing. I stop in on a regular basis to look at their excellent collection of late 19th / early 20th-century hand-embroidered clothing, bedding, tablecloths and night-gowns, all of which you'll find downstairs. They often have very interesting folk costumes at fair prices.

Antik v Dlouhé
LOOK FOR: Toys & Jewelry
Dlouhá 37, Prague 1, Staré Město (Map A)
TEL 774 431 776
HOURS Mon–Fri: 10:00–19:00; Sat: 12:00–18:00
METRO Náměstí Republiky ●
TRAM 5, 8, 14, 26 to Dlouhá třída

While it's not my favorite antique store on Dlouhá, this is certainly worth a stop. They have a good collection of antique toys and lots of other goodies such as jewelry, ceramics, paintings, and often a fabulous chandelier or two. Prices are fair, if a bit higher than at most of my regular haunts, and usually negotiable.

MORAVIAN FOLK COSTUMES, C.1953

MORAVIAN FOLK COSTUMES, C. 1940

Antiques Ahasver

LOOK FOR: Linens & Folk Costumes

Prokopská 3, Prague 1, Malá Strana (Map B)

www.ahasver.com

TEL 257 531 404

HOURS Tue–Sun: 12:00–18:00

METRO Malostranská ●

TRAM 12, 20, 22 to Malostranské náměstí

This store specializes in antique linens and clothing, including some extraordinary folk costumes from 1900–1938, but they also have jewelry, ceramics and other small items. This is one of my regular stops, as there's always something I want to go home with. The owner is delightful and speaks excellent English. Credit cards are accepted, but if you pay in cash, you should be able to negotiate 10% off the price.

Art Deco Galerie

LOOK FOR: 1920s & 1930s-Era Items

Michalská 21, Prague 1, Staré Město (Map A)

www.artdecogalerie-mili.com

TEL 224 223 076

HOURS Mon–Fri: 14:00–19:00; Sat: 14:00–18:00

METRO Můstek ● ●

This shop seems to be closed more often than it's open, which is incredibly annoying. If you do catch them open, however, you'll enter the best Art Deco and First Republic (1918–1938) antique store in Prague. It's a true anomaly among local stores in that it sticks to one period and does so with style and flair. They have an excellent collection of porcelain, ceramics, glass, clocks, lamps, clothing, and various other accessories, all from this period. The prices can be on the high side, but you can bargain with the owner, especially when paying with cash.

Bazar Antik

LOOK FOR: Ceramics, Glassware & Linens

Křemencova 4, Prague 2, Nové Město (Map C)

HOURS Mon–Thurs: 11:00–18:00; Fri 11:00–17:00

METRO Karlovo náměstí ●

TRAM 6, 9, 18, 21, 22 to Karlovo náměstí

If you enjoy sifting through piles of junk in search of a fabulous find, this store is for you. You'll need more patience than money in your treasure hunt here, but the atmosphere is fun and the prices low. I've amassed a wonderful collection of hand-painted ceramic

81

REPRODUCTION OF ORIGINAL CHAISE LOUNGE FROM MÜLLER VILLA (SEE P. 66)
(PHOTO BY DAVID A. LAND, 2006)

bowls from this store, making my morning cereal and afternoon soup consumption that much more fun. I've also had very good luck with hand-embroidered linens here. CASH ONLY

Bazar Antique
LOOK FOR: Glassware, Ceramics & Oddities
Dlouhá 22, Prague 1, Staré Město (Map A)
TEL 222 320 993

HOURS Mon–Sat: 10:00–18:00
METRO Náměstí Republiky ●
TRAM 5, 8, 14, 26 to Dlouhá třída

This shop leans toward the higher end, pricewise, and is my favorite for when I'm feeling slightly indulgent (which seems to be the case all too often). I've purchased interesting artwork and glassware here, but no furniture. The owner is very sweet and definitely willing to negotiate.

Bric a Brac
LOOK FOR: Old Tins, Accessories & Oddities
Týnská 7, Prague 1, Staré Město (Map A)
TEL 224 815 763
HOURS Daily: 11:00–18:00
METRO Můstek ● ●
or Náměstí Republiky ●

Here you will find two shops at the same address. The first, and smaller of the two, I find simply claustrophobic, so unless you really enjoy weeding through mounds of merchandise in the hope of a true find, I recommend you just skip it. The second shop, located in the courtyard, is much more genteel and fun to poke around in; they carry lots of historical items, most of which originate from 1900 and onward. Most of their items, however, are *ridiculously* overpriced. If you find something you absolutely must have, make the effort to negotiate hard, and you should be rewarded with a more reasonable price; if not, walk away in the knowledge that you haven't committed the sin of overspending.

- - - - - - - - - - - - - -
Dorotheum
LOOK FOR: Glassware, Jewelry & Porcelain

Ovocný trh 2, Prague 1, Staré Město (Map A)
www.dorotheum.cz
TEL 224 216 699
HOURS Mon–Fri: 10:00–19:00; Sat: 10:00–17:00
METRO Můstek ● ●
TRAM 3, 9, 14, 24 to Václavské náměstí

This combination antique store / auction house is a frequent stop for me. The quality is always great and the price points are fair, considering they have already done the homework for you. Prices start at 700 CZK and they carry jewelry (including an excellent collection of garnets), ceramics, porcelain, silver, glass, paintings, and furniture. Auctions are held semifrequently (check their website for a complete schedule), but they also have a large section of the store devoted to items for immediate purchase.

- - - - - - - - - - - - - -
Interier Servis
LOOK FOR: Toys, Glass & Costume Jewelry
Opatovická 7, Prague 1, Nové Město (Map C)
TEL 224 930 610
HOURS Mon–Fri: 10:00–17:45
METRO Národní třída ●
TRAM 14 to Myslíkova or 6, 9, 18, 22 to Národní třída

This shop carries a wide assortment of items, including clocks, glassware, jewelry and linens – all at reasonable prices. Ask to see the back room, where the owner keeps some of the best merchandise. I'm still not entirely sure why all this great stuff is off-limits to the average shopper, but owners have their quirks. Typically, you can negotiate 5–10% off the price if you pay in cash.

- - - - - - - - - - - - - -
Military Antiques
Charvátova 11, Prague 1, Nové Město (Map C)
www.vojenskestarozitnosti-praha.cz
TEL 225 379 724
HOURS Mon–Fri: 10:00–18:00; Sat: 10:00–13:00
METRO Můstek ● ● or Národní třída ●

The name says it all, so if you're looking for vintage helmets, weapons and other equipment, be sure to stop in.
CASH ONLY

VINTAGE CZECH TOYS
(PHOTO BY DAVID A. LAND, 2006)

Nanovo

LOOK FOR: **Furniture, Lamps, Watches & Household Objets**
www.nanovo.cz
TEL 603 145 362

This online shop (in Czech with an English option) is excellent resource for vintage finds from the 1960s, 70s and 80s. I always find something fabulous that I am dying to own; lately I've been eyeing an orange plastic analog phone from Tesla for 720 CZK. Furniture, glass, ceramics, lamps, clocks, watches and household objects are all offered on this comprehensive site, and the owners, Jirka and Adam, are both extremely helpful and nice. World-wide shipping is available.

Pražské starožitnosti

LOOK FOR: **Ceramics, Porcelain & Glass**
Mikulandská 8, Prague 1, Nové Město (Map C)
www.starozitnosti-uhlir.cz
TEL 224 930 572
HOURS Mon–Thurs: 10:00–12:00 & 14:00–17:00; Fri: 14:00–17:00
METRO Národní třída ●
TRAM 6, 9, 18, 22 to Národní divadlo

I've been going to this store since I first moved here in 1994. They carry a very wide range of antiques, including one of the best selections of blue and white porcelain and ceramics in Prague. They also have silver, jewelry, paintings and glass from Biedermeier through Art Deco. My most recent purchase was a porcelain bust of T. G. Masaryk, the first president of Czechoslovakia. This had

been on my shopping agenda for two years, and I happily brought it to my country house for immediate installation.
CASH ONLY

Starožitnosti Antiques

LOOK FOR: **Silver, Ceramics, Chandeliers & Jewelry**
Žatecká 14, Prague 1, Staré Město (Map A)
www.czechantiques.cz
TEL 224 812 909
HOURS Mon–Fri: 11:00–18:00; Sat & Sun: 10:00–15:00
METRO Staroměstská ●
TRAM 17, 18 to Staroměstská

I simply love this store. The quality is exceptional and the prices are fair, considering that they've already done the home-work for you and the owner has a great eye. They carry antiques from the 18th, 19th, and 20th centuries, but the 20th-century items (especially from the Art Deco, Art Nouveau, and Wiener Werkstatte eras) are definitely their strong point. Their jewelry is exquisite, and they always have beautiful ceramics, porcelain, silver, glass, paintings, and furniture.

Starožitné hodiny

LOOK FOR: **Clocks & Watches**
Zborovská 31, Prague 5, Smíchov (Map B)
www.kotek-antiques.cz
TEL 257 329 767
HOURS Mon–Fri: 10:00–18:00
METRO Anděl ●
TRAM 6, 9, 12, 20 to Švandovo divadlo

A great source for antique timepieces of any type, including pocket watches, wristwatches, table clocks, mantle pieces, and

grandfather clocks. They focus primarily on pieces from the Empire period, but they stock other periods as well, all the way through Art Deco. Although clocks and watches are the primary reason I stop in this store, they also carry glassware, silver and furniture from periods ranging from Baroque to Biedermeier.
CASH ONLY

Starožitné hodiny Václav Matouš

LOOK FOR: **Clocks & Watches**
Mikulandská 10, Prague 1, Nové Město (Map C)
www.kralovstvihodin.cz
TEL 224 930 172
HOURS Mon–Fri: 09:00–12:00 & 14:00–18:00
METRO Národní třída ●
TRAM 6, 9, 18, 22 to Národní divadlo

This little store focuses specifically on clocks and wristwatches from the Czech Republic, Germany and Austria. During my last visit, the oldest clock on site was a Biedermeier-era wall clock from 1820. They also do repairs. Prices start at 650 CZK.
CASH ONLY

Starožitnosti pod Kinskou

LOOK FOR: **Paintings, Prints, Furniture, & Light Fixtures**
Náměstí Kinských 7, Prague 5, Smíchov (Map B)
www.antique-shop.cz
TEL 257 311 245
HOURS Mon–Fri: 10:00–18:00; Sat 10:00–16:00
METRO Anděl ●
TRAM 6, 9, 12, 20 to Švandovo divadlo

An old favorite of mine, this shop has a very large and

PORCELAIN BUST OF T.G. MASARYK
(PHOTO BY STUART ISETT, 2006)

1907 HUNTING CHAIR WITH HAND-CARVED RELIEF
OF ST. HUBERTUS (PHOTO BY STUART ISETT, 2006)

interesting collection of paintings and prints, and this is the primary reason I visit. My favorite purchase to date is a stately portrait of a cow, in oil, that now hangs above the fireplace in my country house. They often also have very interesting pieces of furniture; a friend of mine found a late 19th / early 20th-century set of hunting furniture with a hand-carved relief portrait of St. Hubertus (patron saint of the hunt) on the back of one of the chairs that reaches a breathtaking level of sculptural brilliance. Additionally, their lighting fixtures – table lamps in particular – are often very good.

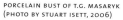

Starožitnosti Ungelt

LOOK FOR: **Glass, Ceramics, Jewelry, & Silver**

Týn 1, Prague 1, Staré Město (Map A)

www.antiqueungelt.cz
TEL 224 895 454
HOURS Daily: 10:00–18:00
METRO Staroměstská ●
or Můstek ● ○
TRAM 17, 18 to Staroměstská

This shop is undeniably expensive, but they do carry very interesting collections of glass, jewelry (including garnets, diamonds, and enamel work), ceramics, and furniture. If you're interested in quality antiques, you should definitely stop in to check out the store – even if it's beyond your budget – as there are always great pieces to see. On my most recent visit I saw a wonderful moldavite (see p. 120) bracelet from the 1850s that was particularly unusual, as this stone was not often used to make jewelry at that time.

(see p. 120)

Vetešnictví

LOOK FOR: **Uniforms, Costume Jewelry & Oddities**

Vítězná 16, Prague 1, Malá Strana (Map B)
TEL 257 310 611
HOURS Mon–Fri: 10:00–17:00; Sat: 10:00–12:00
TRAM 6, 9, 12, 20, 22 to Újezd

Like Bazar Antik (see p. 81), Vetešnictví is a place where you'll need more patience than money as you sift through piles of junk in search of that one special find. They have an excellent collection of Czech military memorabilia, as well as costume jewelry, ceramics, glass, old coins, and vintage toys. The atmosphere is fun and the prices are fair (and always negotiable). Whenever I visit, I always seem to find an item or two that I simply can't leave behind.
CASH ONLY

(see p. 81)

SHOPPING

Czech Auction Houses

In addition to the numerous antique stores I have mentioned, Prague also has several auction houses. If you happen to be in town during a preview or auction, why not add it to your agenda, as there is always something interesting to see.

Cohn Auction – great for furniture, focused primarily on the 20th century. www.cohnauction.cz

Dorotheum – always interesting, great for paintings, prints, furniture, glass, ceramics and jewelry (see p. 83). www.dorotheum.com

Meissner-Neumann – has interesting things and some of them are not too expensive. Great for paintings, prints, silver, glass, ceramics and jewelry. www.aukce-neumann.cz

Sýpka – always interesting and less expensive than the Dorotheum. Great for applied arts, glass, ceramics, small pieces of furniture and antique toys. www.sypka.cz

ART+
This website features a database of auction results – if you're curious what a František Kupka oil painting is currently selling for, they will know. Most of the local auction houses are listed here, and there's also an auction calendar. www.artplus.cz/en/

All websites have an English option.

Slightly Further Afield

Bazar P & J
LOOK FOR: Ceramics, Costume Jewelry, Glassware & Novelties
Anny Letenské 2, Prague 2, Vinohrady (Map E)
www.bazarpj.cz
TEL 224 250 172, 774 576 777
HOURS Mon–Fri: 10:00–18:00
METRO Náměstí Míru ●
TRAM 4, 10, 16, 22 to Náměstí Míru or 11 to Italská
TRAVEL TIME 10 min.

I'm going to let you in on a little secret: this is my all-time favorite shopping haunt for vintage items in Prague. I love sifting through the piles of merchandise here in search of a fabulous find – and there always seems to be one! You'll need more patience than money in your treasure hunt here, but the atmosphere is fun and well organized, and the prices are low. I've had very good luck with costume jewelry and novelties

here, but I encourage you to check out the picture gallery on their website so you can see the full range of purchasing possibilities at this little gem of a shop.
CASH ONLY

Galerie 22
LOOK FOR: Furniture, Lighting & Paintings
Husitská 22, Prague 3, Žižkov
www.galerie22.com
TEL 222 717 633, 602 343 075
HOURS Mon–Fri: 10:00–18:00: Sat & Sun: by appointment
Take a taxi – trust me!
TRAVEL TIME 5 min.

Furniture, paintings, chandeliers, and other decorative art objects from the 18th, 19th, and 20th centuries can be found at this excellent – and expensive – antique store, but their main focus is on the Art Deco period. Everything here is fully restored, and the pieces on offer tend to be very interesting. Worldwide shipping is available, and they also offer restoration services.

Starožitný nábytek Josef Liška
LOOK FOR: Chandeliers, Lighting & Furniture
Vyšehradská 33, Prague 2, Nové Město (Map C)
www.antikliska.byl.cz
TEL 224 919 053
HOURS Mon–Fri: 10:00–18:00
METRO Karlovo náměstí ●
then Tram 18, 24 to Botanická zahrada
TRAVEL TIME 10–15 min.

Located at the far end of a rather crummy courtyard, the entrance to this shop is anything but inviting, but

COMMEMORATIVE POSTCARD FOR PRAGUE JUBILEE 1908, FEATURING A PORTRAIT OF EMPEROR FRANZ JOSEF (ILLUSTRATION BY KOLOMAN MOSER)

the items they carry make it well worth seeking out. They offer lots of interesting furniture and light fixtures, including an extensive collection of chandeliers, as well as miscellaneous small items. This shop is on my regular hit list, and happens to be where I bought my very first antique in Prague, a light fixture that hangs from the ceiling of my bedroom. Hand-painted with a Bohemian floral motif, it remains one of my all-time favorite finds. In addition, I've bought everything from coffee tables and ceramic canister sets for my kitchen to antlers for the entranceway of my country house at this fun establishment.

CASH ONLY

Further Afield

▪ ▪ ▪ ▪ ▪ ▪ ▪ ▪ ▪ ▪ ▪ ▪ ▪ ▪
Buštěhrad

Buštěhrad (near Kladno)
www.bustehradantik.cz
TEL 602 335 834, 608 967 157
HOURS Fri: 06:00–14: 00;
Sat: 06:00–12:00 (second and fourth weekend of each month)
ENTRANCE FEE 20 CZK
PARKING 30 CZK
TRAVEL TIME 30 min.

A thirty-minute drive from the center of town, this is the granddaddy of flea markets in Prague. It's only open on the second and fourth Friday/Saturday of each month, so definitely check their website or have your concierge call before making the trek. You'll find everything at this outdoor market, from knickknacks

to full bedroom suites. All prices are negotiable, so don't be shy about demanding a better one. The market is cash only, and as there is no bank machine close by, be sure to bring enough cash to do a little damage, because there's always something fun and worthy of buying. Try to bring smaller banknotes (100 CZK, 200 CZK, 500 CZK) if possible, as it's difficult to negotiate if you only have large bills. Also, you should try to go on Friday, before the selection of great stuff dwindles over the weekend; indeed, if you're a true die-hard, you'll want to get there by 07:00, while the vendors are still setting up, so you'll be assured of first dibs.

CASH ONLY

ANTIKVARIÁTS

An *antikvariát* is a specific type of antique store that specializes in all things paper-related. In addition to old books, posters and maps, many *antikvariáts* located throughout Prague also feature pick-boxes filled with postcards, banknotes, stamps, and the like – a lovely tradition that has long since disappeared from similar shops abroad.

▪ ▪ ▪ ▪ ▪ ▪ ▪ ▪ ▪ ▪ ▪ ▪ ▪ ▪
Alfafila

LOOK FOR: Stamps & Postcards
Václavské náměstí 28, pasáž U Stýblů (Alfa), Prague 1, Nové Město (Map C)
www.alfafila.cz
TEL 224 235 457
HOURS Mon–Fri: 11:00–18:00; Sat: 11:00–16:00
METRO Můstek ● ●
TRAM 3, 9, 14, 24 to Václavské náměstí

FIRST-ISSUE ENVELOPES, 1946 (top) & 1957 (bottom)

Stamps, postcards, bank notes, and coins are primarily what you'll find at this little hole-in-the-wall shop. If you don't mind weeding through extensive books and boxes (organized by theme), you're bound to find a treasure or two. No English is spoken, but the owner usually manages to figure out what you're interested in and will point you in the right direction. Also, don't be surprised if he offers you a shot of *slivovice* (see p. 184)! This is one of my regular haunts, and I have yet to walk out of the door without buying something; with prices starting at 2 CZK, it's not hard to justify the expenditure.
CASH ONLY

NOTE: This store can also be entered from the Světozor *pasáž* off Vodičkova (see p. 71).

(see p. 184)! ... (see p. 71).

Antikvariát Aurora
LOOK FOR: **Books, Movie Posters & Records**
Spálená 53, Prague 1, Nové Město (Map C)
www.knihkupectvipraha1.cz | www.gramofonove-desky.cz
TEL 222 362 756, 720 498 270
HOURS Mon–Fri: 8:30–18:30; Sat: 10:00–16:00
METRO Můstek ● ● or Národní třída ●
TRAM 6, 9, 18, 22 to Národní třída

This is an amazing *antikvariát* that I've only recently become aware of. They have a large and varied assortment of items, and everything is very well organized and merchandised. In addition to books, they also have extensive collections of vintage records and movie posters. The shop is located in the

back of an arcade – before heading in, be sure to check out the arcade windows, as they are stocked with many of the best items (including an impressive pop-up book collection).

Antikvariát Karel Křenek
LOOK FOR: **Maps, Books & Prints**
Národní 20, Prague 1, Nové Město (Map C)
www.karelkrenek.com
TEL 222 314 734
HOURS Mon–Fri: 11:00–18:00
METRO Národní třída ●
TRAM 6, 9, 18, 22 to Národní třída

This lovely little shop has books and maps dating back to the 1500s, and on my last visit, two items really captured my interest. The first was a Russian book of folk tales from the late 19th / early 20th century illustrated by Ivan Bilibin (think Walter Crane with a Russian flair and sensibility). The second item was a collection of hand-painted prayer books from the 1700s that were as beautiful as they were unusual. If you're interested in folklore and folk art, this store is definitely up your alley, but be forewarned – there are no bargains to be found here.

Antikvariát Galerie Můstek
LOOK FOR: **Maps, Botanical Prints & Books**
Národní 40/34 (Palác Adria), Prague 1, Nové Město (Map C)
TEL 224 949 587
HOURS Mon–Fri: 10:00–19:00; Sat: 10:00–14:00; Sun: 14:00–18:00
METRO Můstek ● ● or Národní třída ●

ADRIA PALACE, 1940

This store features maps dating back to the 17th century, as well as an excellent selection of copperplate engravings and lithographs, including botanical and zoological books. If you do visit this store, be sure to take note of the fantastic Rondo-Cubist building in which it's located (Adria Palace – see photo above).

Antikvariát U Zlaté číše
LOOK FOR: **Books, Advertisements & Records**
Nerudova 16, Prague 1, Malá Strana (Map B)
www.antikvariatnerudova.cz
TEL 257 531 393
HOURS Mon–Fri: 10:00–12:00 & 13:00–18:00; Sat & Sun: 11:00–18:00
METRO Malostranská ●
TRAM 12, 20, 22 to Malostranské náměstí

This is a terrific store that I've only recently begun to patronize. The assortment of items for sale here is large and varied, so although you'll definitely need a bit of time to sort through it all, you might just happen upon a great find! The shop assistants here are most helpful, which, it must be said, is not the norm in most *antikvariáts*.

SHOPPING

89

DANCERS (2006), BY DANIEL PITÍN (OIL ON CANVAS)
(COURTESY OF HUNT KASTNER GALLERY)

ART GALLERIES

Although I'm a designer of fine crystal, I am by no means an art expert. However, I do enjoy visiting art galleries, and Prague has several good ones – I've listed two that I think are noteworthy below.

For more on Prague's contemporary art scene, see the interview with Camille Hunt, owner of Hunt Kastner Artworks, at right.

- - - - - - - - - - - - - -
Galerie U Betlémské kaple
Betlémské náměstí 8, Prague 1, Staré Město (Map C)
www.galerieubetlemske kaple.cz
TEL 222 220 689
HOURS Daily: 10:00–18:00
METRO Můstek ● ○
or Národní třída ○

This gallery focuses exclusively on works on paper, and the artists are primarily Czech, from the late 19th / early 20th century through the end of the First Republic in 1938. Recent shows have

included work by Josef Lada, Vojtěch Preissig (a student of Alfons Mucha), as well as Mucha himself. The prices range from a few thousand crowns on up. They also have antiques in the basement, mostly furniture and lamps from the 1920s and 1930s.

Slightly Further Afield

- - - - - - - - - - - - - -
Hunt Kastner Artworks
Kamenická 22, Prague 7, Holešovice (Map F)
www.huntkastner.com
TEL 222 969 887
HOURS Tue–Fri: 13:00–18:00; Sat: 14:00–18:00
METRO Vltavská ●
TRAM 1, 8, 15, 25, 26 to Kamenická
TRAVEL TIME 15–20 min.

This gallery focuses exclusively on contemporary Czech art. They represent several highly regarded young artists, including Josef Bolf, who is my own favorite Czech painter. Media include

Interview with Camille Hunt: The Contemporary Art Scene in Prague

For a broader perspective on the contemporary art scene here, I spoke with Camille Hunt, the owner of Hunt Kastner Artworks – as she is a true expert.

Karen: How would you describe the art market in Prague?

Camille: It's still very weak even two decades after the fall of communism, and could almost be described as stagnant. There are only a few professional galleries and the city museums and galleries are not very well run. Hence, for my gallery, it is essential that we exhibit abroad.

Karen: What media are most popular here? What artists are on the rise?

Camille: The local market is focused almost exclusively on painting, and installation work is quite popular. Photography, oddly, is not of great interest to Czechs, even though they have a long history in this medium. As for who is hot, there are several Czech artists worth mentioning.

- Ján Mančuška (installation & video)
- Kateřina Šedá (installation)
- Eva Koťátková (installation & drawing)
- Dominik Lang (installation)
- Daniel Pitín (painting)

90

Karen: How successful has Prague been in terms of fostering a local scene?

Camille: The Ministry of Culture supports the art scene with grants that, at least in our case, enable us to participate in art fairs abroad. The gallery system is essential, and more galleries open each year, which is a very positive sign.

Here are some contemporary art venues to know about, along with comments from Camille. Note that not all of these venues offer artwork for sale.

DOX

Poupětova 1, Prague 7, Holešovice (Map F)
www.dox.cz
TEL 295 568 123
HOURS Mon, Sat & Sun: 10:00–18:00; Wed-Fri: 11:00–18:00
ENTRANCE FEE 180 CZK Adults; 90 CZK Children & Seniors
METRO Nádraží Holešovice ●
TRAM 5, 12, 15 to Ortenovo náměstí
TRAVEL TIME 15–20 min.

Camille says: "I am not a huge fan of their program, and the exhibitions are quite mixed, so definitely check the website first to see if what's being shown is of interest to you. The space, however, is quite interesting."

Rudolfinum

Alšovo nábřeží 12, Prague 1, Staré Město (Map A)
www.galerierudolfinum.cz
TEL 227 059 309
HOURS Tue, Wed, Fri–Sun: 10:00–18:00; Thurs: 10:00–20:00
ENTRANCE FEE 130 CZK Adults; 80 CZK Children & Seniors; 5 and under Free
METRO Staroměstská ●
TRAM 17, 18 to Staroměstská

Camille says: "They usually have very interesting shows."

SVIT

Štefánikova 43a (entrance from the courtyard), Prague 5, Smíchov (Map B)
www.svitpraha.org
TEL 608 422 425
HOURS Wed–Sat: 14:00–19:00; or by appointment
ENTRANCE FREE
METRO Anděl ●
TRAM 6, 9, 12, 20 to Švandovo divadlo or Arbesovo náměstí

Camille says: "Very progressive gallery with interesting Czech artists."

Drdova Gallery

Křížkovského 10, Prague 3, Žižkov (Map E)
www.drdovagallery.com
TEL 777 216 416
HOURS Tue–Fri: 13:00–18:00; Sat: 14:00–18:00 (or by appointment)
ENTRANCE FREE
METRO Jiřího z Poděbrad ●
TRAM 11 to Jiřího z Poděbrad
TRAVEL TIME 15 min.

Camille says: "This is a new gallery, but I am confident it will be very interesting."

Tranzitdisplay

Dittrichova 9, Prague 2, Nové Město (Map C)
www.tranzitdisplay.cz
TEL 222 516 982
HOURS Tue–Sun: 12:00–18:00
ENTRANCE FREE
METRO Karlovo náměstí ●
TRAM 3, 4, 7, 10, 16, 17, 18, 24 to Moráň or Palackého náměstí

Camille says: "This gallery often shows very conceptual work, and is very well known and respected internationally."

Hunt Kastner Artworks

(See entry on facing page)

Camille says: "Of course I must recommend my own gallery!"

Galerie Langhans

Vodičkova 37, Prague 1, Nové Město (Map C)
www.langhansgalerie.cz
TEL 222 929 337
HOURS Tue–Sun: 12:00–19:00
ENTRANCE FEE 60 CZK Adults; 30 CZK Children & Seniors
METRO Můstek ● ●
TRAMS 3, 9, 14, 24 to Václavské náměstí

Camille says: "This is a good gallery to check out if you're interested in photography."

Futura: Karlin Studios

Křižíkova 34, Prague 8, Karlín
www.futuraproject.cz
TEL 734 244 581
HOURS Wed–Sun: 12:00–18:00
ENTRANCE FREE
METRO Křižíkova ●
TRAM 8, 24 to Křižíkova
TRAVEL TIME 10–15 min

Camille says: "This space combines a gallery with artist studios."

oil, acrylic, prints and photography. Works on paper and photographs range from 5,000 CZK to 50,000 CZK, while paintings range from 30,000 CZK to 500,000 CZK. Camille Hunt, one of the owners and founders of the gallery, is a native of Toronto and also a long-term expatriate like me. To help put some of the contemporary Czech work in perspective, I'd recommend visiting this gallery in combination with the Veletržní palác, the National Gallery's collection for 19th, 20th and 21st-century art (see p. 60).

ART SUPPLIES

The Czech people are true lovers of the arts, so it's no surprise that Prague has lots of great art supply stores. If you're creatively inclined, here are some good shops that happen to be located within one block from each other....

■ ■ ■ ■ ■ ■ ■ ■ ■ ■ ■

Altamira
Jilská 2, Prague 1,
Staré Město (Map C)
www.vytvarnepotreby.cz
TEL 224 219 950
HOURS Mon–Fri: 9:00–19:00;
Sat: 10:00–17:00
METRO Národní třída ●
TRAM 6, 9, 18, 22 to Národní třída

If you're mostly focused on crafts and hobbies, this is probably the best place to start, as you'll find materials for candle-making, batik, ceramics, decoupage, glass painting, beading, and so on. They also have another store around the corner (at Skořepka 1) that is focused on professional art supplies such as paints, engraving materials, papers, canvases, easels, stretchers, brushes, portfolios and the like.

■ ■ ■ ■ ■ ■ ■ ■ ■ ■ ■

Zlatá loď
Národní 37, Prague 1, Staré Město (in the Platýz *pasáž*) (Map C)
www.zlatalod.cz
TEL 222 220 174

HOURS Mon–Fri: 09:00–19:00; Sat: 10:00–17:00
METRO Národní třída ●
TRAM 6, 9, 18, 22 to Národní třída

You never know when inspiration will strike – or when you'll need to keep the kids occupied with an art project. In either case, this store can supply you with materials for all your artistic needs. Located in the heart of downtown in the same passageway as Kava Kava Kava (a local coffee café that is much better marked than this store), Zlatá loď has an excellent selection of art supplies, and you should be able to find just about anything you need to realize your vision.

BOOKS

Czechs love – and often collect – books. This is not surprising, given the number of great Czech authors and illustrators who have become famous over the years, as well as the exceptional quality of Czech print houses. Most noteworthy, for me, are their architecture and children's books, which you can find at several of the bookshops listed below.

■ ■ ■ ■ ■ ■ ■ ■ ■ ■ ■

Amadito & Friends
Lesnická 6, Prague 5,
Smíchov
www.amadito.com
TEL 257 222 257
HOURS Mon: 09:00–13:00;
Tue–Fri: 09:00–18:00; Sat:
10:00–13:00
METRO Anděl ●
TRAM 4, 7, 10, 14, 16 to Zborovská; 6, 9, 12, 20 to Arbesovo náměstí

ARTMAP!

Planning to check out the local art scene? Check out the ArtMap website (*www.artmap. cz*), which is a great free resource for finding out what exhibitions are currently taking place. They also publish a paper map that is updated six times per year and is available in galleries, museums, and stores throughout the city (including ARTĚL – see p. 116)

Amadito & Friends is an international children's book store, and just visiting this shop is a worthwhile experience in itself: the space is beautifully designed and thoughtfully organized, with a lively yet calming atmosphere – perfect for kids. They offer an excellent selection of books and games in English, French and German for children ages 0-14, as well as original works of art designed for children by local artists. My friend Kate and her kids love the cozy reading and play area, where parents can browse books and drink tea. They host regular story times, author readings, and art workshops featuring oil painting, origami and more. Visit their website for a schedule of events!

KOH-I-NOOR COLORED PENCILS (PHOTO COURTESY OF KOH-I-NOOR)

Koh-i-noor

The České Budějovice-based Koh-i-noor company has been producing high quality art supplies since 1790, including water-soluble colored pencils, graphite pencils, chalks, and paints. In addition to their standard offerings, they also make beautifully packaged gift sets. You can find their products at the art supply stores listed on the facing page, as well as at Hračky (see p. 136) and yes, even ARTĚL (see p. 116). Some department stores also carry the line, usually in the paper section, but their offerings tend to be much more limited.

www.koh-i-noor.cz

■ ■ ■ ■ ■ ■ ■ ■ ■ ■ ■ ■ ■ ■

Ars Pragensis

Malostranské náměstí 27, Prague 1, Malá Strana (Map B)
TEL 257 532 093
HOURS Mon–Fri: 12:00–17:00
METRO Malostranská ●
TRAM 12, 20, 22 to Malostranské náměstí

A great little bookstore in the heart of Malá Strana, Ars Pragensis focuses exclusively on books related to the Czech Republic, including history, architecture and even fairytales translated into other languages. The store also offers a well-edited collection of black-and-white vintage postcard reproductions, most of them Prague-related, as well as a fun selection of writing tools from Koh-i-noor, making it the perfect stop before heading off to a local café for a postcard writing session.

CZECHS ENJOYING A GOOD READ, 1953

Czech Literature Translated Into English

Jaroslav Hašek
The Good Soldier Švejk, Penguin, 1923
By precisely following every order he is given without ever accomplishing anything, Švejk reveals the ludicrous (and hilarious) bureaucracy of war.

Bohumil Hrabal
Closely Watched Trains, Abacus, 1966
Set in Nazi-occupied Czechoslovakia during WWII, this coming-of-age story centers on Miloš Hrma, a young man apprenticing as a signalman at a railway station. This is also a classic Czech film (see p. 196).

I Served the King of England, Vintage International, 1971
The life and ambitions of this novel's protagonist (a waiter-turned-millionaire-turned-prisoner) provide unique insight into the tumultuous history of the Czech nation. This was also recently made into a film (see p. 197).

Milan Kundera
The Joke, Harper, 1967
Ludvik, a bright university student in early 1950s Czechoslovakia, is an active supporter of the country's new Communist regime. Intending to be funny, he sends a postcard to his girlfriend criticizing the government and soon finds his world has turned on him.

The Unbearable Lightness of Being, Harper, 1984
This classic book examines the lives of Czech artists and intellectuals following the Prague Spring political reforms of 1968.

Big Ben Bookshop
Malá Štupartská 5, Prague 1, Staré Město (Map A)
www.bigbenbookshop.com
TEL 224 826 565
HOURS Mon–Fri: 09:30–20:00; Sat: 10:00–20:00; Sun: 11:00–18:00
METRO Náměstí Republiky ●
TRAM 5, 8, 14, 26 to Náměstí Republiky

This English language bookstore has the best selection of guidebooks in town. They also have a wide selection of current fiction and non-fiction best sellers.

Knihkupectví Academia
Václavské náměstí 34, Prague 1, Nové Město (Map C)
www.academia.cz
TEL 221 403 840
HOURS Mon–Fri: 09:00–20:00; Sat: 09:30–19:00; Sun: 9:30-18:00
METRO Muzeum ● ●
or Můstek ● ●
TRAM 3, 9, 14, 24 to Václavské náměstí

Children's Books

Lucie Seifertová
Mysterious Prague
(Slovart, 2003)
This is a wonderfully fun pop-up book that explains the history of Prague.

Josef Lada
Mikeš the Cat
(Albatros, 1936)
A fairy tale made up of four stories about a speaking cat, Mikeš, and his unbelievable adventures with his friends – a pig named Pašík and a goat named Bobeš.

Zdeněk Miler
How Come Little Mole has Trousers (Baset, 1956)
The first book featuring Krtek, the Czech Republic's most famous and beloved animated character (see p. 137 for more information on Krtek's history).

Olga Štruncová (Illustrations by Helena Zmatlíková), *Mother Mouse*, (Albatros, 1961)
A picture book of nursery rhymes with wonderful Bohemian imagery.

PHOTOGRAPHER IN PRAGUE, C. 1930

Maps and books on Prague are the order of the day here, including illustrated coffee table books and Czech children's books translated into English. They also carry lots of interesting postcards, journals, calendars and bookmarks. And as an added bonus, they will also wrap each of your books in paper – a nice old-school touch!

Shakespeare & Sons
U Lužického semináře 10, Prague 1, Malá Strana (Map B)
www.shakes.cz
TEL 257 531 894
HOURS Daily: 11:00–20:00
METRO Malostranská ●
TRAM 12, 20, 22 to Malostranské náměstí

If you're in Malá Strana and looking for the work of a local author translated into English, this is an excellent bet. Shakespeare & Sons carries both new and used titles, and the ambience of the place is wonderfully cozy.

Slightly Further Afield

BenDOX at DOX
Poupětova 1, Prague 7, Holešovice (Map F)
www.dox.cz
TEL 295 568 114, 602 373 874
HOURS Mon, Sat & Sun: 10:00–18:00; Wed–Fri: 11:00–19:00
METRO Nádraží Holešovice ●
TRAM 5, 12, 15 to Ortenovo náměstí
TRAVEL TIME 15–20 min.

BenDOX is a specialized bookstore located in the DOX Centre for Contemporary Art. If you are looking for books on art, architecture and design, including those focused on the Czech Republic, this is the best choice in town. They also have an excellent selection of art-themed coffee table books in English from publishing houses such as Phaidon, Rizzoli, and Thames & Hudson.

CAMERAS

I majored in Fine Art Photography at college, and I also happen to have an extensive vintage camera collection, so I'm somewhat choosy when it comes to camera and photo equipment stores. Here are my two favorites in Prague.

Foto Škoda
Vodičkova 37, Palác Langhans, Prague 1, Nové Město (Map C)
www.fotoskoda.cz
TEL 222 929 029
HOURS Mon–Fri: 09:00–20:00; Sat 10:00–18:00
METRO Můstek ● ○
TRAM 3, 9, 14, 24 to Václavské náměstí

One-stop shopping for all your photography needs: cameras, film (yes, some people still use it!), lenses, cases… You name it, they carry it.

Jan Pazdera

Vodičkova 28, Prague 1,
Nové Město (Map C)
www.fotopazdera.cz
TEL 224 216 197
HOURS Mon–Fri: 10:00–18:00
METRO Můstek ● ●
TRAM 3, 9, 14, 24 to Václavské
náměstí

If you fancy antique cameras, look no further than this store. I usually focus (pardon my pun!) on medium-format cameras that use 120 film, and I particularly like those that were manufactured locally, including brands like Corina, Fex, Folkafex, and Pionýr. The sales staff does not speak English, but with a little patience and perhaps your very best mime performance *ever*, you'll get to see what you want.

CERAMICIST PAINTING BOHEMIAN POTTERY, C. 1941

CAMERAS MADE IN CZECHOSLOVAKIA (top to bottom): PIONYR, C. 1948–1967; CORINA (THE CZECHOSLOVAKIAN EQUIVALENT OF THE FAMED RUSSIAN LOMO), C. 1963–1980s; FLEXARET, C. 1940s

CERAMICS & PORCELAIN

In addition to its world-renowned crystal glassware, the Czech Republic is also known for its high-quality ceramics and porcelain. Although the vast majority is designed on a white background, you may also come upon items with a black background, my personal favorite.

Tupesy Lidová keramika

Havelská 21, Prague 1,
Staré Město (Map C)
TEL 224 214 176
HOURS Daily: 10:00–18:00
METRO Můstek ● ●

This store features hand-made ceramics from Southern Moravia. The style is reminiscent of the kind of Italian ceramics you often see today, but with a unique feeling of Czech folklore and a decorative aesthetic that traces back to the Swiss Protestants who relocated to this region in the first half of the 16th

century. This store has been around for years and carries a wide selection of pieces, many of which make great gifts. Prices range from 70 CZK to 10,000 CZK.

Slightly Further Afield

Dům porcelánu

Jugoslávská 16, Prague 2,
Vinohrady (Map E)
www.dumporcelanu.cz
TEL 221 505 320
HOURS Mon–Fri: 09:00–19:00; Sat: 9:00–17:00;
Sun: 14:00–17:00
METRO Náměstí Míru ●
or I. P. Pavlova ●
TRAM 4, 6, 10, 16, 22, 11 to
I. P. Pavlova
TRAVEL TIME 10–15 min.

If you're interested in Czech porcelain, this is definitely the best place in town. The "blue onion" design made by Český porcelán is the quintessential Czech porcelain motif, its design originating from the first half of the 17th century. It is now back in vogue:

Meissen (the German porcelain firm) produces a version that is about three times more expensive than what you'll find here, and local ultra-hip designer Maxim Velčovský has applied the motif to a fabulous bust of Lenin, as well as the work-boots shown in the photo on p. 106. When I visited Dům porcelánu recently, they also had a great little cow figurine with the blue onion motif for 500 CZK, which in the right setting could definitely be seen as very modern and hip. I was also taken with the work of Haas & Czjzek, another Czech porcelain manufacturer – specifically the decorative pieces with gold ornamental work that are reminiscent of the famous German brand KPM – and they also carry lovely porcelain by Thun and Royal Dux Bohemia. This store is not exactly in the center of town, but it's certainly easily accessible by both metro and tram. Alternatively, hop in a taxi; it will be a very short ride.

GOČÁR CHANDELIER (1913), AVAILABLE AT MODERNISTA (SEE P. 98)

CHANDELIERS & LIGHTING

The excellent reputation enjoyed by Czech crystal glassware also extends to the beautiful chandeliers and light fixtures made here, which are often surprisingly affordable. If you're looking for lighting, here are a few shops that are definitely worth knowing about.

NOTE: Unless stated otherwise, all of the shops listed in this section offer worldwide shipping.

Antikva Ing. Bürger

Betlémské náměstí 8, Prague 1, Staré Město (in courtyard) (Map C)
TEL 602 315 729
HOURS Mon–Sat: 10:00–13:00 & 14:00–18:00
METRO Můstek ● ● or Národní třída ●

If antique lighting fixtures such as chandeliers and lamps are on your shopping agenda, then definitely add this shop to your itinerary. I have not personally bought anything here yet, but I do enjoy stopping in, as they always seem to have an interesting and varied collection.

NO SHIPPING

Art Deco Starožitnosti

Pštrossova 35, Prague 1, Nové Město (Map C)
www.art-deco.cz
TEL 224 931 718
HOURS Mon–Fri: 11:00–18:00
METRO Národní třída ●
TRAM 6, 9, 18, 22 to Národní divadlo

This shop consistently has the most varied and interesting collection of light fixtures in town. I purchased a wonderful Art Deco chandelier here a few years ago; it used to hang in the flagship ARTĚL store (see p. 116) but now graces my living room! They also offer restoration services.

Material Glass

(see p. 118)

In addition to its extensive glassware collection, Material carries a very good selection of contemporary lighting fixtures with clean designs that are anything but fussy. Prices range from 7,000 CZK for wall scones to 500,000 CZK for a very large chandelier.

Modernista

Celetná 12, Prague 1, Staré Město (in shopping arcade) (Map A)
www.modernista.cz
TEL 224 241 300
HOURS Daily: 11:00–19:00
METRO Můstek ● ●

Located in a shopping arcade off one of Prague's busiest streets, Modernista sells reproductions of original designs by prominent Czech Cubist designers like Pavel Janák, Vlastislav Hofman and Josef Gočár. The collection includes a nice reproduction of a really fierce chandelier by Gočár (69,000 CZK), the same architect that designed the interior and chandeliers of the Grand Café Orient at the House of the Black Madonna (see p. 169). In addition to chandeliers, they also offer Cubist table lamps and Functionalist table and floor lamps.

Preciosa

Jáchymova 2, Prague 1, Staré Město (Map A)
www.preciosa.com
TEL 222 247 550
HOURS Mon–Fri: 10:00–19:00; Sat: 10:00–17:00
METRO Staroměstská ●
TRAM 17, 18 to Staroměstská

Preciosa is currently the dominant manufacturer for Czech chandelier production. Prices range from 1,300 CZK for wall scones to 190,000 CZK for a very large chandelier. Custom projects are also possible, and it's quite likely that you'll already have seen their work, since their chandeliers hang in hotels and cultural venues throughout the world, including the Prague Castle and Russia's Bolshoi Theatre. If you're in the market for a new chandelier that is traditional in style, this is definitely an excellent starting point. The sales staff is neither especially friendly nor helpful, but if you seem to be a serious customer, I'm certain they can rise to the occasion.

ST. VOL

Valentinská 11, Prague 1, Staré Město (Map A)
www.stvol.eu
TEL 224 814 099
HOURS Mon-Fri: 10:00–18:00; Sat & Sun: 11:00–17:00
METRO Staroměstská ●
TRAM 17, 18 to Staroměstská

If you're a fan of Bořek Šípek, currently one of the most famous contemporary Czech designers, then you won't want to miss stopping in at ST. VOL, which carries a great many contemporary chandeliers and lighting fixtures that can best be described as colorful, whimsical, and unusual. Prices range from 3,000 CZK for a simple piece to 500,000 CZK for a very large and complex

CHANDELIERS WITH PANTOMIME PRESENTER, 1959
(SOURCE: ČTK / CZECH NEWS AGENCY)

chandelier. Additionally, they offer various items for the home made from glass, porcelain and metal, as well as a few pieces of jewelry.

CHOCOLATE

Czechs love chocolate – just visit a grocery store and you will be shocked to see the disproportionately large amount of shelf space devoted to it. Orion is the most venerable local manufacturer, having been established in 1896, and its products make up over half of the items listed in the *Guide to Czech Chocolate & Candy* that appears in the box at right. That being said, *most* Czech chocolate is nothing very special, so I've listed a single Belgian chocolate store below, which has delicious "luxury" products and a great location.

■ ■ ■ ■ ■ ■ ■ ■ ■ ■ ■ ■ ■ ■

Gold Pralines
Rybná 2, Prague 1, Nové Město (Map A)
www.goldpralines.cz
TEL 222 316 227
HOURS Daily: 09:00–20:00
METRO Náměstí Republiky ●
TRAM 5, 8, 14, 26 to Náměstí Republiky

This small shop happens to make a delicious little dark chocolate truffle filled with Becherovka, a local herbal liqueur (see p. 184), which is a standout among their many offerings and definitely worthy of air travel. If you visit, you'll be just a hop, skip, and half a jump away from the flagship ARTĚL store (see p. 116) – stop in and say hello!

A Guide to Czech Chocolate & Candy

Antiperle (introduced in 1960): The Czechs' minty answer to Tic-Tacs. The retro-fabulous packaging alone makes this a worthy purchase, but the mints are quite tasty, too.

Banány v Čokoládě (introduced c. 1920): Featuring banana-flavored marshmallow mousse dipped in dark chocolate, this candy bar is a perennial favorite among Czechs.

GRANKO BOX, C. 1974.

Fidorka (introduced in 1830): A two-tiered, puck-shaped wafer cookie, stuffed with cream filling and covered in chocolate – no wonder it's a popular favorite. Available in several flavors (each with a different colored wrapper), but coconut is my personal favorite.

BLUE – milk cholocate with coconut filling

BROWN – dark cholocate with chocolate filling

GREEN – milk chocolate with hazelnut filling

RED – dark chocolate with hazelnut filling

YELLOW – white chocolate with white chocolate filling

Granko (introduced in 1979): Just like *Ovaltine* – meant to be mixed with milk and served hot, but the crunchy granules can also also be eaten right out of the box.

Hašlerky (introduced in 1927): Licorice-flavored hard candy.

Kaštany Ledové (introduced in 1966): An affordable chocolate truffle bar – delicous!

Kočičí Jazýčky ("Cat's Tongues" – introduced c. 1900): Cheap, mediocre chocolate, but worth getting just for the fabulous kittens on the box!

KOČIČÍ JAZÝČKY BOX

A Guide to Czech Chocolate & Candy

(continued)

KOFILA CHOCOLATE BAR LABEL, 1962. THE WRAPPER WAS ORIGINALLY DESIGNED IN 1921 AND HAS SURVIVED ALMOST UNCHANGED TO THIS DAY.

Kofila (introduced in 1923): Chocolate truffle bar with coffee-flavored mousse filling.

Koko (introduced in 1986): A drier version of a *Mounds* bar.

Křupky velké arašídové (introduced in 1972): These peanut-flavored *Cheez Doodles* are strangely addictive. You've been warned...

Lentilky (introduced in 1907): Just like *M&Ms* or *Smarties*.

Lion (introduced in 1977): This delightfully crunchy candy bar is neither vintage nor Czech (it's made by Nestlé), but I had to include it here regardless. Consisting of a filled wafer cookie, puffed cereal (think *Rice Krispies*) and caramel, all smothered in chocolate, it's easily the most delicious of the lot.

Margot (introduced c. 1970): "If you like piña coladas..." you'll probably like this, as it's basically a dense coconut-pinapple flavored energy bar covered in chocolate.

Milena (introduced in 1957): A chocolate truffle bar with with a rum / liqueur-flavored mousse filling.

Pedro (introduced in 1968): Sort of like *Bazooka* bubble gum, but with temporary tattoos inside instead of comics.

Piknik (introduced in 1967): Condensed milk in a tube! What more do you need to know? Kids love this straight from the tube, and it can also be added to coffee.

Piškoty (introduced in 1840): These teething biscuits have a form and texture similar to *Nilla Wafers*, with a blander flavor. Equally beloved by Czech children and dogs!

Sójové řezy (introduced c. 1970): This one is tough to describe. The texture is somewhere between halva and compressed stale cornbread, with a *soupçon* of coconut essence... definitely not for everyone, but some Czechs swear by it.

Studentská pečeť (introduced in 1975): A *Cadbury*-ish chocolate bar with raisins, peanuts and candied fruit – dark chocolate is my favorite.

Tatranky (introduced in 1945): A six(!)-layer wafer cookie bar with a creamy cholocate filling and chocolate coating on the sides. This is the quintessential Czech treat, a staple of childhood here for decades.

CHRISTMAS ORNAMENTS

Czechs have a long history of making Christmas ornaments. Sadly, today it seems that the bulk of this work is done for export, and it's difficult to find interesting new pieces for purchase here in Prague. However, I've listed two of the stores where I've consistently had good luck. I also encourage you to look for ornaments in antique stores and bazaars (see p. 80–87), as that's where I often pick up some of my most cherished finds.

- - - - - - - - - - - - - - -

Dana Bohemia
Národní 43, Prague 1, Staré Město (Map C)
www.danabohemia.cz
TEL 224 214 655
HOURS Mon-Sat: 09:00–19:00; Sun: 11:00–18:00
METRO Můstek ● ● or Národní třída ●

While this store also sells ceramics, porcelain and chandeliers, I tend to come here mainly for their Christmas ornaments, stopping in throughout the year to check out their inventory, which is always prominently displayed at the counter. I should

GINGERBREAD COOKIES CHRISTMAS, 2006 (MADE BY KATEŘINA PAVLITOVÁ, AS A GIFT TO THE AUTHOR)

GINGERBREAD PRODUCTION, 1990

TRADITIONAL HAND-PRINTED TEXTILE, 1939 (SOURCE: EVA MAGAZINE)

PAINTING EASTER EGGS IN A BOHEMIAN VILLAGE, 1940

mention that if you're looking for handcrafted ornaments made from natural materials, this shop is *not* for you. What you will find here are wonderfully colorful and glittering ornaments in all shapes and sizes ranging from classic ball shapes to my personal favorite, the Christmas hedgehog! Prices start at 30 CZK per ornament.

NOTE: You will need to enter by walking through the passageway.

- - - - - - - - - - - - - - -
Manufaktura
Melantrichova 17 and Železná 3a, Prague 1, Staré Město (Map A)
www.manufaktura.cz
TEL 221 632 411
HOURS Sun–Thurs: 10:00–20:00; Fri & Sat: 10:00–21:30
METRO Můstek ● ●

You'll see this chain of stores throughout downtown Prague. They offer a wide range of Czech traditional handicrafts, including old-fashioned Christmas ornaments made from either straw or varnished gingerbread, as well as hand-painted eggs which are used for decoration both at Christmas and Easter.

CZECH HANDICRAFTS

If you're seeking an authentic souvenir from Prague, why not consider a Czech-made handicraft? Some of the best items to look out for are ceramics, textiles, wood toys and Christmas ornaments. You can find these – and more – in the shops listed below.

Czech Glass Beads

Czech glass beads are synonymous with excellent quality and variety. Over the past few years several stores that focus exclusively of the sale of loose beads and beading materials have opened in Prague. The slightly-further-afield Vinohrady neighborhood (10 to 15 minutes from the center of town, see Map E) has a cluster of great bead shops in a very small radius, making it a very convenient destination for the avid bead enthusiast — you can easily visit all of the stores listed below in a morning or afternoon. Prices start at 1 CZK! Happy shopping...and beading!

Koralky
Vinohradská 76, Prague 3, Vinohrady (Map E)
www.koralky.cz
TEL 605 351 573
HOURS Mon—Fri: 10:00—19:00; Sat & Sun: 10:00—18:00
METRO Jiřího z Poděbrad ●
TRAM 11 to Jiřího z Poděbrad

Korallo
Italská 27 (entrance on Mánesova), Prague 2, Vinohrady (Map E)
www.korallo.cz
TEL 223 008 565
HOURS Mon, Tue & Thurs: 11:00—19:00; Wed: 11:00—20:00; Fri: 11:00—18:00
METRO Muzeum ● ● or Náměstí Míru ●
TRAM 11 to Vinohradská tržnice or Italská

Robinson
Blanická 26, Prague 2, Vinohrady (Map E)
www.robinsonbeads.com
TEL 222 515 323
HOURS Mon—Fri: 10:00—18:00; Sat: 10:00—16:00
METRO Náměstí Míru ●
TRAM 11 to Vinohradská tržnice or Italská

Rooya
Italská 13, Prague 2, Vinohrady (Map E)
www.praha.rooya.cz
TEL 773 699 503
HOURS Mon 12:00—18:00; Tue, Thurs & Fri: 10:00—18:00; Wed: 10:00—19:00; Sat: 10:00—16:00
METRO Muzeum ● ● or Náměstí Míru ●
TRAM 11 to Vinohradská tržnice or Italská

MAKING GLASS BEAD NECKLACES AT HOME, 1947
(SOURCE: ČTK / CZECH NEWS AGENCY)

KOTVA, 1983

KOTVA DEPARTMENT STORE GRAND OPENING, 1975
(SOURCE: ČTK / CZECH NEWS AGENCY)

DEPARTMENT STORES

Whether you're a local or a tourist, sometimes you just need a department store; Prague has two that will be sure to satisfy.

■ ■ ■ ■ ■ ■ ■ ■ ■ ■ ■ ■ ■

Kotva

Náměstí Republiky 8, Prague 1, Staré Město (Map A)
www.od-kotva.cz
TEL 224 801 111
HOURS Mon–Fri: 09:00–20:00; Sat: 10:00–19:00; Sun: 10:00–18:00
METRO Náměstí Republiky ●
TRAM 5, 8, 14, 26 to Náměstí Republiky

When Prague was under communism, the Kotva department store, built in 1975, was the chicest in town. Sadly, this is no longer true – and it's not even a real department store anymore. Instead, it is now made of up various independently run kiosks offering everything from cosmetics, costume jewelry and clothing to sporting goods and major appliances. I tend to pop in every now and then to check out the stationery section on the ground floor, which has a good selection of office and school supplies (Europeans always have great plastic folders and binders, so if you are obsessively organized, you'll love it). A kiosk on the third floor offers the most comprehensive selection of Schleich plastic animals and figurines I've ever seen; these toys are surprisingly realistic and extremely well made. Also on this floor is an excellent kitchen supply shop – should you be seeking

■ ■ ■ ■ ■ ■ ■ ■ ■ ■ ■ ■ ■

Botanicus

Ungelt – Týn 3, Prague 1, Staré Město (Map A)
www.botanicus.cz
TEL 234 767 446
HOURS Daily: 10:00–20:00
METRO Náměstí Republiky ●
or Můstek ● ●
TRAM 5, 8, 14, 26 to Náměstí Republiky

Botanicus features organically produced handmade products with exceptional packaging, making it an ideal resource for gift buying. The product range includes soaps, bath oils, shampoos, handmade paper, candles and condiments – all made in the Czech Republic.

■ ■ ■ ■ ■ ■ ■ ■ ■ ■ ■ ■ ■

Manufaktura

See p. 101

In addition to old-fashioned Christmas ornaments and Easter decorations, Manufaktura offers a wide range of Czech traditional handicrafts including wooden toys, printed textiles, embroidered table-cloths, ceramics, kitchen utensils, bath products, sweaters, and rugs. They also offer beautiful packaging, making them a terrific resource for gifts.

locally made cooking tools such as enamelware, poppy seed grinders, dumpling slicers, or uniquely Czech Christmas cookie forms, you will definitely want to take a look. There's also a rather good sewing department on the top floor, and an Albert supermarket can be found in the basement.

▪ ▪ ▪ ▪ ▪ ▪ ▪ ▪ ▪ ▪ ▪ ▪ ▪

Tesco – MY
Národní 26, Prague 1, Nové Město (Map C)
www.itesco.cz
TEL 222 815 111
HOURS Mon–Fri: 07:00–21:00; Sat: 07:00–21:00; Sun: 08:00–20:00
METRO Národní třída ●
TRAM 6, 9, 18, 22 to Národní třída

Tesco is the largest department store in downtown Prague and my personal favorite, as its layout is more logical and better labeled than Kotva's. Here, too, you will find an excellent selection of office and school supplies, as well as cosmetics, clothing, shoes, sporting goods, household items and electronics. In the basement is a Tesco supermarket.

NOTE: In October 2006, the building in which Tesco is housed became a cultural monument, cited as an excellent example of 1970s Communist architecture. You might question my fact checking after seeing the building for yourself; however, I can assure you, it's true. The review committee must have focused on the escalators, which are indeed rather chic.

DESIGN SHOPS

As the owner of a design company – and someone who is, to say the least, passionate about good design – I've spent a lot of time and effort seeking out the best design stores in town. Other than the two ARTĚL shops (see p. 116), which you really shouldn't leave town without visiting, these are the ones to know about....

▪ ▪ ▪ ▪ ▪ ▪ ▪ ▪ ▪ ▪ ▪ ▪ ▪

ARTĚL
(see p. 116)

In addition to the handmade luxury crystal glassware for which ARTĚL is globally renowned, both of the ARTĚL shops carry a wide range of eclectic design items from the Czech Republic, ranging from hard-to-find vintage pieces to cutting-edge work from contemporary designers.

▪ ▪ ▪ ▪ ▪ ▪ ▪ ▪ ▪ ▪ ▪ ▪ ▪

Futurista Universum
Betlémské náměstí 5a, Prague 1, Staré Město (Map C)
www.futurista.cz
TEL 725 128 660
HOURS Daily: 11:00–19:00
METRO Můstek ● ● or Národní třída ●

Futurista Universum focuses exclusively on contemporary Czech design and is one of the best design stores in Prague. They offer a wide selection of glassware, porcelain and jewelry by some of the best Czech designers working today, as well as very cool Prague maps focused on Cubist architecture, Art Nouveau architecture, and the Prague metro. The one

TESCO – MY ESCALATORS, 1980
(PHOTO BY JAROSLAV VEBR)

ARTĚL DESIGN STORE IN MALÁ STRANA
(PHOTO BY FILIP ŠLAPAL, 2010)

downside is that the customer service leaves something to be desired – but this should not deter you from visiting if you are a fan of great design, as many of the items on offer are truly exceptional.

■ ■ ■ ■ ■ ■ ■ ■ ■ ■ ■ ■ ■ ■ ■
HARD DE CORE
(see p. 108)

In addition to the chic clothing, shoes and costume jewelry sold here, this eclectic shop also offers funky tableware and innovative household design items – all created by young Czech designers and produced locally.

■ ■ ■ ■ ■ ■ ■ ■ ■ ■ ■ ■ ■ ■ ■
Kubista
Ovocný trh 19, Prague 1, Staré Město (Map A)
www.kubista.cz
TEL 224 236 378
HOURS Tue–Sun: 10:00–18:30
METRO Náměstí Republiky ●
TRAM 5, 8, 14, 26 to Náměstí Republiky

Located in the ground floor of the Museum of Czech Cubism at the House of the Black Madonna (see p. 58), Kubista sells replicas of original designs by prominent Czech Cubist designers like Pavel Janák, Vlastislav Hofman and Josef Gočár. The offerings include ceramics, furni-

CUBIST BOX WITH LID BY
PAVEL JANÁK (1911)

PORCELAIN WELLIES WITH BLUE ONION MOTIF
(PHOTO BY DAVID A. LAND, 2006)

ture, metalwork, and paper goods, including some very cool Cubist wrapping paper. They also offer an excellent selection of literature related to Czech Cubist painting, architecture and applied arts.

■ ■ ■ ■ ■ ■ ■ ■ ■ ■ ■ ■ ■

Mumray
Náplavní 3, Prague 2,
Nové Město (Map C)
www.mumray.cz
TEL 602 211 052
HOURS Mon–Fri: 11:00–18:00
METRO Karlovo náměstí ●
TRAM 14, 17 to Jiráskovo náměstí

Mumray offers handbags, totes, book bags and "man purses" – all designed and manufactured onsite by the very talented Lucie Michalcová. The design style can best be described as "1960s airline tote bag

Czech 100 Design Icons
(CzechMania, 2005)
This wonderful paperback book by Tereza Bruthansová and Jan Králíček focuses exclusively on 20th-century design in the Czech Republic and includes excellent images and captions in English. It is a fabulous resource for anyone interested in design. You can pick up a copy at Kubista (see p. 105), or simply check out the website: www.czech100.com.

DOLCE VITA MAGAZINE
COVER (COURTESY OF
DOLCE VITA)

Dolce Vita Magazine
Far and away the best local design magazine, Dolce Vita is so hip it hurts. The closest comparison would be Wallpaper. For anyone interested in design, fashion, or interior design, this publication will give you great insight to what is happening in the Czech market today.

meets British schoolboy book bag," for a result that is at once modern and retro-chic. The bags are offered in lots of interesting shapes and fun colors, but – most excitingly – she *also* offers the possibility of creating your own! You choose the style you want and then select your colors, decide on a lining, and even add extra inside pockets if you like; production only takes one week. Prices range from 550 CZK to 1600 CZK.

CASH ONLY

■ ■ ■ ■ ■ ■ ■ ■ ■ ■ ■ ■ ■

Tuzeks
Benediktská 11, Prague 1, Staré Město (Map A)
www.tuzeks.eu
TEL 222 318 319
HOURS Mon–Fri: 10:00–18:00
METRO Náměstí Republiky ●
TRAM 5, 8, 14, 26 to Dlouhá třída

If you love Czech glass from the 1960s, you will definitely want to add this store to your must-hit list. Tuzeks focuses on vintage items from the 1960s and 1970s, ranging from glass vases, ashtrays and figurines to costume jewelry, toys and accessories. The owner has a keen eye for good design and the store is thoughtfully curated. Prices range from 100 CZK to 4,000 CZK.

CASH ONLY

Slightly Further Afield

■ ■ ■ ■ ■ ■ ■ ■ ■ ■ ■ ■ ■

DOX by Qubus
Poupětova 1, Prague 7, Holešovice (Map F)
www.dox.cz | www.qubus.cz
TEL 295 568 114, 608 658 587
HOURS Mon, Sat & Sun: 10:00–18:00; Wed-Fri: 11:00–19:00
METRO Nádraží Holešovice ●
TRAM 5, 12, 15 to Ortenovo náměstí
TRAVEL TIME 15–20 min.

DOX by Qubus focuses on high end contemporary design, with many of the pieces being one-of-a-kind. They offer a wide selection of glassware, porcelain and jewelry by some of the best Czech designers working today, including František Vízner, Maxim Velčovský and Eva Eisler. Although the customer service is rather standoffish, the exceptional quality of the merchandise makes this a worthwhile destination for design lovers. Qubus also has a much smaller shop downtown, offering a more limited selection of similar merchandise, which is worth a stop if you're in the neighborhood (Qubus Design Studio – Rámová 3, Prague 1, Staré Město, Mon–Sat: 11:00–19:00).

FASHION

Although Prague is not particularly well known as a fashion center like Milan or Paris, there are some noteworthy fashion shops here that offer great clothing designed and manufactured in the Czech Republic.

For more on the current fashion scene, see the interview with local fashionista Věra Korandová on p. 112.

A Gift Idea for Your Gay Friend or Lover...

Kostelecké párky
This brand of hot-dogs-in-a-can has the best packaging ever! My friend's father works for the company and assures me that they don't see what could possibly be humorous about this little gem.

THE KOSTELECKÉ PÁRKY PACKAGING DESIGN WAS CREATED IN 1917, WHEN THE COMPANY WAS FOUNDED, AND HAS SURVIVED ALMOST UNCHANGED TO THIS DAY.

Women's Fashion

Boheme

Dušní 8, Prague 1, Staré
Město (Map A)
www.boheme.cz
TEL 224 813 840
HOURS Mon–Fri: 11:00–
19:00; Sat: 11:00–17:00
METRO Staroměstská ●
TRAM 17, 18 to Staroměstská
or 17 to Právnická fakulta

The Boheme brand was
started in Sweden, where
Czech designer Hana
Stocklassová studied for a
year at the University of
Design and Craft in
Gothenburg. In 2002 she
opened her first store in
Prague. The collection now
includes knitwear, sepa-
rates, leather and suede,
with designs that are
classic yet fresh.

E.daniely Gallery

Na struze 1, Prague 1,
Nové Město (Map C)
www.edaniely.cz
TEL 257 324 296
HOURS Mon–Fri: 10:00–
19:00; Sat: 10:00–17:00
METRO Národní třída ●
TRAM 6, 9, 17,18, 21, 22 to
Národní divadlo

Designers Daniela
Flejšarová and Eva
Janoušková have been
working as a team for over
20 years. The store focuses
on locally made clothing
designed for women aged
35 and over, made from
interesting and comfor-
table fabrics that are
perfect for everyday wear.
For spring and summer
they utilize mostly linen,
cotton and jersey, and in
the winter wool is the
primary material. They
also offer a small collection

of hats and accessories.
Prices range from 1,600 CZK
to about 14,000 CZK.

HARD DE CORE

Senovážné nám. 10, Prague 1,
Nové Město (Map A)
www.harddecore.cz |
www.chi-chi.cz
TEL 777 094 421
HOURS Mon–Fri: 11:00–
19:00; Sat: 11:00–17:00
TRAM 3, 9, 14, 24 to
Jindřišská; 3, 5, 14, 24, 26 to
Masarykovo nádraží

If I'm in the mood for one-
stop shopping where I
can find everything from
chic clothing, shoes and
costume jewelry to funky
tableware and innovative
household design items –
all created by young Czech
designers and produced
locally – the HARD DE
CORE gallery, which also
includes the Chi-Chi
clothing boutique, is always
my first stop. Prices for
clothing start at around 750
CZK and go up to 6,500 CZK.
This store is super fun and
absolutely worth a visit,
and the merchandise is
totally unique.

Julius Fashion Shop

Ostrovní 20, Prague 1,
Nové Město (Map C)
www.juliusfashion.com
TEL 731 419 953
HOURS Mon–Fri: 11:00–
19:00; Sat: 11:00–18:00
METRO Národní třída ●
TRAM 6, 9, 18, 21, 22 to
Národní divadlo

This is a great store to
know about if you're
interested in modern Czech
design. Filled with very
fun and totally unique
items, including fashion
for men and women,
costume jewelry, access-

ories, and even some
original works of art, it's
definitely worth a visit
for fashion-conscious
hipsters and contemporary
design aficionados alike.
Prices range from 50 CZK
to around 3,000 CZK.

Klara Nademlynska

Dlouhá 3, Prague 1,
Staré Město (Map A)
www.klaranademlynska.cz
TEL 224 818 769
HOURS Mon–Fri: 10:00–
19:00; Sat: 10:00–18:00
METRO Staroměstská ●
TRAM 17, 18 to Staroměstská

Super-chic high fashion
designed by a local talent
is what you'll find at Klara
Nademlynska. The
proprietress of this very
refined establishment
worked in Paris before
establishing her own brand
in Prague. There's lots of
great stuff here, but if
you're any bigger than a
size 8, you may be out of
luck.

Móda Original

Jungmannova 4, Prague 1,
Staré Město (Map C)
www.originalmoda.com
TEL 222 514 136
HOURS Mon–Fri: 10:00–
18:00; Sat: 10:00–13:00
METRO Můstek ● ● or
Národní třída ●
TRAM 3, 9, 14, 24 to Lazarská
or Vodičkova

This store offers perfect
one-stop shopping for gifts,
as their range of merchandise includes dresses,
blouses, skirts and pants –
all made from natural
fabrics, including linen,
silk and wool – as well as
tablecloths, jewelry, and
ceramics made by local
designers. Most of the

FASHION SAMPLER SWATCHES, C. 1940

items are sold exclusively in this store. They even have a modern version of a *zavinovačka*, a very traditional wrap for a baby, used for carrying a baby or placing it in a pram.

Navarila

Eliška Krásnohorské 4/11, Prague 1, Staré Město (Map A)
www.navarila.cz
TEL 271 742 091
HOURS Daily: 10:00–19:00
METRO Staroměstská ●
TRAM 17, 18 to Staroměstská

This shop focuses on everyday knitwear designed by Czech designer Martina Nevařilová, who designs two collections annually that are manufactured locally. The quality and workmanship is uniformly excellent. The store also carries a linen collection by another local designer named Iva Šimandlová, as well as leather handbags and jewelry by various local designers. Clothing prices range from 600 CZK to 3,000 CZK and they accept most credit cards, but *not* American Express.

Pietro Filipi

Národní 31, Prague 1, Staré Město (Map C)
www.pietro-filipi.com
TEL 222 365 239
HOURS Daily: 10:00–20:00
METRO Národní třída ●
TRAM 6, 9, 18, 21, 22 to Národní třída

Given its name, it would be easy to assume that Pietro Filipi is an Italian firm, as I had for years. In fact, it's a Czech-owned company that was started in 1993, just four years after the fall of communism, and has grown to the point where they now have over 70 stores in nine former eastern bloc countries. They offer seasonal collections for men, women and children, and their target audience is the thirty-and-over set. Their clothing tends to have a classic look, the materials are always of excellent quality, and everything (except for leather goods) is manufactured locally. Clothing prices range from 1,100 CZK to 10,000 CZK. In addition to clothing, they also offer

shoes, accessories and costume jewelry – all of their own design. Their flagship store, designed by the leading Czech design firm Olgoj Chorchoj, is the most interesting of their several locations in Prague, which include Václavské náměstí 14, NC Palladium (Náměstí Republiky 1) and OD Kotva (Náměstí Republiky 8).

STEFAN

Národní 37, Prague 1, Staré Město (in the Platýz *pasáž*) (Map C)
www.ivko-stefan.cz
TEL 224 242 631
HOURS Mon–Fri: 10:00–19:00; Sat: 10:00–16:00
METRO Národní třída ●
TRAM 6, 9, 18, 21, 22 to Národní třída

This small shop focuses on knitwear made by a Serbian company named IVKO. The designs tend to be a very creative and colorful mix of Swedish and Bohemian design – two styles that I love! Needless to say, I own more than a handful of sweaters from this store. The quality and workmanship is excellent. They offer winter and summer collections, but I always seems to prefer their winter items. They also carry a small collection of handbags from Oilily. Prices start at 1,990 CZK.

MEN'S FASHION SHOW, LUCERNA PALACE, 1948

Tatiana Boutique

Dušní 1, Prague 1, Staré Město (Map A)
www.tatiana.cz
TEL 224 813 723
HOURS Mon–Fri: 10:00–19:00; Sat: 11:00–16:00
METRO Staroměstská ●
TRAM 17, 18 to Staroměstská

Started in 1995 by two Czech designers, Tatiana offers classic lines with a definite element of glamour in more than a few pieces. For spring / summer 2012 the use of jersey and cotton was seen throughout the collection. A very cute jersey dress with obvious 1940s inspiration, for instance, was 6,900 CZK.

Timoure Et Group TEG

V kolkovně 6, Prague 1, Staré Město (Map A)
www.timoure.cz
TEL 222 327 358
HOURS Mon–Fri: 10:00–19:00; Sat: 11:00–17:00
METRO Staroměstská ●
TRAM 17, 18 to Staroměstská

Designers Alexandra Pavalová and Ivana Šafránková have been working as a design team since 1992 and opened this store in 2001. Here you will find classic clothing with great lines that is perfect everyday wear for even the chicest customer. For spring and summer they utilize mostly linen and cotton, and in the winter wool is primary. Prices begin at 2,400 CZK for skirts and 2,500 CZK for trousers. TEG also has a second location at Martinská 4, Prague 1, Staré Město (tel 224 240 737).

Men's Fashion

Adam Steiner

Politických vězňů 10, Prague 1, Nové Město (Map C)
www.adamsteiner.cz
TEL 224 231 853
HOURS Mon–Fri: 10:00–18:00
METRO Muzeum ● ●
TRAM 3, 9, 14, 24 to Václavské náměstí

If you're curious about where Prague's power players go to have their suits made, now you know. Bespoke suits at Adam Steiner start at 21,400 CZK, not including material. You'll also find their line of ready-to-wear suits in the back of the store. Additionally, on the off chance that you've managed to plan a day of golf at Karlštejn (the Winged Foot of the Czech Republic; see p. 216), they can, of course, provide you with just the right outfit to tee-off in. Golf attire includes women's wear as well.

Hedva

Na Příkopě 16, Prague 1, Staré Město (Map C)
www.hedva.cz | www.ties.cz
TEL 224 212 566
HOURS Daily: 10:00–18:30
METRO Můstek ● ●
or Náměstí Republiky ●

This little tie shop opened in 1926. All of the ties, scarves and accessories (including cufflinks) are Czech-made. Even if ties don't happen to be one of your Prague visions, you might want to reconsider, as many of the styles are actually rather chic! Who knew? And the prices make these ties the bargain of the century (the "expensive" ties are 700 CZK). Eat your heart out, Paul Smith! I will, however, warn you that their merchandising is *terrible*, so you'll need to hunt through the display cases that are organized by color. The window display will prove very helpful for cross-referencing.

Jozef Sloboda
Rytířská 11, Prague 1,
Staré Město (Map C)
www.jozefsloboda.cz
TEL 224 248 971
HOURS Daily: 11:00–19:00
METRO Můstek ● ●

A real rarity in Prague, this young Czech designer's store caters exclusively to men. And if you would describe your fashion sensibility as metro-sexual, then you'll definitely want to stop in to check out their fun, unique, and actually quite affordable collection of casual wear, including t-shirts, jeans, dress shirts and jackets. All items are made in limited editions not exceeding 25 pieces and often limited to as few as three. They also offer bespoke suits, with a lead time of two to three weeks, starting at 15,000 CZK (price is dependent on the type of material chosen). This store has the best customer service of any store I've visited in Prague; I only wish his staff worked for *me*. Ask if Petr is working when you stop in, as he's my favorite, and his English is exceptional.

Pietro Filipi
(See p. 109)

Children's Fashion

Brána k dětem
Náplavní 11, Prague 2,
Nové Město (Map C)
www.branakdetem.cz
TEL 725 811 631
HOURS Mon–Fri: 10:00–18:00
METRO Karlovo náměstí ●
TRAM 14 to Myslíkova; 3, 4, 6, 10, 16, 18, 22, 24 to Karlovo náměstí

SHOPPING

CZECH PAPER DOLL POSTCARDS, C. 1974

Interview with Věra Korandová: The Prague Fashion Scene

Věra Korandová is easily the most fashionable person I know in Prague. Having studied textile design in high school, she designed and sold clothing for several years, and currently works exclusively as an interior designer. Věra's interest in fashion started early; she began dyeing her shoes and applying buttons to them at age 15. By the time she was 16 she had started designing her own clothing, often working with wonderful old dresses her grandmother would find for her. "People under communism were very creative about what they wore," Věra points out. "They had to be, since no fashion was available in stores." Under communism, Věra created 60% of her wardrobe, as it was the only way to be

original. Věra feels that the need to make one's own clothes during the Communist era ultimately proved beneficial to the development of Czech fashion design, as it forced people to be very creative in finding a way to "make it work."

Karen: Who is currently your favorite Czech fashion designer?

Věra: Hana Zárubová. She works with interesting materials in a very original way. Her Air Force collection, introduced in 2011, was made from a combination of neoprene (more closely associated with wetsuits and laptop sleeves), wool, and parachute silk. She used the neoprene to create wonderful round, smooth sculpture-like shapes, and the silk is so fine and soft that her long dresses seem to fly when the wearer walks around – truly impressive. She also designs the Leisure Time collections for Pietro Filipi (see p. 109),

which are both elegant and comfortable.

Karen: What are your favorite stores that focus on Czech fashion?

Věra: My absolute favorite is No.fashion, which is not an actual shop but the atelier ("studio") of Hana Zárubová. Visits are by appointment only, which can be made in advance via her website (*www.hanazarubova.cz*). TIQE, with designs by Petra Balvínová, is another interesting place where one can find really original pieces. Pour Pour, a store in the Vinohrady district, sells clothes from up-and-coming young designers, so they often have very original pieces that are not too expensive. Another favorite shop is Leeda; I would describe their look as casual and minimalist with playful details – many of their pieces feature original prints or embroidery. Leeda offers a men's collection as well.

Karen: All of the stores you mentioned are definitely off-the-beaten track of the Prague fashion center on Dlouhá, Dušní, and V kolkovně streets. Are you less interested in the Czech designers based there?

Věra: No, I'm definitely interested in them, too. I particularly like the work of Klára Nademlýnská and Timoure Et Group (TEG, see p. 110), but I often find their clothing too expensive for my own budget. From time to time I'll purchase

STORE WINDOW, C. 1980 (PHOTO BY IRENA STEHLÍ)

pieces at these stores and combine them with pieces from other stores.

Stores Recommended by Věra:

Leeda
Bartolomějská 1, Prague 1, Staré Město (Map C)
www.leeda.cz
TEL 775 601 185
HOURS Mon–Sat: 11:00–19:00
METRO Národní třída ●
TRAM 6, 9, 17, 18, 22 to Národní divadlo

No.fashion
Jánský vršek 9/325, Prague 1, Malá Strana (Map B)
www.nofashion.eu
HOURS Mon–Fri by appointment only
METRO Malostranská ●
TRAM 12, 20, 22 to Malostranské náměstí

Pour Pour
Vinohradská 74, Prague 3, Vinohrady (Map E)
www.pourpour.cz
TEL 777 830 078
HOURS Mon–Fri: 11:00–19:00, Sat 10:00–15:00
METRO Jiřího z Poděbrad ●
TRAM 11 to Jiřího z Poděbrad
TRAVEL TIME 10 min.

TIQE
Benediktská 9, Prague 1, Staré Město (Map A)
www.tiqe.cz
TEL 608 519 656
HOURS Mon–Fri 10:00–18:00
METRO Náměstí Republiky ●
TRAM 5, 8, 14, 26 to Náměstí Republiky

If the words "Montessori," "Waldorf," or "organically grown" speak to your heart, you will love this off-the-beaten-track children's store that focuses on children up to three years old. If I had a little tyke, I would certainly make this a regular shopping stop. They carry everything from clothing, shoes, and baby carriers to toys, nursing supplies, and all-natural cosmetics, so it truly is one stop shopping for busy parents! And if, like many eco-conscious parents, you're seeking reusable diapers, you will be mesmerized by the wide range of styles and designs on offer here – including several with traditional Czech pictorial themes such as hedgehogs, ladybugs, apples, and cherries! The majority of the items sold here are Czech and Slovak, although they do have products from other countries as well.

La Femme Mimi
Štěpánská 51, Prague 1, Nové Město (Map C)
www.lafemmemimi.com
TEL 224 214 106
HOURS Mon–Fri: 10:00–19:30; Sat: 11:00–17:00
METRO Muzeum ● ● or Můstek ● ●
TRAM 3, 9, 14, 24 to Václavské náměstí

This children's fashion store offers a very fun and colorful collection of clothing for kids ranging from six months up to six years old. The designer, Nguyen Hoang Lan, has lived in Prague for over 15 years but originally hails from Hanoi – and you can definitely see the influence of Vietnamese style in her clothing design and fabric choices. What caught my eye were the appliqued hoodies and shirts – the lion and the zebra are my favorite! Prices range from 350 CZK to 1,100 CZK.

NOTE: They also have a women's fashion boutique, which is located right next door, but I find their children's collection to be much more interesting.

Pietro Filipi
(See p. 109)

FASHION (Vintage)
People are always asking me to recommend vintage clothing shops in Prague. Unfortunately, unlike in the US, there are hardly any to be found. The reason for this is that during the Communist era, clothing was not mass-produced; instead, it was most often homemade and worn until it was threadbare. That being said, in the past few years several vintage clothing stores have opened around town, although the word "vintage" is rather broadly interpreted, as at several stores you'll find clothing from last season mixed in with true vintage gems. Nevertheless, each of the stores listed below are worth a look if you love vintage fashion and accessories.

SHOPPING

Laly

Štupartská 3, Prague 1,
Staré Město (Map A)
www.laly.cz
TEL 775 076 326, 608 227 561
HOURS Mon–Sat: 11:00–
20:00; Sun: 12:00–19:00
METRO Můstek ● ○

Located right off of Old
Town Square, this vintage
clothing shop sells items
from the Czech Republic
and abroad, from the 1940s
through the 1990s. Here
you will find shoes and
handbags, fashion for men
and women, as well as
costume jewelry. It's more
upscale than Bohemian
Retro (see below), and the
merchandising is more
thoughtful and sophis-
ticated – and their higher
prices reflect this
difference.

FASHION SHOOT, C. 1970

Vintage Boutique

Michalská 18, Prague 1,
Staré Město (Map A)
www.vintage-clothes.cz
TEL 774 273 238
HOURS Mon–Fri: 11:00–
19:00; Sat: 11:00–18:00; Sun:
12:00–17:00
METRO Můstek ● ○

Vintage Boutique
specializes in vintage
clothing from the 1950s
through the current
decade, including women's
and men's wear, as well as
costume jewelry, handbags
and accessories. Here is
where you can score some
of the best vintage finds
in town – especially from
the 60s and 70s – and they
always have super cute
dresses. Their buying
is done both locally and
abroad. The shop also
boasts their own label
called Kiss My Valentine,
which specializes in very

cute replicas of 50s and 60s
party dresses – think puffy
skirts with large polka
dots and bold stripes!

Slightly Further Afield

Bohemian Retro

Čajkovského 22, Prague 3,
Žižkov (Map E)
www.bohemianretro.com
TEL 607 914 992
HOURS Tue–Fri: 11:00–19:00;
Or by appointment
METRO Jiřího z Poděbrad ●
TRAM 5, 9 or 26 to Lipanská
TRAVEL TIME 15–20 min

Located just outside of the
city center in Žižkov, this is
one of the best places to
find retro fashion in
Prague. They specialize in
Czech vintage items from
the 1920s through the
1980s, including handbags,

hats and sunglasses. You'll
also find an extensive
collection of women's and
men's fashion, as well as
costume jewelry, key-
chains, buttons and other
interesting trinkets, all
handpicked by the British
owner, Rebecca. Hipsters
will love this store and the
prices are very reasonable.
CASH ONLY

FUR & LEATHER

Fur shops have a long
history here in the Czech
Republic, which makes
sense when you consider
the extraordinarily high
quality of fur and leather
goods available in this
region. If you're a fan of
fur, which I must admit
I am, here are a few shops
you'll want to stop by...

Kreibich kožešiny & rukavice
Michalská 14, Prague 1,
Staré Město (Map A)
www.kreibich.cz
TEL 224 222 522
HOURS Mon–Fri: 10:00–
18:00; Sat & Sun: 10:00–
17:00
summer **HOURS** Mon–Fri:
10:00–12:00 & 14:00–18:00
METRO Můstek ● ●

Looking for some fabulous fur? How about a sheepskin or a rabbit pelt that has been dyed bright pink? Perhaps a vibrant blue fox throw or a natural cowhide from South America? If so, this is your dream store. I recently had them make two rabbit fur carpets and a luxurious sheepskin rug for my country house in southern Bohemia. The owner is more than willing to accommodate special orders, but he also has lots of smaller items in stock and available for immediate purchase, including scarves, hats, and coats made of various furs. Baby slippers are 340 CZK, gloves start at 660 CZK, longhaired sheepskin pillows are 2,400 CZK, and an absolutely delicious chinchilla scarf is 24,000 CZK.

COUNTESS OSTHEIM IN AN ERMINE FUR, 1909
(SOURCE: ČTK / CZECH NEWS AGENCY)

Liška
Železná 1, Prague 1,
Staré Město (Map A)
www.liskapraha.cz
TEL 224 239 457
HOURS Mon–Fri: 10:00–
19:00; Sat: 10:00–15:00
METRO Můstek ● ●

Mink, sable, chinchilla, and fox are among the furs you can find at this Austrian store right off Old Town Square. Prices begin at 28,000 CZK and run up to about 250,000 CZK, though there are some excellent sales during the summer season. Accessories are on the ground floor and coats are upstairs, along with the best selection of Wolford stockings in town. Thankfully, they offer tax-free shopping, which can provide substantial savings if you're as big a fan of chinchilla as I am.

RUKAVICE
Železná 1/548,
Prague 1, Staré Město
(Map A)
TEL 224 221 920
HOURS Daily: 10:00–20:00
METRO Můstek ● ●

RUKAVICE has been in business, in this location, for over 40 years. If you are looking for a pair of fabulous leather gloves, this is your dream store. The variety of colors, shapes, styles and sizes is mind-boggling and most items are made locally. This small shop also offers a limited selection of fur scarves, hats, and other accessories – but trust me, their gloves are the reason to visit. Prices range from 750 CZK to 2,500 CZK for gloves.

ARTĚL STORE IN OLD TOWN (PHOTO BY ESTER HAVLOVÁ, 2007)

GLASS

The Czechs are renowned for their beautiful handmade crystal glassware, and the history of glassmaking in the Czech Republic dates back to the 13th century. My fascination with this centuries-old tradition inspired me to launch my own Czech glass company, ARTĚL, in 1998. While I will admit to being perhaps just a little biased, I truly feel that the two ARTĚL shops (see below) are where you will find some of the most uniquely beautiful crystal in town. Having said that, I've also listed a few other firms that do high quality work. The difference between the shops listed here and the dozens of generic souvenir shops hawking Bohemian glassware all over town will become immediately apparent once you see it for yourself.

■ ■ ■ ■ ■ ■ ■ ■ ■ ■ ■ ■ ■ ■ ■
ARTĚL
Celetná 29 (entrance on Rybná), Prague 1, Staré Město (Map A)
www.artelglass.com
TEL 224 815 085
HOURS Daily: 10:00–19:00
METRO Náměstí Republiky ●
TRAM 5, 8, 14, 26 to Náměstí Republiky

U Lužického semináře 7, Prague 1, Malá Strana (Map B)
TEL 251 554 008
HOURS Daily: 10:00–19:00
METRO Malostranská ●
TRAM 12, 18, 20, 22 to Malostranská

Founded (by me!) in 1998, ARTĚL fills a niche in the luxury crystal market, not only in Prague but throughout the world, by producing whimsically elegant glassware that offers a modern twist on traditional crystal design. All of our glass is mouth-blown and hand-engraved by highly skilled Czech artisans – and while, certainly decorative, all of our pieces are intended to be functional as well.

Our work has been acquired for the permanent collections of three major museums and is sold in boutiques, galleries, and design stores in 26 countries around the world. Please visit our website to view our entire collection.

ARTĚL'S *POE* VASE

ARTĚL'S *GLACIER* VODKA GLASSES

ARTĚL'S *GRAPHIC* COLLECTION

The flagship ARTĚL Design Shop in Old Town was launched in 2007, and our second store – located just below the Charles Bridge in Malá Strana – opened in 2010. Both are worth a visit, in my humble opinion, and also happen to be very conveniently located right in the heart of the main tourist areas, so stop by anytime! Our staff is very knowledgeable about Prague and always happy to help out with directions or offer recommendations on what to do and see around town.

In addition to our crystal glassware, both shops carry one of the best jewelry collections by Czech designers in Prague, with over 30 local designers represented, as well ARTĚL's own line of costume jewelry. Also on display (and for sale) are an eclectic assortment of vintage items that I've acquired throughout the Czech Republic, ranging from 1960s bath toys to glorious Bohemian textiles and even some very chic taxidermy. There's truly something for everyone (well, everyone who enjoys reading this book, anyway...).

ARTĚL'S *SAKURA* BOWL

Galerie Meridian

Široká 8, Prague 1,
Staré Město (Map A)
www.galeriemeridian.cz
TEL 224 819 154
HOURS Mon-Fri: 11:00—17:30
METRO Staroměstská ●
TRAM 17, 18 to Staroměstská

If the idea of 'form over function' rings true to your heart, then stopping into this glass gallery is a must. Prices begin at 65,000 CZK, with some pieces even exceeding 2,000,000 CZK, so this is for serious collectors only. Tomáš Hlavička, Pavel Hlava and Stanislav Libenský are among the artists whose work is carried. Galerie Meridian also exhibits annually at SOFA (Sculpture Objects & Functional Art) in New York City.

NOTE: On a recent visit, the staff of the shop was neither helpful nor friendly, and the English speaking ability of the saleslady helping me was, frankly, less than terrific. So, if you're serious about buying something, you might want to bring along a translator to assist.

Material Glass

Ungelt-Týn 1, Prague 1,
Staré Město (Map A)
www.i-material.com
TEL 608 664 766
HOURS Daily: 10:30—20:00
METRO Můstek ● ● or
Staroměstská ●

The store features work by Ajeto (the firm formerly owned by Bořek Šípek), "forest" glass (the type of glassware Juliska makes – often green and either inspired by or copied from medieval drinkware from Central Europe) and Peter Rath (of the Lobmeyer family). The items include glassware, vases, plates, bowls and a very good selection of contemporary chandeliers (see p. 98).

Moser

Na Příkopě 12, Prague 1,
Staré Město (Map C)
www.moser-glass.com
TEL 224 211 293
HOURS Mon—Fri: 10:00—
20:00; Sat & Sun: 10:00—
19:00
METRO Můstek ● ●

Moser, established in 1857, is without question the most renowned Czech crystal manufacturer. The store on Na Příkopě, which opened in 1925, was Moser's first shop. The dark wood-paneled showroom, with alluringly elaborate inlay work, is well worth a look, regardless of your interest in glass. And while Moser is certainly available throughout the world, it's only in this store that you'll be able to see the very widest selection of merchandise. My favorite set is called "Bar." Originally designed in 1934 by Rudolf Eschler, it looks every bit as contemporary today as it did then, and comes in a variety of delicious colors. Moser's founder, Ludwig Moser, who was Jewish, fled the Czech Republic when the Nazis invaded, and the company was later seized by the Communists; nevertheless, Moser is one of a handful of Czech companies that did not suffer a serious decline in either quality or reputation during this period.

GLASS CUTTING, 1969 (SOURCE: ČTK / CZECH NEWS AGENCY)

Umělecké sklenářství

U Milosrdných 14, Prague 1,
Staré Město (Map A)
www.vitraz.cz
TEL 737 666 851
HOURS Mon–Fri: 08:00–16:00
METRO Náměstí Republiky ●
TRAM 5, 8, 14, 26 to Dlouhá
třída

This stained-glass
workshop was established
in 1935, and the founder's
claim to fame was
executing the windows
designed by Alfons Mucha
for the St. Vitus Cathedral
at Prague Castle. The
workshop currently offers
significantly less monu-
mental pieces for purchase,
including new works and
antiques, with prices
starting at around 2,000
CZK. I've found the staff
extraordinarily helpful and
extremely nice.
CASH ONLY
NOTE: Don't be intimidated
by the less-than-inviting
entryway; this is a work-
shop, not a store. Just knock
on the door, and someone
will come to open it.

HATS

Hat-making has been a
tradition in the Czech lands
since the 13th century, and
TONAK, a firm dating back
to the second half of the 19th
century, is still producing
its traditional felt hats
today – as softly textured as
velvet. They are one of only
eight remaining felt hat
manufacturers in the world,
as a matter of fact, and
their customers are every
bit as varied as the hats
themselves, including the
Czech Army, Hasidic Jews in
Brooklyn, Muslims in Saudi
Arabia... and me! So if you're
in the market for a fez,
fedora, knit cap, or even a
top hat, I can only encourage
you to seek out the store
listed below.

TONAK

Koruna Palace
Václavské nám. 1, Prague 1,
Nové Město (Map C)
www.tonak.cz
TEL 224 218 506
HOURS Daily: 10:00–20:00
METRO Můstek ● ●

The TONAK hat company,
based in Nový Jičín (about
3.5 hours east of Prague),
has been in business for
over 200 years. Their flagship Prague store opened in
2008, and it offers the
widest selection of TONAK
hats in town – so if you
only have time to stop in
one hat shop, this should
be it. They carry men's and
women's styles in all
shapes and sizes, and the
quality is exceptional.
They also offer a wide range
of scarves, umbrellas,
handbags and handker-
chiefs. Hat prices range
from 250 to 4,750 CZK.

JEWELRY (Fine)

Garnets are the official gem
of the Czech Republic, and
you'll find them just about
everywhere in downtown
Prague. They were first
found in the Czech lands in
the 11th century, and the
first garnet craftsmen's guild
was established in 1715
in Turnov (about an hour's
drive north of Prague),
which is still the center of
garnet production today.
　　If you've already been
window-shopping and have
started to notice that all the
new garnet items, regardless
of the store, look exactly the
same, I can assure you that
you're not going crazy,
and, in fact, have a wise eye.
They all look the same
because they are all — yes,

FEZ HATS IN PRODUCTION, 1948

119

all of them — made by Granát Turnov, a collective established in 1953. This collective is responsible for getting the products from the ground all the way to the display cases, including excavating, sorting, cleaning, cutting, and setting the stones in one of the 6,500 designs that they currently offer. Barring the very infrequent exception, I find virtually all of the new products to be rather boring and unoriginal, which is why I must encourage you to consider the idea of purchasing antique garnets at any of the shops listed below; I'm confident you'll find something far worthier this way.

Moldavite is the other local gemstone that you might have read about or seen. Olive green in color, it is unique to the Czech Republic, having been formed by the impact of a meteorite in southern Bohemia millions of years ago. The stones are some-times cut and polished as precious stones, and when finished this way, they often look similar to Russian green garnets; this is how I prefer them. More often they are left in their natural state, with a meteorite-like wrinkled surface.

Antique Vladimír Andrle

Platnéřská 6, Prague 1, Staré Město (Map A)
www.antiqueandrle.cz
TEL 222 311 625
HOURS Mon–Sat: 10:00–19:00; Sun: 10:00–18:00
METRO Staroměstská ●
TRAM 17, 18 to Staroměstská

If your taste in garnets is similar to mine, and you

favor antique jewelry rather than new, this shop will be a good starting point. They have a wide selection of earrings, brooches, necklaces, bracelets and even some unusual (albeit expensive) hair ornaments. The pieces are well curated, and while prices are on the high side, negotiation is definitely possible. As a matter of fact, they have emphasized their willingness to negotiate on each of my visits, so haggling 25% off the price here feels especially satisfying (most stores won't budge more than 10%).

BeldaFactory

Mikulandská 10, Prague 1, Nové Město (Map C)
www.belda.cz
TEL 224 933 052
HOURS Mon–Fri: 11:00–18:00
METRO Národní třída ●
TRAM 6, 9, 18, 21, 22 to Národní divadlo

While offering an assort-ment of items, this shop specializes in contemp-orary jewelry designed by the owner, Jiří Belda, utilizing various metals (including silver, tita-nium, stainless steel, platinum and white and yellow gold) combined with precious stones, as well as onyx, turquoise and even plastics such as Perspex and Corian.

Dorotheum

(see p. 83)

This great antique store and auction house has an extensive section devoted to jewelry, including an excellent collection of garnets.

Halada

Pařížská 7, Prague 1, Staré Město (Map A)
www.halada.cz
TEL 222 311 868
HOURS Mon–Sat: 10:00–19:00; Sun: 11:00–19:00
METRO Můstek ● ○ or Staroměstská ●

While you can now find Cartier, Tiffany & Co. and Bulgari in Prague, if you're looking for fine jewelry I think Halada is a much more interesting stop, as many of the pieces are designed by the owner, Lia Halada, and made onsite in their workshop at the back of the store. The jewelry here includes bracelets, earrings, necklaces, and rings set in precious metals and accented with diamonds and colored gemstones. They also offer an extensive collection of beautiful pearls, which I always find myself eyeing whenever I visit, but what really wins me over is their exceptional customer service. Prices range from 3,500 CZK to 400,000 CZK. I believe they are absolutely trustworthy; hence this is the *only* store in Prague where I would *ever* feel comfortable leaving my diamonds for cleaning or repairs.

STUDIO ŠPERK

Dlouhá 19, Prague 1, Staré Město (Map A)
www.drahonovsky.cz
TEL 224 815 161
HOURS Mon–Fri: 10:00–19:00; Sat: 10:00–18:00
METRO Náměstí Republiky ●
TRAM 5, 8, 14, 26 to Dlouhá třída

This small store is an anomaly among garnet

shops, because many of the settings they offer are absolutely contemporary, with clean, modern lines. One item that caught my eye was a necklace strung with Japanese pearls interchanged with hand-cut, hand-polished garnets, at 40,000 CZK. If this is too steep for your pockets, the store has other pearl and garnet pieces that begin at 4,000 CZK. Garnets set together with diamonds are another unusual find here. The store is owned by the Drahoňovský family, who have been involved in the garnet industry since the late 1800s, and the family designs and manufactures all of the pieces in the store, making this a very unique find.

JEWELRY (Costume)

The Czech costume jewelry industry dates back some 300 years. Like the Austrian firm Swarovski, Czech factories also produce machine-cut faceted beads, and while it's truly impossible to detect any difference, they sell for substantially less than Swarovski beads. Within the industry, "Czech beads" are synonymous with excellent quality and variety, regardless of their manufacturer. Stop by any of the shops listed below and you'll see why.

Want to make your own costume jewelry? Loose Czech beads and beading supplies can be found at the shops listed on p. 102.

▪ ▪ ▪ ▪ ▪ ▪ ▪ ▪ ▪ ▪ ▪ ▪

ARTĚL
(see p. 116)

In addition to our crystal

LEAF CHOKER WITH SMALL & LARGE FLOWER EARRINGS BY ARTĚL (1999)

OVAL CLUSTER RINGS BY ARTĚL (2000)

collection, ARTĚL designs a line of costume jewelry. The matte stones used throughout the collection lend a look that's classic with a contemporary edge. The collection includes earrings, necklaces, rings, brooches and hair accessories, with a dazzlingly wide array of colors. We also offer collections from other well-known costume jewelry designers from the Czech Republic and elsewhere, including Alexis Bittar.

FOXTROT

Kotva Department Store –
3rd Floor
Náměstí Republiky 8, Prague
1, Staré Město (Map A)
www.foxtrotbizu.com
TEL 224 801 520
HOURS Mon–Fri: 09:00–
20:00; Sat: 10:00-19:00; Sun:
10:00-18:00
METRO Náměstí Republiky ●
TRAM 5, 8, 14, 26 to Náměstí
Republiky

Definitely worth a stop if
the look you're after is
"beyond glamorous." They
actually carry a better
beaded jewelry collection
then Jablonex (see below).

Frey Wille

Havířská 3, Prague 1,
Staré Město (Map A)
www.frey-wille.com
TEL 272 142 228
HOURS Mon–Sat: 10:00–
19:00; Sun: 12:00–18:00
METRO Můstek ● ●

The jewelry produced by
this Austrian brand (OK, so
it's not Czech, but pretty
close!) includes enameled
bracelets, earrings, necklaces rings and cufflinks,
set in gold, silver, or silver-
plate. Their 2012 collection
honors Alfons Mucha and
Sarah Bernhardt, which is,
of course, very apropos, as
Prague is indeed the land
of Mucha. What caught my
eye here on a recent visit
were the wide rings
(although at 5,000 CZK they
are hardly inexpensive),
and the bracelet cuffs
(9,000 CZK).

Jablonex

DŮM MÓDY Department
Store
Václavské náměstí 58, Prague
1, Nové Město (Map C)

Spejbl & Hurvínek

A father and son marionette duo who made their
debut in the 1920s, Spejbl and Hurvínek are
the best-known puppets in the Czech Republic.
They even have their own theatre in Prague
(unfortunately, their performances are only in
Czech). Rounding out the crew is Žeryk, their
beloved dog; Mánička, Hurvínek's friend;
and Mrs. Kateřina, her *babička* (grandmother).
In addition to their stage shows, they appear
regularly on TV and have become beloved
characters throughout the nation. It's not hard to
find good reproductions, and they make great
souvenirs for adults and kids alike. You'll also
find stuffed animals, coloring books, and bedding
featuring the famous duo.

SPEJBL & HURVÍNEK WITH THEIR CREATOR, PROF. JOSEF
SKUPA, C. 1940 (SOURCE: SUPRAPHON RECORD)

www.jablonex.inshop.cz
TEL 234 101 114
HOURS Mon–Fri: 09:00–
20:00; Sat: 10:00–20:00; Sun:
10:00–19:00
METRO Muzeum ● ●
TRAM 11 to Muzeum

Jewelry production in
Czechoslovakia peaked just
before World War II, when
it was the center for
worldwide production.
Although it no longer holds
this position, the

manufacture of costume jewelry is still significant in the Czech Republic today. Jablonex was founded in 1952 and remains the country's leading exporter. Among its many baubles are imitation pearls and diamonds in positively every size and color.

▪ ▪ ▪ ▪ ▪ ▪ ▪ ▪ ▪ ▪ ▪ ▪ ▪ ▪

Pietro Filipi
(see p. 109)

This Czech fashion house carries a small but worthy collection of contemporary and very fashionable costume jewelry, designed in house and made in the Czech Republic, at affordable prices. Definitely worth a look.

MARIONETTES
Home of the International Puppetry Association (UNIMA), established in 1929, Prague is famous for its marionettes and puppets – and the local history of this art form dates back much further. Foreign troops during the Thirty Years War (1618–1648) first introduced Bohemia to the magic of puppetry, and toward the end of the 18th century Czechs began to make their own puppets. By the turn of the 20th century, puppet theatre underwent a renaissance here, with famous artists and designers of the day supporting it as a valid form of art. Hundreds of theatres and even schools for puppetry formed during the golden age of the First Republic (1918–1938). While there are puppets for all budgets sold throughout Prague, what's really

Make Your Very Own Marionette (In Just 3 Hours!)

Are you curious about how marionettes are made? Here's your chance not only to find out, but also to make one yourself. This ingenious activity was thought up by Pavel Truhlář, the owner of Obchod Pod Lampou (see p. 124). With 22 unique wooden characters to choose from, you'll be set up at your own workstation, and either Pavel or his wife will help you complete all the necessary steps. In addition to making your own marionette, you'll also have an opportunity to tour his professional workshop and view his collection of vintage marionettes – plus, beverages and cookies will be served!

▪ ▪

Pavel Truhlář
Boleslavská 16, Prague 3, Vinohrady (Map E)
www.marionety.com
TEL 606 924 392
HOURS Daily: 10:00–17:00
METRO Flora ●
TRAVEL TIME 15 min.
COST 1, 200 CZK per marionette
RESERVE 48 hours in advance, maximum 6 people
COURSE TIME 3–4 hours (ages 6 and up)

Can I Have a Marionette Made that Looks Just Like Me?

MY MINI ME AND ME – LOOK, EVEN OUR SHOES MATCH!

Of course! Simply provide Pavel Truhlář, listed above, with the following photographs:
• Head Shot (a close-up)
• Profile Shot (a close-up)
• Full Body Shot

The marionette will be made of wood and will stand 45 cm (18 inches) tall! The lead-time is one month, and they are, of course, happy to ship your finished marionette anywhere in the world. Prices are available upon request; for more information, write to Pavel at ptruhlar@marionety.com.

amazing to see are the pieces that could just as easily be classified as fine sculpture, with no two exactly the same. So, even if you're not interested in purchasing any puppets, I encourage you to stop into a few stores to see the truly impressive levels of workmanship out there.

- - - - - - - - - - - - - -
Obchod s loutkami

Nerudova 51, Prague 1, Malá Strana (Map B)
www.loutky.cz
TEL 257 533 035
HOURS Daily: 10:00–19:00
METRO Malostranská ●
TRAM 12, 20, 22 to Malostranské náměstí

The traditional marionettes carried at this store are not as well executed as those at Obchod Pod Lampou (see below); however, they do have an excellent selection of simple felt puppets starting at 290 CZK. They also have a Prague Castle Guard doll in a very charming box for 790 CZK, and this is an item I haven't seen in any other store.

- - - - - - - - - - - - - -
Obchod Pod Lampou

U Lužického semináře 5, Prague 1, Malá Strana (Map B)
www.marionety.com
TEL 602 689 918
HOURS Daily: 10:00–21:00
METRO Malostranská ●
TRAM 12, 20, 22 to Malostranské náměstí

This shop offers a very broad range of puppets, from simple, generic 300 CZK puppets to one-of-kind creations that cost 60,000 CZK. Needless to say, it was the one-of-a-kind selection that did it for me. Ask to

see puppets designed and made by Antonín and Martin Müller, as these two brothers are my personal favorites. Jan Růžička is another renowned artisan to seek out. In total, this shop carries the work of over 60 Czech artisans. The store has a very small workshop located right on the premises, so you can even see the puppets being carved! They have a second location near Old Town Square at Ungelt-Týn 1, but I prefer the store in Malá Strana.

MUSIC & MUSICAL INSTRUMENTS

The history of Czech music is long and illustrious, with the first significant pieces of Czech music dating back to the 11th century. While Mozart, Smetana and Dvořák are the classical composers most often associated with Czech music, Czechs are passionate about traditional folk music – and, oddly, many have a deep love of American country music as well. If music is of interest to you, these are some fun stores to know about.

- - - - - - - - - - - - - -
Bontonland Megastore

Palác Koruna
Václavské náměstí 1, Prague 1, Nové Město (Map C)
www.bontonland.cz
TEL 224 473 080
HOURS Mon–Fri: 09:00–20:00; Sat: 10:00–20:00; Sun: 10:00–19:00
METRO Můstek ● ●
TRAM 3, 9, 14, 24 to Václavské náměstí

A GUIDE TO CZECH MUSIC

Classical: Antonín Dvořák, Bedřich Smetana, Leoš Janáček

Country: "I See America" by Noví Zelenáči (in English)

Country: "Nashle-danou!" by Banjo Band Ivana Mládka (in Czech, but don't worry, it's really all about the music, which is terrific)

Swing: Originální Pražský Synkopický Orchestr (any of their CDs are great)

Rock: Monkey Business (funky rock – super popular in the Czech Republic)

Rock: Tata Bojs (rock with electronic effects, samples and loops)

Rock: J.A.R (hugely influenced by Prince)

Looking for vintage vinyl records? See p. 127. Also, for more on Prague's jazz scene, see the interview on p. 195.

Located in the basement of Prague's famed Koruna Palace (see p. 70), Bontonland is the largest music and video store in the Czech Republic. You'll find all music genres here and every sort of media, including DVDs and video games. They also have a mini Apple store, so if you need a new iPod, travel

JIŘÍ ŠLITR & ORCHESTRA IN LATERNA MAGIKA, C. 1958 (SEE P. 211)

ACCORDION PRODUCTION, 1953

speakers or even a laptop, this is a great resource to know about – but as noted in the introduction to the Shopping section, be forewarned that prices for electronics are generally much higher here than in the US and western Europe.

■ ■ ■ ■ ■ ■ ■ ■ ■ ■ ■ ■ ■
Petrof Pianos
Jungmannovo náměstí 17, Prague 1, Nové Město (Map C), 3rd floor
www.petrof.com
TEL 224 222 501
HOURS Mon–Fri: 10:00–19:00; Sat: 10:00–15:00
METRO Můstek ● ● or Národní třída ●

Petrof has been making pianos in the Czech Republic since 1864. If you can't afford a Steinway, but are in the market for a high performance piano, Petrof might be just the ticket. Uprights range from 99,000 CZK to 260,000 CZK while grand pianos range from 500,000 CZK to 2,000,000 CZK. It's also worth noting that they

have several dealers worldwide, so feel free to try one out here and purchase it back home.

■ ■ ■ ■ ■ ■ ■ ■ ■ ■ ■ ■ ■
Talacko
Rybná 29, Prague 1, Staré Město (Map A)
www.talacko.cz
TEL 224 813 039
HOURS Mon–Fri: 10:00–18:00; Sat: 10:00–16:00
METRO Náměstí Republiky ●
TRAM 5, 8, 14, 26 to Dlouhá třída

From Dvořák and Hayden to the Beatles and even Iggy Pop, this is one-stop shopping for all your sheet music needs. Rumor has it that such stores are now a scarcity in the United States, so if you're seeking a hard-to-find piece of music, this shop might just be worth a look.

■ ■ ■ ■ ■ ■ ■ ■ ■ ■ ■ ■ ■
U Zlatého kohouta
Michalská 3, Prague 1, Staré Město (Map A)
www.violin-hron.cz
TEL 224 212 874
HOURS Mon–Fri: 10:00–12:00 13:30–18:00
METRO Můstek ● ●

If you're the string instrument type, this store is for you. What you will find here is a wide range of antique and new violins, cellos, double basses, and guitars; I'm fascinated by this store and I can't even *play* an instrument! Most of the instruments on offer are made in the Czech Republic; prices range from 10,000 CZK to 5,000,000 CZK and worldwide shipping is available.

OUTDOOR MARKETS

Outdoor markets are always a fun and interesting way to gain insight into local culture, and Prague's markets will not let you down. Below are a few the local outdoor markets that are most noteworthy.

- - - - - - - - - - - - -

Farmers' Market

Výtoň - Rašíno nábřeží, Prague 2, Nové Město (Map C)
www. farmarsketrziste.cz
TEL N/A
HOURS Sat: 08:00–14:00
METRO Karlovo Náměstí ●
TRAM 3, 7, 17, 21 to Výtoň or 3, 4, 7, 10, 16, 17, 21 to Palackého náměstí

This lively farmers' market is located right on the riverbank. To be honest, the produce will be a letdown – except for the mushrooms, which are fabulous. Baked goods, however, are excellent and abundant; I encourage you to seek out a *maková kobliha* (poppy seed donut) – trust me, your 15 CZK will be well spent. You will also find great fruit preserves, as well as lots of pickled items – Czech's love to pickle! I encourage you to arrive as early as possible, as the market becomes very crowded by around 09:00.
CASH ONLY

- - - - - - - - - - - - -

Old Town Square

Staroměstské náměstí Prague 1, Staré Město (Map A)
METRO Staroměstská ●
During the Christmas and Easter seasons, Old Town Square is transformed into a bustling holiday market, complete with vendors, seasonal music and enter-

OUTDOOR MARKET, 1938
(SOURCE: ČTK / CZECH NEWS AGENCY)

tainment. The vendors sell holiday-themed handicrafts and as well as lots of *grog* (hot rum and water) and *svařené víno* (hot red wine spiced with cinnamon, sugar, dried oranges and other goodies).
CASH ONLY

- - - - - - - - - - - - -

Prague Flea Market

Various locations; check website.
www.prazsketrhy.cz | www.facebook.com/prazsketrhy.cz
HOURS Sat: 09:00–16:00
This roving flea market operates in several locations around town, so you will definitely want to check their website or Facebook page to confirm where it will be the week of your visit. Many local antique stores and individuals display their finds at this market, making it extremely useful for one-stop shopping. On my last visit I picked up a several pieces of vintage Czech costume jewelry ranging in price from 100–250 CZK, as well as a fun little plastic mushroom bank for 150 CZK. I was also completely enamored with a huge late-1800s porcelain doll head, but at 30,000 CZK the price was just too steep.
CASH ONLY

■ ■ ■ ■ ■ ■ ■ ■ ■ ■ ■ ■ ■ ■

Buštěhrad
(see p. 87)

POSTERS

From Alfons Mucha's iconic theater advertisements to Communist-era propaganda posters, the Czech Republic has a long history of outstanding graphic design. Why not take home a piece of history for your wall?

■ ■ ■ ■ ■ ■ ■ ■ ■ ■ ■ ■ ■ ■

Agentura Pro Vás
Rybná 21, Prague 1,
Staré Město (Map A)
www.AgenturaProVas.cz
TEL 224 819 359
HOURS Mon–Fri: 10:00–18:00
METRO Náměstí Republiky ●
TRAM 5, 8, 14, 26 to Náměstí Republiky

Would your trip to Prague be complete without a Communist-era image of Stalin? Or perhaps one or two early Czech advertisements? Surely not, so put this hidden gem on your must-hit list. Original posters start at 300 CZK and run up to 50,000 CZK. The store offers copies of original posters for either 80 CZK or 120 CZK, depending on size. The owner, Vojtěch Sedláček, is charming. His English is terrific, and, most importantly, he is a true capitalist, as he advised me "everything is for sale." That was a first for me in the Czech Republic, so, needless to say, he charmed his way into my heart immediately. Oddly, the store shares its space with a children's store for clothing and toys, so don't be misled if the window

WOODCUT, C. 1946

František Hrubín CHLÉB S OCELÍ

happens to be featuring children's shoes rather than Stalin; you *are* indeed in the right place!

RECORDS

Vintage vinyl seems to be a hot item these days, as I have received numerous requests from readers seeking information on where to get their hands on some hot wax. Although vintage records can be found at several of the *antikvariáts* I have recommended (see p. 87–89), here are a few stores that specialize in this niche item.

■ ■ ■ ■ ■ ■ ■ ■ ■ ■ ■ ■ ■ ■

Happyfeet
Lucerna Palace *pasáž*
Vodičkova 36, Prague 1,
Nové Město (Map C)
www.happyfeet.cz
TEL 606 722 655
HOURS Mon–Thurs: 12:00–19:00; Fri: 12:00–18:00
METRO Můstek ● ●
TRAM 3, 9, 14, 24 to Václavské náměstí

This great little hole-in-the-wall record shop opened in 2010 and offers a very eclectic mix of vintage vinyl from the 1950s–90s, with prices starting at 30 CZK. Additionally (and somewhat randomly), they have a small but excellent selection of vintage Czech-

RECORD SHOPPING AT KOTVA DEPARTMENT STORE, 1975
(SOURCE: ČTK / CZECH NEWS AGENCY)

made PRIM watches from the 60s, 70s and 80s – I got one for myself and I love it! The shop is located in the Lucerna Palace *pasáž* (shopping arcade, see p. 70) and will be on the right-hand side if you've entered via Vodičkova; if you run into David Černý's sculpture of St. Wenceslas mounted on an upside-down steed, you've gone too far.

▬▬▬▬▬▬▬▬▬▬▬▬
Národní muzeum - České muzeum hudby
Karmelitská 2, Prague 1, Malá Strana (Map B)
www.timemusic.cz
TEL 777 671 570
HOURS Mon, Tue, Thurs, Sat & Sun: 10:00–18:00; Wed: 10:00–20:00; Fri: 09:00–18:00
METRO Malostranská ●
TRAM 12, 20, 22 to Hellichova

Located in the café at the National Music Museum,

this store is a bit fancier than most record shops; they offer a wide range of musical styles and also sell CDs, DVDs, books, calendars, and music-themed gift items.

▬▬▬▬▬▬▬▬▬▬▬▬
Phono.cz
Opatovická 24, Prague 1, Nové Město (Map C)
www.phono.cz
TEL 222 521 448
HOURS Tue-Fri: 13:00–19:00
METRO Národní třída ●
TRAM 6, 9, 18, 21, 22 to Národní třída or Národní divadlo

This is one of the few record stores in Prague that offers both new and used vinyl. They offer a wide selection of genres but specialize in Funk, Soul, Reggae, Jazz, Afro-Latin, and Hip Hop. They also sell and repair vintage turntables, rent DJ equipment, and offer a wide selection of vinyl-related accessories.

Plus, if you want to make your own records, they do custom vinyl pressing. The staff is both friendly and knowledgeable – a real rarity in Prague. They have an excellent English website and offer world-wide shipping.

SHOES
If you're looking for shoes made in the Czech Republic, the two brands worth seeking out are Baťa and Botas; the best places to find them are listed below.

▬▬▬▬▬▬▬▬▬▬▬▬
Baťa
Václavské náměstí 6, Prague 1, Nové Město (Map C)
www.bata.com
TEL 221 088 478
HOURS Mon–Fri: 09:00–21:00; Sat: 09:00–20:00; Sun: 10:00–20:00
METRO Můstek ● ●
TRAM 3, 9, 14, 24 to Václavské náměstí

Founded by Tomáš Baťa in 1913 in the town of Zlín, Baťa has long since become nothing less than a shoe empire, one of the first truly global companies. Their flagship store on Václavské náměstí, built in 1927, originally sold Baťa shoes exclusively. Today the store sells other brands as well, although Baťa certainly remains the primary brand carried. Baťa's shoe quality is not what it once was, so I'd only indulge if the shoes you have your eye on are really cute and cost 1,500 CZK or less, so you won't need to worry if they only last one season. The building, however, is Functionalist perfection, and should not be missed, especially at night when it's lit up all the way to its roof!

BAŤA, WENCESLAS SQUARE, 1940

■ ■ ■ ■ ■ ■ ■ ■ ■ ■ ■ ■ ■ ■ ■

Botas Concept Store
Konviktská 30,
Prague 1, Staré Město
(Map C)
www.botas66.cz
TEL 224 281 148
HOURS Daily: 11:00–20:00
METRO Můstek ● ●
or Národní třída ●

Hipsters and sneaker fans alike will love this store. If you are dying to get your hands on (and your feet in) a pair of retro-fabulous Czech-made sneakers, look no further. The Botas 66 Classic was originally designed in 1966 and has been in production ever since; in 2005 it was ranked among the top 100 Czech design icons (see p. 106). In 2008, for a school project, two local art students updated the original design with wildly fun color combinations

A PROUD BOTAS FACTORY WORKER, C. 2008
(PHOTO COURTESY OF BOTAS)

(I have the pink and red ones). The manufacturer was impressed, and as the saying goes, the rest is history – the company now produces the sneaker in a wide range of color combinations (see the website for a sample), and they are available here. Prices range from 1,099 CZK to 1,699 CZK depending on the year of the collection.

SPECIALTY SHOPS

When I first moved to Prague from the US in 1994, I was struck by the prevalence of stores around town specializing in one specific category of merchandise – rope, rubber, paper goods, and even beekeeping and hunting supplies – that had remained in business after the fall of communism. Simply put, I love visiting these little shops. I appreciate their focus, as well as the old-school atmosphere found in most of them. I will be honest, as a tourist – or even as a local – it's unlikely that you will make a purchase at some of the more obscure spots listed below; however, I still feel they are worth a visit, due to their wholehearted uniqueness.

Bee Keeping

■ ■ ■ ■ ■ ■ ■ ■ ■ ■ ■ ■ ■ ■

Včelařské potřeby

Křemencova 8, Prague 1, Nové Město (Map C)
www.vcelarskaprodejna.cz
TEL 224 934 344
HOURS Mon–Thurs: 08:30–12:30 & 13:00–17:00; Fri: 08:30–12:30 & 13:00–14:00
TRAM 6, 9, 18, 22 to Karlovo náměstí or Národní třída

Have you always dreamed of becoming a beekeeper? If so, Včelařské potřeby provides you with the ideal opportunity to get your feet wet and stock up on all of the required accessories. Additionally, they carry a generous selection of gifts, including *medovina* (a local honey wine), beeswax candles, and a broad range of cosmetics.

Butcher Shop

■ ■ ■ ■ ■ ■ ■ ■ ■ ■ ■ ■ ■ ■

The Real Meat Society

Náplavní 5, Prague 2, Nové Město (Map C)
www.trms.cz
TEL 739 022 597
HOURS Tue & Wed: 11:00–17:00; Thurs & Fri: 11:00–18:00; Sat: 09:00–12:00
METRO Karlovo náměstí ●
TRAM 14 to Myslíkova or 3, 4, 6, 10, 16, 18, 22, 24 to Karlovo náměstí

This fantastic butcher shop was founded in 2012 by Paul Day, the owner of Sansho Restaurant (see p. 163), and I'm a regular patron. If you are curious to see (and sample) the best fresh meat in town, look no further.

WOODEN BUTCHER SHOP, C. 1880

SHOPPING

All of the meat is raised humanely, and they take a nose-to-tail approach in butchering whole animals and selling interesting cuts. An extra added bonus is that the entire staff speaks English, so if you are curious about the different meats on offer they will actually be able to answer.

Dancewear

Grishko

Mikulandská 4/122, Prague 1, Nové Město (Map C)

www.grishko.cz

TEL 224 933 027

HOURS Mon–Fri: 10:00–18:00; Sat: 10:00–14:00

METRO Národní třída ●

TRAM 6, 9, 18, 21, 22 to Národní třída or Národní divadlo

I've always dreamed of having a tutu, and I don't even dance! Should you, on the other hand, be an actual ballerina (or have a child with an interest in dance), you absolutely must stop into this brilliant dancewear emporium, as they feature a huge selection of tutus, ballet slippers, leotards, leg warmers, and tights. Although the company is Russian, the tutus are made locally, with prices ranging from 180–14,000 CZK, and sizes small enough to fit a two-year-old (how's *that* for healthy early encouragement?!). Should you desire a color that is not available, they can create custom designs with a lead time of 2–45 days, depending on the complexity of the tutu and the materials in stock.

Dental Hygiene

PROFIMED

Ječná 2, Prague 2, Nové Město (Map C)

TEL 257 535 544

www.profimed.cz

HOURS Mon–Fri: 08:00–18:30; Sat: 10:00–14:00

METRO Karlovo náměstí ●

TRAM 4, 6, 10, 16, 22 to Štěpánská or 3, 4, 6, 10, 16 18, 22, 24 to Karlovo náměstí

Dental hygiene fanatics, this is the store for you. PROFIMED focuses exclusively on all things related to tooth care and maintenance. Not surprisingly, they offer a very extensive collection of manual and electric toothbrushes for children and adults, toothpaste, toothpicks, floss and even toothbrush sanitizers in fun shapes and colors. As an extra added bonus, they offer a touch-and-feel display for each toothbrush, so you can feel how soft the bristles are before making a selection.

Hardware

GUMA

Ječná 24, Prague 2, Nové Město (Map C)

www.gumapraha.cz

TEL 224 918 411

HOURS Mon–Thurs: 09:00–18:00; Fri: 09:00–17:00

METRO Karlovo náměstí ●

TRAM 6, 10, 16, 22 to Štěpánská or 6, 9, 10, 16 18, 21, 22 to Karlovo náměstí

I am just going to start off by saying I LOVE THIS STORE! It has been here forever, and focuses exclusively on all things rubber. Rubber flooring, rubber pipes, rubber floats, rubber blow-up toys – you name it, they've got it. Frankly, I will be shocked if you actually make a purchase here, but it's worth a quick visit simply to experience the old-school Communist-era atmosphere.

CASH ONLY

KUTIL

Vítězná 10, Prague 1, Malá Strana (Map B)

www.kutilujezd.cz

TEL 257 310 477

HOURS Mon–Fri: 09:00–18:00

TRAM 6, 9, 12, 20, 22 to Újezd

I have come to think of this as this as the "rope store," and should you have an opportunity to see their window display you will know why. Beyond their extensive offerings of all things rope-related, this little gem of a store also happens to have a surprisingly brilliant collection of metal western-style belt buckles and leather belts, all sorts of replacement zippers and snaps, as well as a few handy tools for the home. As with GUMA, the Communist-era rubber store listed above, there are few items here that would appeal to the average tourist (unless you are a big fan of cowboy belt buckles), but the overall vibe is so old-school and unique that it's worth stopping in for a quick visit – especially since it's so close to Café Savoy (see p. 158) and several other worthwhile shops, and just steps away from the Legií Bridge.

CASH ONLY

Železářství, potřeby pro řemeslníky

Dlouhá 25, Prague 1,
Staré Město (Map A)
TEL 222 324 734
HOURS Mon–Fri: 10:00–18:00; Sat: 09:00–14:00
METRO Náměstí Republiky ●
TRAM 5, 8, 14, 26 to Dlouhá třída

As with the rubber and rope shops listed on the previous page, I highly doubt that you will purchase anything at this old-school, retro-fabulous hardware store in the heart of downtown, but I nevertheless encourage you to stop in and take a look. Hardware stores, like grocery stores, can provide great insight into a foreign culture – and this one definitely does not disappoint. Brooms, brushes and buckets are offered here in more shapes and sizes than you can imagine. They also offer an extensive range of belts, buckles and chain link, as well as everything you might need to start a career in stuccoing. By the way, if you need them, nails, screws, nuts, and bolts can be purchased individually – a relic of bygone era indeed!
CASH ONLY

Hunting Supplies

Česká Zbrojovka

Opletalova 37, Prague 1,
Nové Město (Map C)
www.czub.cz
TEL 225 375 800
HOURS Mon–Fri: 09:00–18:00; Sat: 09:00–13:00
METRO Muzeum ● ● or Můstek ● ●
TRAM 3, 9, 14, 24 to Václavské náměstí

Hunters (or Fans of Taxidermy), Put This Castle on Your Must-Hit List!

Konopiště Castle, which appears in the photo on the back cover, is located an hour outside of Prague and features a jaw-droppingly huge collection of 100,000 hunting trophies (see p. 55).

HUNTING PARTY, 1906

Although I am most definitely NOT a hunter, I nevertheless decided to sneak a peek at this sportsman's emporium, and – to my great surprise – found lots of goodies that piqued my interest in all things hunting! The store is focused on weaponry, including an extensive range of guns made by Česká Zbrojovka, which was established in Moravia in 1936 (prices range from 7,000 CZK to 350,000 CZK), as well as a wide selection of knives and bullets. If you're an avid hunter – or just seeking a truly unique souvenir from your visit to Prague – you'll be interested to know that they make custom guns upon request; the lead time is approximately three months but might be more or less, depending on the intricacy of the engraving and type of wood requested. Please note, however, that in order to get it out of the country, Czech law requires you to dismantle the gun and export it yourself, so some advance planning will be necessary. In addition to the practical tools of the trade, Česká Zbrojovka also offers a wide selection of hunting attire, trophy mounts, and hunting-themed items like pins, pipes, glassware and even baseball caps! I fully enjoyed my visit to this store (and even bought myself a baseball cap with an embroidered image of a Labrador holding a dead pheasant) and I'll definitely be back.

A second store is located in the Pánská *pasáž* (shopping arcade), Ovocný trh 12, Prague 1, Staré Město (open Mon–Fri 10:00–20:00, weekends from 10:00–18:00). This location, however, is much smaller and only carries hunting attire, knives, and a few novelty items, so I highly recommend that you visit their flagship store instead; it is a bit less convenient but much more interesting.

■ ■ ■ ■ ■ ■ ■ ■ ■ ■ ■ ■ ■
Myslivost
Jungmannova 25, Prague 1, Nové Město (Map C)
www.myslivost.cz
TEL 224 949 014
HOURS Mon–Fri: 09:00–18:00; Sat: 09:00–12:00
METRO Můstek ● ○ or Národní třída ○

This is one-stop shopping for all things hunting – except for guns, which you can get at Česká Zbrojovka (see listing on the facing page). The lower floor here is devoted primarily to clothing, including formal hunting hats by TONAK (see p. 119), starting at 290 CZK, as well as pants, shirts, sweaters, socks, and even ties. Upstairs, you'll find glassware, porcelain, flatware and pewter, all decorated with hunting motifs. One liqueur set with decaled motifs, including a decanter and

six glasses, bordered on kitsch and sold for a mere 370 CZK. Other items that caught my fancy included a wood carving of St. Hubertus, the patron saint of hunting, at 3,870 CZK, and Saint Hubertus Liqueur, which is not available everywhere, at 390 CZK a bottle.

Slightly Further Afield

■ ■ ■ ■ ■ ■ ■ ■ ■ ■ ■ ■ ■
Zbraně a střelivo Brymová
Nádražní 7, Prague 5, Smíchov
www.zbranebrymova.com
TEL 222 310 773
HOURS Mon–Fri: 10:00–17:00; Sat: 09:00–13:00
METRO Anděl ●
TRAM 4, 12, 14, 20 to Na Knížecí
TRAVEL TIME 10–15 min.

This store is focused on weaponry, including an extensive range of guns, knives (medieval as well as modern) and bullets. They also offer proper hunting attire, trophy mounts, as well as hunting-themed items like cufflinks, pins, pipes, and glassware. I fully enjoyed my visit to this store (even purchasing a pair of cufflinks with Irish Setters on them for a friend), and will definitely be back.

Office Supplies

■ ■ ■ ■ ■ ■ ■ ■ ■ ■ ■ ■ ■
Rossa Bella Papírnictví
Palackého 10/725, Prague 1, Nové Město (Map C)
www.rossabella.com
TEL 224 946 072
HOURS Mon–Fri: 08:30–18:00; Sat: 09:00–15:00

METRO Můstek ● ○ or Národní třída ○
TRAM 3, 9, 14, 24 to Václavské náměstí or 6, 9, 18, 21, 22 to Národní třída

This is my favorite office supply store in downtown Prague, as it is super old-school in appearance and function (don't forget to grab a basket when you enter), but modern enough that you'll be able to shop without a problem. They have a great selection of plastic folders and binders, as well as an impressive number of options for books for writing receipts. If you're curious to see what office supply stores looked like under communism and in the early 90s (or simply have a fetish for office supplies as I do), you will love this place. As a random added bonus, they also happen to have an excellent collection of locally made masks and party hats.

Paper Goods

■ ■ ■ ■ ■ ■ ■ ■ ■ ■ ■ ■ ■
Jan Petr Obr
Palác Kinských, Staroměstské náměstí 12, Prague 1, Staré Město (Map A)
www.bohemianpaper.cz
TEL 266 712 566, 775 150 464
HOURS Mon, Tue, Thu & Fri: 10:00-18:00; Wed: 10:30-18:00
METRO Můstek ● ○

Although this wonderful paper shop is located right on old town square, it is a bit hard to find - but trust me, it's well worth the effort. Jan Petr Obr creates fabulous hand-engraved stationery, and the quality is easily comparable to that of legendary US paper-makers Crane & Co. They offer an extensive collection of greeting cards, note cards, place cards and gift cards; monogrammed stationery, birth announcements and invitations can be custom ordered and take approximately 10 working days to produce.

■ ■ ■ ■ ■ ■ ■ ■ ■ ■ ■ ■ ■ ■ ■ ■

Papelote

Vojtěšská 9, Prague 1, Nové Město (Map C)
www.papelote.cz
TEL 774 719 113
HOURS Mon–Fri: 11:00–19:00; Sat: 12:00–18:00
METRO Národní třída ●
TRAM 6, 9, 18, 21, 22 to Národní divadlo or 14 to Myslíkova

Papelote was started in 2010 by three young Czech designers. They offer a wonderfully original collection of paper and paper-related products, ranging from journals to book covers to creatively designed pencil holders, almost all of which are locally made. I love to pop in to their off-the-beaten-track flagship store every so often to see what fun new items are in stock. Without fail, I always seem to walk out with a bag of fabulous finds.

Pet Supplies

■ ■ ■ ■ ■ ■ ■ ■ ■ ■ ■ ■ ■ ■ ■ ■

ZOO BOHOUŠ

Spálená 10, Prague 2, Nové Město (Map C)
www.zoobohous.cz
TEL 222 543 663, 604 804 042
HOURS Mon–Fri: 09:00–19:00; Sat: 10:00–16:00
SUMMER HOURS Mon–Fri: 10:00–18:00
METRO Národní třída ●
TRAM 6, 9, 18, 21, 22 to Národní třída

Ok, I'll admit it: I love shopping for my dog. Whenever I travel, I always make it a priority to stop in at least one pet shop in the hope of finding him a special little something. If you're the same way, this is a shop to know about, as they have a wide range of unique pet treats. I love their "penny candy" self-serve bins in the front of the store, and they also have a great selection of spectacularly gruesome dehydrated animal tidbits, including pig ears, snouts, and more – all of which seem to be quite delicious, according to my puppy. In addition to the extensive dog treat selection, they also offer food, collars, clothing and toys for all types of animals.

Slightly Further Afield

■ ■ ■ ■ ■ ■ ■ ■ ■ ■ ■ ■ ■ ■ ■ ■

Dog Town

Letenské náměstí 1, Prague 7, Bubeneč (Map F)
www.dogtown.cz
TEL 233 313 288
HOURS Mon–Fri: 10:00–19:00; Sat: 10:00–17:00
METRO Hradčanská ● or Vltavská ●
TRAM 1, 8, 15, 25, 26 to Letenské náměstí
TRAVEL TIME 15–20 min.

If luxury is what you seek for your four-legged friend, there's no better store in Prague than Dogtown. They have a great selection of dog clothing, beds, carrier bags, feeding bowls, collars, and leashes from a range of international brands. They also offer locally made pet food and treats, with flavors ranging from rabbit to venison, as well as an onsite grooming spa – so your pooch can be perfectly primped and pampered.

Produce

■ ■ ■ ■ ■ ■ ■ ■ ■ ■ ■ ■ ■ ■ ■ ■

frutapura

Rámová 1, Prague 1, Staré Město (Map A)
www.frutapura.cz
TEL 775 719 436
HOURS Mon–Fri: 09:00–19:00; Sat: 09:00–16:00
METRO Náměstí Republiky ●
TRAM 5, 8, 14, 26 to Dlouhá třída

Located in the heart of downtown, this cute little market – really more like a beautifully curated vegetable gallery – is great to know about in this city where fresh produce is something of a rarity. If you're dying for a fabulous juicy peach, thirsty for a bit of watermelon juice, or in need of some fresh cilantro, this is where you'll want to come. Opened in 2012, frutapura represents the growing trend of new specialty food shops in Prague, a development I am most thankful for.

University Paraphernalia

■ ■ ■ ■ ■ ■ ■ ■ ■ ■ ■ ■ ■ ■ ■ ■

UK Point

Speciality Shop – Charles University Paraphernalia
Celetná 14, Prague 1, Staré Město (Map A)
http://point.cuni.cz
TEL 224 491 842
HOURS Mon–Thurs: 10:00–17:30; Fri: 10:00–16:00; Sat & Sun: 11:00–17:00
METRO Můstek ● ●

If you're after an official Charles University (Univerzita Karlova v Praze) sweatshirt or baseball cap, look no further, as this is the place to go. However, do not expect a college bookstore like those found in the US – this one is far more modest and the selection is tiny in comparison. What you will find are t-shirts starting at 240 CZK, baseball caps for 190 CZK and a super-cute book bag for 220 CZK. They also sell lots of other goodies, including scarves, mugs, water bottles and, of course, pens and pencils.

SPORTS PARAPHERNALIA

Nearly all Czechs are passionate about sports – particularly hockey and football (soccer). If you're a sports fan seeking a truly unique souvenir from your visit to Prague, these are some shops to seek out.

▪ ▪ ▪ ▪ ▪ ▪ ▪ ▪ ▪ ▪ ▪ ▪ ▪

JB Sport
Dlážděná 3, Prague 1, Nové Město (Map C)
www.jbsport.cz
TEL 224 210 921
HOURS Mon–Fri: 10:00–19:00; Sat: 10:00–14:00
METRO Náměstí Republiky ●
TRAM 3, 9, 14, 24 to Jindřišská; 3, 5, 14, 24, 26 to Masarykovo nádraží

JB Sport is one-stop shopping for all of your hockey needs, including pads, skates and helmets, but what I think may really interest you is their jersey collection in the back of the store. You can get the official Czech or Slovak Olympic or World Cup jersey for 2,200 CZK, or alternatively, be a bit more creative and get one of the official shirts from the local teams for 1,290 CZK, including Kladno, Jaromír Jágr's hometown team; Pardubice, Dominik Hašek's hometown; or the local favorite and current champs, Sparta. For an additional fee and a one day lead time, you can have your favorite number and name put on the jerseys (45 CZK per number and 10 CZK per letter). XL is the only size available, I'm afraid. Obviously, they assume you're a player and intend to wear it while playing. Hah!

▪ ▪ ▪ ▪ ▪ ▪ ▪ ▪ ▪ ▪ ▪ ▪ ▪

Sparta Praha Association Club
Na Perštýně 17, Prague 1, Staré Město (Map C)
www.acspartapraha.cz
TEL 222 220 424
HOURS Mon–Fri: 10:00–17:00
METRO Můstek ● ● or Národní třída ●

This place can pretty accurately be described as a hole in the wall, but if you're desperate for official team paraphernalia from AC Sparta and SK Slavia, then look no further. They have all the usual gear: jerseys, hats, scarves, banners, key chains, and so on. You name it, they have a sports logo on it!
CASH ONLY

Slightly Further Afield

▪ ▪ ▪ ▪ ▪ ▪ ▪ ▪ ▪ ▪ ▪ ▪ ▪

SK Slavia Praha Fotbal
SYNOT Tip Arena
U Slavie 1540/2a, Prague 10, Vršovice
www.proslavisty.cz
TEL 724 013 521
HOURS Fri–Mon: 10:00–17:00; Wed: 10:00–17:00; Thurs: 10:00–19:00 (on match days, shop closes one hour after match ends)
METRO Strašnická ● then
TRAM 7 to Slavia
TRAM 6, 7, 22, 24 to Slavia
TRAVEL TIME 20–25 min.

If you're after an *official* Czech football (soccer) jersey from Slavia, one of the local favorites, as opposed to one of the knockoffs that can be found practically anywhere downtown, this is the place to go. You can get one right there on the spot for 1,200 CZK, and for an additional 100 CZK you can put a name and number of your choosing on it – though this takes approximately one week, so you might want to ask your hotel to assist you with coordinating this in advance and then simply pick it up while you're here. I have to say, they are very cool. I got one for a Canadian football

MERKUR

The MERKUR company has been producing children's toys – including trains, erector sets (see p. 9), steam engines, and robotics – since the 1920s. My favorite is their "Retro" line of erector sets – reproductions of original kits from the 1920s and 1930s, complete with period packaging and manuals – any of which would make a brilliant gift for a boy. They are available at Hračky (see p. 136).

www.merkurtoys.cz

(soccer) fanatic with Czech heritage, who also happens to have worked for ARTĚL, and I just may have won him over for life. They also sell lots of other goodies, including official soccer balls, t-shirts, mugs, and scarves. The official jerseys are only available in adult sizes.

TOYS & MODELS

The Czech Republic has a long history of toy making, especially toys made from wood and tin. Needless to say, if you're seeking a present for a child – or simply want to indulge your own inner child – you should definitely seek out the stores listed below, as they offer a wide range of toys for children *and* adults.

ABREX

Václavské náměstí 28, Prague 1, Nové Město (Map C)
www.abrex.cz
TEL 224 247 332
HOURS Mon–Sat: 09:00–19:00; Sun: 10:00–16:00
METRO Muzeum ● ● or Můstek ● ●
TRAM 3, 9, 14, 24 to Václavské náměstí

Have you been longing for an antique or contemporary Škoda, Tatra or Jawa (see p.138) to add to your car collection? Well, you're in luck! In this great store, located in a shopping arcade, you can pick up a 1:18, 1:43 or 1:72 model of your favorite. Among the classic models on offer are a perfect pint-size replica of a 1938 Škoda Superb 913 for 605 CZK, a 1963 Škoda Felicia Roadster (see back cover) for 318 CZK, or a 1966 Jawa 350 "Kývačka" Automatic for 244 CZK. A brilliant store for car lovers young and old! If you enter the arcade from Václavské náměstí, ABREX is on your right.

Hračky

Loretánské náměstí 3, Prague 1, Hradčany (Map D)
TEL 603 515 745
HOURS Daily: 09:30–18:30
TRAM 22, 25 to Pohořelec

Despite its prime location near the Prague Castle, this toy store charges extremely fair prices, and happens to have the best selection of Czech-made tin toys that I've seen in Prague, as well as an excellent collection of wooden toys (including a marvelous Noah's Ark with exquisitely carved animals, some of which verge on being Cubist in design). Also be sure to check out the magnetic marionette sets, including dioramas – an excellent item for a 5 to 7 year old. Definitely worth a stop.

IVRE

Jakubská 3, Prague 1, Staré Město (Map A)
TEL 775 667 148
HOURS Daily: 11:00–18:00
METRO Náměstí Republiky ●
TRAM 5, 8, 14, 26 to Náměstí Republiky

IVRE focuses exclusively on wonderfully colorful hand-sewn fabric toys and accessories ranging from animals and puppets to beanbags and rattles. They offer fabric wall hangings for children's rooms with nature and transportation themes, among others. All of the items in the store have a very appealing homemade feel to them.

MPM Plastikové modely

Myslíkova 19, Prague 1, Nové Město (Map C)
www.mpmshop.cz
TEL 224 930 257
HOURS Mon–Fri; 09:00–18:00; Sat: 09:00–13:00
METRO Karlovo náměstí ●
TRAM 14 to Myslíkova; 3, 4, 6, 10, 16, 18, 22, 24 to Karlovo náměstí

Another excellent model shop, MPM is actually a bit larger than its competitors. Here you'll find miniature Škodas and Fiats, a Russian MiG-29MS aircraft, and an interesting collection of Czech-made wooden hobby kits from which to build miniature structures such as a fort, house, windmill or cottage.

SHOPPING

Old Toys

www.oldtoys.cz

This e-shop is certainly a bit overpriced, and it's sad that they no longer have a retail outlet in downtown Prague. However, this is the only e-shop I'm aware of that focuses exclusively on vintage children's toys from the Czech Republic, Central Europe, and the former Soviet Union, so I always make an effort to take a look at their website whenever I have a free moment. I bought a fabulous Russian penguin here that walks, lights up, flaps its wings, and opens its mouth – an obvious gem. They also have the best selection of vintage Igráček (the Czech equivalent of Playmobil) figures, which feature some very atypical professions (for toys), such as coalminers and chimneysweeps (see photo on p. 79). If you're interested in old toys ranging from dolls to metal trains to miniature furniture and appliances, it's definitely worth checking out.

Pecka Modelář

Karolíny Světlé 3, Prague 1, Staré Město (Map C)
www.peckamodel.cz
TEL 224 230 170
HOURS Mon–Fri: 09:30–18:00; Sat: 09:00–12:00
METRO Národní třída ●
TRAM 6, 9, 18, 21, 22 to Národní divadlo

Prague boasts more model stores per capita than any other city in the world. Perhaps this phenomenon can be explained by the fact that under communism, there was only one

Beloved Czech Fictional Characters

Krtek Created in 1956 by Zdeněk Miler

As the story goes, Zdeněk Miler was having trouble inventing a character that Disney hadn't already come up with. Then, one day, while pondering the idea, he tripped over a molehill and *voilà* – Krtek was born. This little mole does not talk and is constantly surprised by the outside world, since he lives underground. All his friends are animals native to the Czech Republic — Zajíc the hare, Myška the mouse, and Ježek the hedgehog. Krtek is now an international star, well known throughout Europe, as well as parts of Asia.

Pat & Mat Created in 1976 by Lubomír Beneš and Vladimír Jiránek

(SOURCE: ČTK / CZECH NEWS AGENCY)

Pat and Mat are the stars of *"A je to!"* ("And that's it!"), a stop-motion animated series in which these two bumbling handymen face an endless number of self-made problems. Their attempted solutions inevi-

tably lead to even more problems – and hilarity ensues – but in the end, with their optimistic can-do spirit, they always manage to figure things out.

Spejbl & Hurvínek Created in 1920 (Spejbl) and 1926 (Hurvínek) by Josef Skupa

This father and son marionette duo are the stars of the best-known puppet show in the Czech Republic. See p. 122 for more information.

Večerníček Created in 1967 by Radek Pilař

Večerníček is a nightly tv program featuring children's stories, broadcast at 18:45, when Czech children are supposed to go to sleep. The animated host, Večerníček, says good evening (*"dobrý večer"*) to the children at the beginning and goodnight (*"dobrou noc"*) at the end. Much beloved.

Cartoons featuring these characters can be found on YouTube, and purchased in DVD form here in Prague. Additionally, each of them has begotten countless spin-off products, including stuffed animals, coloring books, and clothing, any of which would make a wonderful gift for a child.

Czech Vehicles — Škoda, Tatra, and Jawa

The Czech motoring industry dates back to the end of the 19th century, and its most famous manufacturers are Škoda, Tatra, and Jawa.

ŠKODA ADVERTISEMENT, C. 1964

Škoda, which ironically means "it's a pity" in Czech (though for some reason Czechs don't seem to find the humor in it), dates back to 1899, when a company called Laurin & Klement produced their first motorcycle. Their first car, the Voiturette, debuted in 1905, making them the first car manufacturer in the Austro-Hungarian Empire. In 1925, Laurin & Klement merged with a machinery company named Škoda in order to stay afloat during the severely weakened market after World War I.

Want to see some? Visit the Škoda museum (see p. 63)!

Tatra is the third oldest car maker in the world after Daimler and Peugeot. Although they are known for building the cars driven by high-ranking Communist officers, they focus primarily on trucks these days. In their heyday, however they produced one of the first aerodynamic cars, the Tatra 77, which is beyond fabulous.

Want to see some? Visit the Tatra museum (see p. 64)!

Jawa is the most famous Czech motorcycle manufacturer. It began in 1929, when the founder bought the motorcycle division of the Wanderer company, and then changed the name to the unforgettable one it still sports today.

VINTAGE JAWA ADVERTISEMENT

Want to see some? Along with Škodas and Tatras, the National Technical Museum (see p. 59) has an extensive Jawa collection.

See p. 136 (ABREX) if you're interested in acquiring toy versions of any of these Czech classics.

1969 TATRA 77

(above) VELOREX RALLY, C. 1965; (below) TRABANT ADVERTISEMENT, 1962 (SOURCE: WWW.TRABANT.CZ)

The Velorex

In 1953, Velorex, a Czech manufacturer, introduced a crazy little car that has been referred to as a "Flying Tent" due to the vinyl that was stretched over its cage-like structure. The Velorex has three wheels, four gears and an engine that can run backwards! This means it doesn't have a conventional reverse gear, but the handy option of four reverse speeds. Under communism, disabled "invalids" received subsidies to buy these primitive but well-liked cars, which enjoyed a very long production run (until 1971). They have since become highly collectible, and an annual rally is held in Hradec Králové, the manufacturer's hometown.

The Trabant

Trabants, or "Trabis," as they are affectionately called, have, like the Beetle and the Mini, passed into motoring legend. What sets this East German car apart, though, is that they were made from Duraplast, a composite of Phenolic resin and cotton fibers (similar to Formica, Bakelite or fiberglass) developed at the end of World War II, when steel was in limited supply. The sedan and station wagon styles that you'll find in toy stores (miniatures of miniatures!) were in production from 1964 through 1991, and retained the same basic shape throughout that entire period.

See p. 140 (Sparkys) if you're interested in acquiring the toy version.

SHOPPING

ABC TECHNICAL MAGAZINE COVER, 1981

include jewelry and toys made of wood and metal; the top floor features toy Trabant cars (see p. 139), as well as plastic figurines of local hockey team players. They also carry a vast array of Krtek, Večerníček, and Spejbl & Hurvínek goodies (see box on p. 137).

▪ ▪ ▪ ▪ ▪ ▪ ▪ ▪ ▪ ▪ ▪ ▪ ▪

U Krále Železnic
Mánesova 42, Prague 2, Vinohrady (Map E)
www.ukralezeleznic.cz
TEL 222 252 525
HOURS Mon–Fri: 11:00–18:00; Sat: 09:00–12:00
METRO Muzeum ● ●
TRAM 11 to Italská

Attention, electric train fanatics: this small, off-the-beaten-track shop is stocked to the brim with treasures from big firms, such as Roco and Faller, as well as smaller Czech brands like MB and SVD. They also stock a full range of accessories, including trees, houses and little-itty-bitty-teeny-weeny people to help create the perfect diorama for your train. On a recent visit I picked up a very cool plastic apartment building, gutters and all, for 120 CZK.
CASH ONLY

WATCHES

If you're a wristwatch collector – or just appreciate fine timepieces – be sure to add this shop to your must-hit list.

(yes, one) magazine for boys – ABC (see photo above), which was entirely devoted to engineering and modeling. So, if you happen to be a model enthusiast, you'll have ample opportunity to purchase models made by local manufacturers all over town, but this shop is the best, in my opinion. Smer is my favorite brand, featuring all kinds of fighter jets, tanks, and cars. Additionally, Pecka carries some wonderfully creepy hand-painted Styrofoam heads in varying sizes that are meant to be installed in the model jets as pilots – I bought a few of these for a little installation in my flat, as they

were simply too strange to leave behind....

▪ ▪ ▪ ▪ ▪ ▪ ▪ ▪ ▪ ▪ ▪ ▪ ▪

Sparkys
Havířská 2, Prague 1, Staré Město (Map A)
www.sparkys.cz
TEL 224 239 309
HOURS Daily: 10:00–19:00
METRO Můstek ● ●

The Toys "R" Us of the Czech Republic, Sparkys carries a wide variety of good quality Czech-made toys. Items to look out for on the ground floor

TOY TRAM SET, 1960 - AVAILABLE AT ARTÉL (SEE P. 116)

PRIM

Pánská pasáž, Na Příkopě 23, Prague 1, Staré Město (Map A)

www.prim.cz

TEL 774 877 090

HOURS Mon–Fri: 10:00–20:00; Sat & Sun: 10:00–18:00

METRO Můstek ● ● or Náměstí Republiky ●

PRIM has been making watches in the Czech Republic since 1949. Under communism their focus was producing watches for the masses (think Casio or Seiko), and just about every Czech owned at least one or two of their watches back in the day. I own several, and I love them! These days, they have gone upscale, making all of their mechanisms by hand. Their standard collections start at 6,000 CZK; prices for high-end

BOOK COVER ("*PRECISE TIME*"), 1942

WINE BOTTLING, C.1930

models go up to 100,000 CZK. Uniquely, it is even possible to have them create a one-of-a-kind watch just for you, and you can participate in the design process from start to finish! How cool is that? The lead time for custom watches is six to eight weeks. If you enter the *pasáž* (shopping arcade) from Na Příkopě, PRIM is on the left-hand side.

Interested in owning a vintage PRIM watch? Be sure to check out Happyfeet (see p. 127).

WINE SHOPS

Although the Czech Republic is best known for beer, there are several decent wines produced here as well – especially white wine from Moravia – and these shops are the best place to find them.

■ ■ ■ ■ ■ ■ ■ ■ ■ ■ ■ ■ ■

Cellarius Vinotéka

Lucerna Palace *pasáž*
Štěpánská 61, Prague 1,
Nové Město (you can also
enter from Vodičkova)
(Map C)
www.cellarius.cz
TEL 224 210 979
HOURS Mon–Fri: 09:30–
20:00; Sat: 11:00–20:00
METRO Můstek ● ●
TRAM 3, 9, 14, 24 to Václavské
náměstí

A serious yet unpretentious wine store located on the ground floor of the Lucerna Palace (see p. 70), Cellarius offers an extensive and diverse collection of Czech wines and spirits, as well as some foreign choices. They also offer a wide range of decorative wood boxes with which to create handsome presentation packaging, and the sales staff is always extremely helpful.

■ ■ ■ ■ ■ ■ ■ ■ ■ ■ ■ ■ ■

Dům vína U Závoje

Havelská 25,
Prague 1, Staré Město
(Map A)
www.uzavoje.cz
TEL 226 006 126
HOURS Mon–Fri: 11:00–
19:00
METRO Můstek ● ●

Dům vína U Závoje opened in 2004 as part of a food and beverage-oriented commercial passageway. It's obvious that the people working in this shop are serious wine lovers with a broad knowledge to draw upon. The shop, however, is surprisingly small, compared with the wine bar in the same passageway. Indeed, if the store does not have what you're looking for, you might try to purchase it directly from the wine bar, as the latter's selection is much more extensive.

What's the Deal with the VAT Refund?

Added to the price of all merchandise that you see in stores is a Value Added Tax (VAT) of 21%. However, if you spend over 2,000 CZK (on the same day) in a store that participates in the VAT refund program, you will be entitled to get most – though not all – of the tax back (there is small processing fee). Lots of people will advise you that it's not worth your time and effort, but if you're a spender like I am, it is indeed worthwhile – hey, 21 percent is 21 percent, right?

Here's what you need to do:

1. Request a TAXFREE form from the merchant. They may ask to see your passport when filling out the form. From my experience, however, Czech stores are very lenient about this; I have yet to know anyone who has had to show their passport (as one must in, say, Paris, where it really is a requirement).

2. You will want to fill out the form before you get to the airport, as it will save time in executing your claim.

3. At the airport, before you check your luggage, go to turn in your paperwork at the "TAXFREE for Tourists" desk, located right next to "Oversize Luggage." At this time you will need to give the inspector your:
• TAXFREE form
• Airplane ticket
• Passport

The inspector will then review the form and might ask to see a specific item as proof that the merchandise is actually being exported; this does not happen often, but better safe than sorry (this is why I recommend you stop here *before* checking in). The inspector will then stamp your document, after which you can proceed to check in.

4. If the Czech Republic is your last stop in the EU, then, once you've checked in and passed through passport control, you can proceed to the "Global Refund" desk to collect your refund.

Be sure to advise them what currency you want to receive the refund in.

NOTE: I strongly recommend that you take the cash refund versus having the amount applied to your credit card.

5. If the Czech Republic is *not* your last stop in the EU, you will not be able to get your refund at the Prague airport. Instead, you will need to submit your stamped TAXFREE form at your *last* stop in the EU and collect your refund there.

Exceptions to be aware of:
• Paperwork must be turned in within 90 days of purchase.
• You must be over 15 years of age to file a claim.
• The VAT tax does not apply to antiques – hence, no refund.
• You cannot claim a VAT refund on food, alcohol or cigarettes.
• The VAT tax on books varies (15% or 21%, depending on the type of book); in either case, however, a claim can be made.

CZECH CURRENCY, C. 1929

Services

SPA TREATMENT IN KARLOVY VARY, 1940

There's nothing I find more relaxing and enjoyable than indulging in services such as massages, facials or pedicures. If, by some strange coincidence, you *also* enjoy these things, you'll be pleased to know that Prague will not let you down – there are many excellent options to choose from. Below I have included a few of my favorites.

SPAS

▪ ▪ ▪ ▪ ▪ ▪ ▪ ▪ ▪ ▪ ▪ ▪ ▪ ▪
Augustine Hotel
Letenská 12/33, Prague 1,
Malá Strana (Map B)
www.theaugustine.com
TEL 266 112 242
HOURS Daily: 09:00–21:00
METRO Malostranská ●
TRAM 12, 18, 20, 22 to
Malostranská

The Augustine Hotel spa is my go-to option in the winter months, as I love to take advantage of their wellness area, which includes a great sauna and a fabulous aromatherapy / color therapy steam room. On my most recent visit, I opted for the "Surrender" treatment (90 minutes for 3,300 CZK), which left me feeling, well, surrendered – but I must admit I'm dying to try their "St. Thomas Beer Body Ritual," utilizing beer brewed by the in-house monks! (90 minutes for 3,900 CZK.) Reservations are absolutely essential, and I recommend you try to make them before you arrive in Prague. For a full menu of spa services, visit the website listed above, as they offer several different treatments including massages, facials, scrubs and nail care.

▪ ▪ ▪ ▪ ▪ ▪ ▪ ▪ ▪ ▪ ▪ ▪ ▪ ▪
L'Institut Guerlain
Dlouhá 705/16, Prague 1,
Staré Město (Map A)
www.guerlain-linstitut.cz
TEL 227 195 330
HOURS Mon–Fri: 09:00–
21:00; Sat 10:00–19:00

If it's a facial that you fancy, there's no better location in Prague then L'Institut Guerlain. The prices here are unquestionably high, but if you want to splurge, the experience is is well worth it. I recommend you opt for one of their 90-minute facial offerings – "Intensive Facial" (3,900 CZK) is my personal favorite: In addition to the standard cleaning, steaming, and mask, it also includes eyebrow shaping, facial waxing, and a 25-minute face, neck and shoulder massage – plus, if you need it, paraffin for your hands and touch-up make-up before you go. Without fail, I end up falling asleep (and snoring), as I am so relaxed by the end of the massage. My friend Blanka has also raved about their dry manicure and pedicure. For a full menu of spa services, visit the website listed above. Appointments required.

■ ■ ■ ■ ■ ■ ■ ■ ■ ■ ■ ■ ■
Mandarin Oriental Hotel

Nebovidská 459/1, Prague 1, Malá Strana (Map B)
www.mandarinoriental.com/prague
TEL 233 088 888
HOURS Daily: 10:00–20:30
METRO Malostranská ●
TRAM 12, 20, 22 to Hellichova

From the moment it opened in September 2006, the Mandarin Oriental Hotel spa has established itself as, quite simply, the best in Prague. The calm tranquil setting of the reception area, originally a Gothic church (the remains of which can be seen through a glass floor), immediately sets a relaxed tone for your visit. The hotel is renowned for customer service and attention to detail, and my first visit only confirmed this. From their wide selection of massages, facials and scrub options, I opted for the "Oriental Harmony" treatment (120 minutes for 8,500 CZK), which began with a soothing footbath, followed by a linden-blossom scrub (linden being the national tree of the Czech Republic), followed by a four-hand massage with two masseurs working in perfect unison. I followed the massage with a relaxing soak in the Vitality Pool located in my spa suite, which was called *Vltava*. In a word, it was perfect! Request this suite, if possible, as I found it to be the prettiest – they're all lovely, actually, but the *Vltava* is the only one with a Vitality Pool. Reservations are absolutely required, and I recommend that you try to make them before you arrive in Prague, as this spa is currently the hot ticket in town, especially on weekends. For a full menu of spa services, visit the website listed above.

■ ■ ■ ■ ■ ■ ■ ■ ■ ■ ■ ■ ■
Thai Foot Massage

Rytířská 19, Prague 1, Staré Město (Map C)
TEL 608 743 491
HOURS Daily: 12:00–22:00
METRO Můstek ● ●

As long as you don't mind being worked on in a very informal and communal room, this is a great place to know about, as walk-ins are more than welcome. You'll have a choice of two options, the Foot Massage (400 CZK) and the Full Body Massage (600 CZK). Without question, go for the Full Body – I assure you your money will be well spent! First, they hand you a pair of shorts to change into, then you just sit back in your own comfy reclining chair and let them go to work. I have to say I was pleasantly surprised by the quality of the massage. Ladda was my girl, and I can attest to her talents by mentioning that I was not in the least bit distracted by all the relentless Thai chattering in the background. To take full advantage of the Full Body massage, be sure to take a T-shirt or camisole to change into, as it will allow them to work more comprehensively on your upper body.

CASH ONLY

■ ■ ■ ■ ■ ■ ■ ■ ■ ■ ■ ■ ■
Zen Asian Wellness @ Maximilian Hotel

Haštalská 14, Prague 1, Staré Město (Map A)
www.planetzen.cz
TEL 225 303 116
HOURS daily: 10:00–22:00
METRO Náměstí Republiky ●
TRAM 5, 8, 14, 26 to Dlouhá třída

Sabai is Thai for "relaxed," and that is precisely how you'll feel in this serene Thai-style environment with Art Deco accents deep within the Maximilian Hotel. They offer 20 different massages, ranging from the "Footjoy," a 60-minute massage that focuses solely on feet

(900 CZK), to the "Bali Blossom," a 90-minute Balinese oil massage that is followed by a relaxing bath in coconut milk (1,895 CZK). During my most recent visit, I went for the aptly titled "Back Special" (60 minutes for 1,395 CZK), which left me very satisfied. Topping off your massage with a visit to one of their two 'floating rooms'—basically enormous seven-meter bathtubs —is certain to melt the stress away. The water is enriched with natural salt and mineral crystals for what they call 'The Dead Sea Effect,' by which you virtually float on the water, experiencing a unique feeling of weightlessness, absolute silence, deep relaxation and peace. Perfect after a long flight or an endless day of sightseeing. Floating 50 minutes will run you 890 CZK, but if you combine it with a massage, it's discounted approximately 30%. Reservations required.

"SUN" TREATMENT AT THE LUHAČOVICE STATE SPA FOR CHILDREN, 1957 (SOURCE: ČTK / CZECH NEWS AGENCY)

Slightly Further Afield

Cordeus

Na Dlouhém lánu 11, Prague 6, Vokovice
www.cordeus.cz
TEL 251 097 311, 411
HOURS Mon–Fri: 08:00–21:00; Sat: 08:00–20:00
METRO Dejvická ●
TRAM 20, 26 to Horoměřická
TRAVEL TIME 20–25 min.

Have you been dreaming of visiting the famous spas in Karlovy Vary but simply don't have the time? If so, Cordeus might just be the answer, as it is

the best representation of a true Czech-style spa in Prague. The experience will be clinical as opposed to luxurious, and the atmosphere modest (not to say hospital-like) as opposed to posh, but the price is highly affordable. If you can accept the lack of plush terry robes and changing rooms, as well as the therapists' minimal English skills (although communication is not a problem – trust me, you'll work it out), this place has quite a lot to offer. My six hours of treatments set me back a mere 4,370 CZK and included a seaweed bath and body wrap, an Amatsu massage, hydrocolon therapy (what can I say, I was curious), and a 120-minute facial that featured a divine paraffin treatment of my hands and feet. Reservations are

required, and I recommend that you try to make them by email before you arrive in Prague. Their excellent English website includes a full spa menu / price list, and Iveta, the front desk receptionist, speaks excellent English.

Pure Spa @ Hotel Le Palais

U Zvonařky 1, Prague 2, Vinohrady (Map E)
www.palaishotel.cz
TEL 234 634 111
HOURS Daily: 10:00–21:00
METRO I. P. Pavlova ● or Náměstí Míru ●
TRAM 6, 11 to Bruselská
TRAVEL TIME 15 min.

The Pure Spa at Hotel Le Palais is my go-to option when I want a luxury spa experience but simply can't afford the Mandarin Oriental or Augustine. It's is also a great place to spend a morning or afternoon in the winter months, when I love to take advantage of their health club, which includes a whirlpool, sauna, steam room, mood lighting, and the quirkiest thing yet: aromatic showers! I got to test eucalyptus and orange (eucalyptus was my preferred scent). Of the various massages, facials, and peelings offered here, the "Stone Infinity" treatment (60 minutes for 2,190 CZK) is my personal favorite – it involves a combination of hot stone therapy and massage and leaves me feeling both revived and relaxed. Reservations are absolutely required, and I recommend that you try to make them before you arrive in Prague. For a full menu of spa services, visit the website listed above.

Further Afield

■ ■ ■ ■ ■ ■ ■ ■ ■ ■ ■ ■ ■

Chateau Mcely

Mcely 61, Mcely
www.chateaumcely.com
TEL 325 600 000
HOURS Daily: 09:00–20:00
TRAVEL TIME 1 hour

Why not escape to the Bohemian countryside for a day at the spa? The Chateau Mcely spa is the perfect destination and definitely worth the effort to get there – trust me, you will not be disappointed. The spa features three spa suites, each with its own distinct personality. The *Honey Pavilion* is my favorite: located amidst the Chateau's gardens, this hexagonal wood structure features a wonderful wooden bathtub for two, as well as a fireplace – in the winter and autumn months, it is simply magical. This tranquil setting created the ideal atmosphere for enjoying the "Royal Ritual of Nine Flowers" (150 minutes for 5,890 CZK), which began with a cleansing sage-salt peeling, followed by a body wrap, a facial massage with a fabulous rose serum, a relaxing soak in the wooden bathtub laced with lavender crystal and rose petals, and – finally – a full-body massage with warm herbal pouches. Needless to say, this heavenly procedure left me limp, drooling, and thoroughly satisfied. Other treatments worth noting are the locally inspired "Beautifying Poppy Seed" (150 minutes for 5,200 CZK) – the Czech Republic is a poppy seed-loving nation – as well as the "Mcely Glow Facial" (90 minutes for 2,890 CZK). Before or after your treatment, you can also take advantage of the Chateau's private beach and lake, sauna building,

"CARBON BATHS" SPA TREATMENT, 1953

outdoor Jacuzzi, steam bath, health trail and sports grounds. Reservations are absolutely required, and I recommend that you try to make them before you arrive in Prague. For a full menu of spa services, visit the website listed above.

NOTE: All of the products used in their treatments are blended by hand in the Chateau's own "alchemical" laboratory, located on the property, using exclusively local ingredients. The full range of skin and body care products is available for purchase at the spa or at their online store.

NAIL CARE

■ ■ ■ ■ ■ ■ ■ ■ ■ ■ ■ ■ ■ ■
Express Elite Nails
Palladium Shopping Center náměstí Republiky 1078/1, Prague 1, Nové Město (Map A)
TEL 222 313 286
HOURS daily: 09:00–21:00
METRO Můstek ● ● or Náměstí Republiky ●
TRAM 5, 8, 14, 26 to Náměstí Republiky

Should you need a quick-fix manicure, this will be your best option, as no appointments are required. Located in a kiosk across from the Starbucks in Level -1 of the Palladium Shopping Center, the setting is less than relaxing, to say the least: you will be sitting on a bar stool in the middle of a mall with a terrible infomercial about nail care playing in the background, so brace yourself for that. I also found the prices a bit steep, given the setting . That said, the dry manicure they offer will do the trick if you need your nails done right away and don't have time to make an appointment at the other places I've recommended.

Manicures: 770 CZK including nail polish
CASH ONLY

■ ■ ■ ■ ■ ■ ■ ■ ■ ■ ■ ■ ■ ■
Four Seasons Hotel
Veleslavínova 2a, Prague 1, Staré Město (Map A)
www.fourseasons.com/prague
TEL 221 427 000
HOURS Daily: 08:00–20:00
METRO Staroměstská ●
TRAM 17, 18 to Staroměstská

This place is a real hidden gem. The pedicurist, Monika, is rumored to be among the best in town, and her English is as exceptional as the service she provides. The wet pedicure here is as close to a American pedicure experience as I have found in Prague. I must say that I was a bit disappointed by the lack of hot towels or a substantial foot and leg massage, but overall I was satisfied with the experience. Additionally it's worth noting that you can utilize the sauna and health club before or after your appointment – a major bonus – and they offer free valet parking. The health club is right next door to the manicure/pedicure room, so it can be somewhat noisy if people are on the treadmill during your appointment. Making an appointment is absolutely necessary, though calling in the morning for an afternoon appointment will usually suffice.

NOTE: Be sure to bring your own flip-flops or sandals if you want polish, as these are not provided.

Manicures: 1,470 CZK including nail polish
Pedicures: 1,920 CZK including nail polish

■ ■ ■ ■ ■ ■ ■ ■ ■ ■ ■ ■ ■ ■
Mandarin Oriental Hotel
Nebovidská 459/1, Prague 1, Malá Strana (Map B)
www.mandarinoriental.com/prague
TEL 233 088 888
HOURS Daily: 10:00–20:30
METRO Malostranská ●
TRAM 12, 20, 22 to Hellichova

As noted earlier, the Mandarin Oriental Hotel spa has established itself as the best in Prague – as well as the most expensive. I was a bit leery of spending 2,600 CZK on a pedicure; to say the price is steep is an understatement. However, believe it or not, I actually think it was money well spent, as they quite simply provided me with the *best* pedicure I've ever had. It was far more of a spa experience than a basic pedicure. First, they will ask you to change into a robe, which seems unnecessary but, trust me, it is not. The 75-minute pedicure is executed while you are lying down on a massage table and the experience is beyond relaxing; so much so that I found myself nodding off several times. It was also utterly peaceful, so if you hate the chit chat that normally accompanies manicures and pedicures you will love it here. I also encourage you to opt for the paraffin treatment, which costs an additional

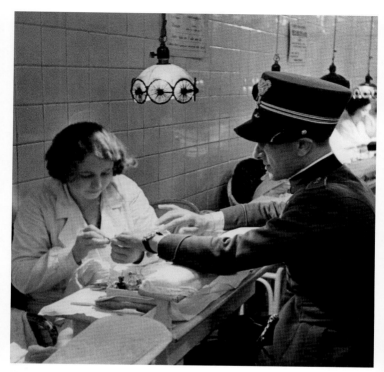

POLICEMAN HAVING A MANICURE, 1933
(SOURCE: ČTK / CZECH NEWS AGENCY)

500 CZK – but seriously, if you're already spending so much, does another 500 CZK really make a difference?

Making an appointment is absolutely necessary, though calling in the morning for an afternoon appointment will usually suffice.

NOTE: Be sure to bring your own flip-flops or sandals if you want polish, as these are not provided.

Manicures: 2,400 CZK including nail polish
Pedicures: 2,600 CZK including nail polish
Paraffin: 500 CZK

■ ■ ■ ■ ■ ■ ■ ■ ■ ■ ■ ■ ■
The Nail Shop / Darphin Salon

Slovanský dům, Na Příkopě 22, Prague 1, Nové Město (Map A)
www.opi.cz
TEL 221 451 800
HOURS Daily: 09:00–20:00
METRO Můstek ● ● or Náměstí Republiky ●
TRAM 5, 8, 14, 26 to Náměstí Republiky

The Nail Shop is a favorite of mine. If you're looking for a little TLC for your nails before hitting the town for the night, a stop here might be just what the doctor ordered. Iva is my go-to gal, and her English is exceptional (she worked in a Wisconsin salon for two years). They also offer facials and waxing. Appointments are absolutely necessary. The shop is located on the right-hand side of the courtyard in Slovanský dům, a building with several other retail shops and restaurants, directly across from Kogo Ristorante (see p. 160).

Manicures: 730 CZK including nail polish
Pedicures: 1,040 CZK including nail polish

Dining & Drinking

A few words before we begin: the good news is that dining out in Prague has become a tastier and more pleasant prospect in the last few years, and it continues to improve all the time. Indeed, I can assure you that you'll be pleasantly surprised by the quality, diversity, and sophistication you'll find.

One particularly noteworthy trend is the recent increase in the number of restaurants offering "artisanal" food: organically raised meats, local cheeses, and surprisingly fresh local produce are finding their way onto menus around town, providing a much wider range of options for "foodie" tourists and locals alike.

The bad news? It may surprise you to learn that dining in Prague is *definitely* no bargain. Indeed, some restaurants are actually incredibly expensive. Even after living here for so long I still find it shocking that meals here can cost more than dining out in New York City – especially at some of the fancier places in town.

That said, there are many yummy options all over the city, spanning a wide range of international cuisines, so if you're hungry, read on...

OLD HRADČANY TOWN HALL, 1958

A Few Pieces of Basic Advice

CHECK THE BILL

It's always wise to check the bill before paying, as mistakes do happen. I myself have actually had very *few* problems with overcharging; however, I've heard plenty of reports from other expats and visitors, so take a minute to double-check.

PAYING THE BILL

Except where noted, all of the restaurants listed below accept credit cards. You may find that some restaurants try to prohibit you from using your credit card for tips (or will include the words "tips in cash appreciated" on the credit card receipt); however, if they accept credit cards for the meal, there is no reason why you should not be able to add a tip to the final bill.

TIPPING

Tips are rarely included in the bill, so the assumption is that you'll add one yourself. A 10% tip is more than acceptable from foreigners; Czechs themselves tend to leave about half that. It's up to you whether you want to tip based on the price of the meal only or on the full cost, including the 21% VAT tax. I tend to tip based on the meal only, unless the service has been really exceptional.

DRESS CODE

Dress code at most Prague restaurants is generally informal. Even the chicest places will be happy to seat men without a jacket, and ties are simply never required.

TABLE SHARING

At more informal restaurants, it's absolutely acceptable to share a table if no other free ones are available.

RESERVATIONS

Strongly recommended for dinner; usually not necessary at lunchtime or at any of the Cafés / Quick Bites listed below.

RESTAURANTS

■ ■ ■ ■ ■ ■ ■ ■ ■ ■ ■ ■ ■
Bellevue
INTERNATIONAL
Smetanovo nábřeží 329/18, Prague 1, Staré Město (Map A)
www.bellevuerestaurant.cz
TEL 222 221 443
HOURS Daily: 12:00–15:00, 17:30–23:00
METRO Staroměstská ●
TRAM 17, 18 to Karlovy lázně

Table Request: Ask to sit near the window overlooking Prague Castle – simply a must!

Bellevue has been renowned for years as one of the best restaurants in town; it also happens to have a fantastic location, offering one of the all-time great views of Prague Castle and the Charles Bridge. Its reputation is well earned, and I can assure you a meal here will not let you down. Although the menu's descriptions of the food are not so exciting, the food itself is outstanding. The dining room is sophisticated and elegant in design, making Bellevue a perfect choice for a special evening on the town. The Bellevue Sea Degustation, a mixed seafood starter, is a real standout, and the seared foie gras is exceptional and vast. Ordering is made easy by their pricing structure: all starters, mains and deserts have the same price per category, so there's no need to labor over the dreaded "Can I afford the lobster?" dilemma.

Starters: 345 CZK
Main courses: 745 CZK
Dessert: 295 CZK
Wine: 790 CZK (3 glasses of wine paired to your order)
Wine: 890–30,000 CZK
Pilsner beer: 80 CZK

■ ■ ■ ■ ■ ■ ■ ■ ■ ■ ■ ■ ■
The Blue Duck
U Modré kachničky
CZECH
Nebovidská 6, Prague 1, Malá Strana (Map B)
www.umodrekachnicky.cz
TEL 257 320 308
HOURS Daily: 12:00–16:00 & 18:30–23:30
METRO Malostranská ● then
TRAM 12, 20, 22 to Hellichova

Table Request: Ask to sit in the upstairs dining room.

If you're after authentic Czech cuisine, this is a charming and pleasant place to get it. The décor upstairs is especially quaint, and is warmed up with antique furnishings. The duck, perhaps not surprisingly, is as traditional as you can get, and when you pair it with lots of potato and bread dumplings and cabbage, you'll be dining in classic Czech style. There are two locations for this restaurant, including another in the Old Town, but I prefer the one listed above.

Starters: 215–475 CZK
Main courses: 445–595 CZK
Dessert: 195 CZK
Wine: 375–9,490 CZK
Pilsner beer: 55 CZK

DINING

155

Foods You Really Should Try While You're In Prague

ENJOYING ICE CREAM POPS, 1973
(SOURCE: ČTK / CZECH NEWS AGENCY)

Breakfast and Lunch

Chlebíčky: These open-faced sandwiches are a staple of Czech cuisine. Classic options include *chlebíček se šunkou a vejcem* (ham and egg) and *chlebíček s herkulesem* (salami), all of which can usually be eaten while standing at small tables or counters at a *lahůdky* (delicatessen).

Soups

Bramboračka: Thick, creamy potato soup.

Česnečka: Garlic soup garnished with croutons and shredded cheese.

Hovězí vývar s játrovými knedlíčky: Beef bouillon with liver dumplings.

Main Courses

Guláš: Pieces of beef or pork cooked in a hearty sauce and served with bread dumplings.

Kachna s bramborovými knedlíky a zelím: Roast duck with cabbage and potato dumplings.

Ovocné knedlíky: Warm bread dumplings stuffed with fruit and topped with an ample amount of melted butter, powdered sugar and crumbled *tvaroh* (quark cheese). Flavors include *jahodové* (strawberry), *meruňkové* (apricot) and švestkové (plum). Czechs actually do eat these for dinner, but you might prefer trying them for dessert.

Řízek s bramborovým salátem: Breaded and fried fillets of chicken or pork (a.k.a. wiener schnitzel) served with potato salad.

Svíčková: Roast beef slices served in a cream sauce, garnished with cranberries and lemon and served with bread dumplings.

Vepřo, knedlo, zelo: Pork with cabbage and bread dumplings.

Vepřové koleno: Roasted pig's knee served on the bone with mustard, horseradish and rye bread – imposing!

Side Dishes

Bramborové knedlíky: Steamed potato dumplings – rather lead-like.

Houskové knedlíky: Steamed and sliced bread dumplings – great for soaking up sauce or gravy.

Krokety: Fried mashed-potato balls. A personal favorite.

Street Food

Sold at stalls on Wenceslas Square, Národní třída, and elsewhere.

Bramborák: Potato pancake.

Klobásy: Traditional grilled sausages served with mustard and a slice of rye bread.

Párek v rohlíku: A hot dog slid into a hollowed-out roll with the condiment of your choosing (mustard or ketchup).

Smažený sýr: Fried cheese, a true Czech specialty, served either alone or in a roll with tartar sauce. The perfect way to end a heavy night of drinking, with a grease level that can only be called impressive.

Trdelník: Rolled dough, wrapped around a stick, then rotisserie-baked and topped with a cinnamon, sugar and walnut mixture.

SAUSAGE PRODUCTION, 1957
(SOURCE: ČTK / CZECH NEWS AGENCY)

SVÍČKOVÁ (SERVED ON BLUE ONION CHINA)
(PHOTO BY JAN FISHER, 2012)

Sweets

Bábovka: Pound cake.

Kobliha: Jelly doughnut.

Koláč: The closest thing to a cheese danish from a Jewish bakery that you're going to find here. Other fillings include apricot, poppy seed and plum.

Lívaneček: Thick pancakes, resembling blinis, served with blueberries and whipped cream.

Medovník: Layered honey cake.

Míša: A *tvaroh* (quark cheese) ice cream pop covered with chocolate. Yum!

Palačinka: Czech-style crêpe often served with ice cream, fruit and whipped cream.

Závin / štrůdl: Good old-fashioned strudel – apple is the most popular, but *mák* (poppy seed) and *tvaroh* (quark cheese) are usually available too.

Soda

Kofola: Sort of like Coke.

Malinovka: Carbonated raspberry lemonade.

TopTopic: Sort of like Sprite.

Café Imperial

INTERNATIONAL / CZECH
Na Poříčí 15/ Prague 1, Nové Město (Map C)
www.cafeimperial.cz
TEL 246 011 440
HOURS Daily: 07:00–23:00
METRO Náměstí Republiky ●
TRAM 5, 8, 14, 26 to Náměstí Republiky

Table Request: Ask to sit in back of the main dining room, ideally at a banquette; I find these to be the best place from which to appreciate the incredible interior design.

Café Imperial is worthy of a visit not just for their food, which is delicious, but also for the original mosaic tile walls from 1914 that have recently been renovated to perfection. The space is simply incredible – I always feel like I am dining in some surreal Art Deco spa – so you should definitely try to pop in and sneak a peek even if you are not hungry. The menu combines both International and Czech options; I always seem to choose the Czech items, with the schnitzel and mashed potatoes being my personal favorite. The staff, to be honest, is less than charming – often acting as though serving your food is a major inconvenience – yet somehow I always forgive them, as the space is so wholly unique.

Starters: 85–199 CZK
Main courses: 205–355 CZK
Dessert: 127–147 CZK
Wine: 445–1675 CZK
Pilsner beer: 61 CZK

DINING

157

WORKERS FROM THE UNITED AGRICULTURAL COOPERATIVE ARE REWARDED WITH A MEAL IN KARLOVY VARY, 1960 (SOURCE: ČTK / CZECH NEWS AGENCY)

■ ■ ■ ■ ■ ■ ■ ■ ■ ■ ■ ■ ■ ■ ■

Café Savoy

CZECH / INTERNATIONAL
Vítězná 5, Prague 5, Malá
Strana (Map B)
www.ambi.cz
TEL 257 311 562
HOURS Mon–Fri: 8:00–22:30;
Sat & Sun: 9:00–22:30
TRAM 6, 9, 12, 20, 22 to Újezd

Table Request: For dinner, ask to sit in the back room, ideally at the center banquette facing the main dining room. For breakfast or lunch, request a table in the front room, facing the street (so you can watch the trams go by).

Housed in a handsome Neo-Classical space, this café is a real find, as it serves breakfast, lunch and dinner, not to mention the best cake in town. Many people, including myself, have wondered why Czech café culture generally falls so far short of the Viennese model; but thankfully, with Café Savoy, I'm able to get around that problem without a six-hour drive to Demels. The food here is terrific, especially the soups, and priced very fairly. They also have a very good wine list. I would recommend this restaurant for breakfast, lunch, or dinner, as it's one of the very few places in Prague that is actually good with all three. If you do go for breakfast, make sure to try a few of the classic Czech pastry offerings, as you won't see them at many other places. These include: *bábovka* (pound cake); *koláč* (similar to a Danish, with fillings that include tvaroh [cheese] and mák [poppyseed]); apple strudel; and *rebarborový koláč* (rhubarb pastry so rich and complex, it verges on the savory).

Starters: 125–208 CZK
Main courses: 185–325 CZK
Dessert: 45–195 CZK
Wine: 455–11,450 CZK
Pilsner beer: 55 CZK

Breakfast: 08:00–11:00; average price 280 CZK.

DINING

■ ■ ■ ■ ■ ■ ■ ■ ■ ■ ■ ■ ■

Coda

INTERNATIONAL
Tržiště 9, Prague 1,
Malá Strana (Map B)
www.codarestaurant.cz
TEL 225 334 761
HOURS Daily: 12:00–24:00
METRO Malostranská ●
TRAM 12, 20, 22 to
Malostranské náměstí

Table Request: Ask to sit on
the terrace, facing the
Prague Castle and St.
Nicholas Church.

Located on the roof terrace
of the Aria Hotel (see p. 25),
Coda has become my place
of choice for terrace dining,
as it's nestled among the
rooftops of Malá Strana—
about as charming as it gets
in Prague. The menu is
mainly international, with
a few Czech classics thrown
in, and the food is consistently right on the mark. If
you choose to dine inside,
you should ask to be seated
at the beautiful original
green Art Deco dining table.

Starters: 360–490 CZK
Main courses: 490–750 CZK
Dessert: 290–390 CZK
Wine: 590–15,900 CZK
Pilsner beer: 150 CZK

■ ■ ■ ■ ■ ■ ■ ■ ■ ■ ■ ■ ■

CottoCrudo Restaurant at the Four Seasons Hotel

ITALIAN
Veleslavínova 2a, Prague 1,
Staré Město (Map A)
www.cottocrudo.cz
TEL 221 426 880
HOURS Daily: 12:00–22:30
METRO Staroměstská ●
TRAM 17, 18 to Staroměstská

Table Request: If the weather
allows, ask to sit on the
outdoor terrace; otherwise,
request a table next to the
window overlooking the
river.

Located inside the lovely
Four Seasons Hotel (see p.
30), CottoCrudo opened in
late 2011. Unlike its
predecessor, Allegro, I can
actually afford to eat here
– and I often do, as I love
the chic décor almost as
much as the menu. Misto
CottoCrudo, a cold anti-
pasto platter, is my starter
of choice, followed by the
pan-fried cod with
chickpea puree – both are
simply exceptional. Once
you're seated, it's easy to
forget you're at a hotel;
indeed, more than half of
the people dining there on
any given night are not
hotel guests. The food is
excellent, and the riverside
location overlooking the
Charles Bridge and the
Prague Castle is nothing
short of dreamy. I also love
to indulge in a drink or two
at their bar / lounge, which
offers fabulous booths –
always my preferred
seating. A live DJ plays on
Thursday and Friday nights
from 21:00–24:00.

Starters: 100–380 CZK
Main courses: 440–640 CZK
Dessert: 180 CZK
Wine: 580–41,000 CZK
Budvar beer: 70 CZK

■ ■ ■ ■ ■ ■ ■ ■ ■ ■ ■ ■ ■

Grosseto Marina Ristorante

ITALIAN
Alšovo nábřeží, Prague 1,
Staré Město (Map A)
www.grosseto.cz
TEL 605 454 020
HOURS Daily: 11:30–24:00
METRO Staroměstská ●
TRAM 17, 18 to Staroměstská

Table Request: Ask for a
riverside table, no matter
what – and if the weather
is good, ask to be seated
upstairs.

As the saying goes, when it
comes to real estate, what
matters most is "location,
location, location" – and it's
quite possible that this
restaurant has the best one
in town. Located on a
beautifully decorated barge
in the river, it offers one of
the all-time great views of
Prague Castle and Malá
Strana – simply magical.
It's one of my own personal
favorites, so I'm a regular
customer. The menu
includes pizzas, pastas, and
salads, as well as an
excellent selection of fresh
fish and meats. The food is
consistently good – I usually
opt for a pizza – and the
prices are extremely
reasonable, considering the
prime location. Please note
that it's only possible to
make table reservations for
the downstairs seating
area, but the wait for a
table upstairs is usually
only 10-15 minutes and you
can enjoy a glass of prosecco
while you wait.

Starters: 55–249 CZK
Main courses: 270–590 CZK
Pizza: 189–229 CZK
Pasta: 165–2255 CZK
Dessert: 110–145 CZK
Wine: 460–11,000 CZK
Staropramen beer: 55 CZK

■ ■ ■ ■ ■ ■ ■ ■ ■ ■ ■ ■ ■

Hergetova Cihelna

INTERNATIONAL
Cihelná 2b, Prague 1,
Malá Strana (Map B)
www.kampagroup.com/en/
TEL 296 826 103
HOURS Daily: 11:30–24:00
METRO Malostranská ●
TRAM 12, 20, 22 to
Malostranské náměstí

Table Request: Ask to sit on
the terrace next to the wall.

This restaurant boasts a
fabulously expansive

terrace right next to the river and a prime view of the Charles Bridge. Less expensive than Kampa Park (see below) but with an equally inspiring riverside view, it's certainly a great option, though hardly on par with the former in terms of either culinary sophistication or total execution. The food is international, with a little bit of everything, and the wine list is fairly expensive relative to the rest of the menu, with bottles starting around 500 CZK.

Starters: 235–445 CZK
Main courses: 395–595 CZK
Dessert: 195–295 CZK
Wine: 475–21,950 CZK
Pilsner beer: 75 CZK

■ ■ ■ ■ ■ ■ ■ ■ ■ ■ ■ ■ ■ ■

Kampa Park
INTERNATIONAL / MEDITERRANEAN
Na Kampě 8b, Prague 1, Malá Strana (Map B)
www.kampagroup.com/en/
TEL 296 826 112
HOURS Daily: 11:30–24:00
METRO Malostranská ●
TRAM 12, 20, 22 to Malostranské náměstí

Table Request: Ask for the riverside terrace downstairs, which is open year-round.

Everything here is outstanding: food, service, and location. They really don't miss a trick, which is why this has been one of my favorite places in town for years. It's equally popular among locals, tourists and even A-list celebrities. The best things about this restaurant is its location, which is literally *on* the river, beneath the strikingly lit arches of the Charles Bridge, making it very possibly the most

MEAL PREPARATION, 1964
(SOURCE: ČTK / CZECH NEWS AGENCY)

romantic spot in town for dinner. Even if you're not able to get a table on the terrace, it's still *highly* recommended, as the food itself here is simply outstanding.

Starters: 395–595 CZK
Main courses: 425–895 CZK
Dessert: 295 CZK
Wine: 595–24,950 CZK
Pilsner beer: 55 CZK

■ ■ ■ ■ ■ ■ ■ ■ ■ ■ ■ ■ ■ ■

Kogo Ristorante
ITALIAN
Slovanský dům, Na Příkopě 22 (in the courtyard), Prague 1, Nové Město (Map A)
www.kogo.cz
TEL 221 451 258
HOURS Daily: 11:00–23:00
METRO Můstek ● ● or Náměstí Republiky ●
TRAM 5, 8, 14, 26 to Náměstí Republiky

Table Request: Ask to sit either under the covered terrace or in the winter garden.

If you're curious as to where the locals lunch, well, now you know. This also happens to be one of

my own personal favorites, so I'm a regular. The food is always great and the service is outstanding. An added bonus is the location in a very large, quiet courtyard right in the middle of downtown Prague, which gives you the pleasure of eating outside without the hassle of being bombarded by tourist traffic. The menu includes pastas, pizzas, and salads, as well as an excellent selection of fresh fish.

Starters: 240–745 CZK
Main courses: 195–950 CZK
Pasta: 245–395 CZK
Dessert: 105–170 CZK
Wine: 490–11,500 CZK
Pilsner beer: 55 CZK

■ ■ ■ ■ ■ ■ ■ ■ ■ ■ ■ ■ ■ ■

Nostress Café
ASIAN FUSION / FRENCH
Dušní 10, Prague 1, Staré Město (Map A)
www.nostress.cz
TEL 222 317 007
HOURS Daily: 10:00–24:00
METRO Staroměstská ●
TRAM 17, 18 to Staroměstská

DINING

Table Request: There's a great table with four leather club chairs located in the back room on the ground floor – see if it's available.

While this definitely wins the prize for the Worst Restaurant Name in Prague, the café itself is actually lovely. Located in the Old Town, close to the Jewish Quarter (Josefov), it's especially good for lunch, and both the chicken salad and fried shrimp with coconut sauce are yummy. The atmosphere here is great – it feels like they're going for a vibe reminiscent of Buddha Bar in Paris – and I can definitely recommend it for a before-dinner drink or a nightcap.

Starters: 220–480 CZK
Main courses: 230–460 CZK
Dessert: 150–180 CZK
Wine: 550–3,690 CZK
Pilsner beer: 60 CZK
Breakfast: 10:00–11:30; average price 250 CZK.

■ ■ ■ ■ ■ ■ ■ ■ ■ ■ ■ ■

La Degustation Boheme Bourgeoise
CZECH / FRENCH
Haštalská 18, Prague 1, Staré Město (Map A)
www.ladegustation.cz
TEL 222 311 234
HOURS Daily: 18:00–24:00
TRAM 5, 8, 14, 26 to Dlouhá třída

Table Request: Ask for a table in the corner with a view of the open kitchen, so you can watch the chefs prepare your meal.

If haute cuisine is what you are after – and you have at least three hours to spare – La Degustation will not let you down. Each evening they offer two different seven-course tasting menus, with an optional wine pairing menu for each. The *Degustation Boheme Bourgeois* menu presents traditional Czech cuisine inspired by an 1894 cookbook by Marie B. Svobodová; the *Degustation du Chef* menu tends to include French dishes. Uniquely, should you happen not to like any of the items in the menu, they are happy to make substitutions. Both menus change daily based on ingredient availability; all ingredients are sourced from Czech organic farms and small local producers. This would be an exceedingly worthwhile destination restaurant in any major city around the globe, which makes its presence here in Prague that much more remarkable. Reservations are absolutely required and should be made well in advance if possible.

Degustation du Chef: 2,750 CZK
Wine Pairing: 1,890 CZK

Degustation Boheme Bourgeois: 2,250 CZK
Wine Pairing: 1,390 CZK

BREAKFAST, 1933
(SOURCE: ČTK / CZECH NEWS AGENCY)

DINING

La Finestra In Cucina

ITALIAN

Platnéřská 13, Prague 1,
Staré Město (Map A)
www.lafinestra.cz
TEL 222 325 325
HOURS Daily: 12:00–23:00
METRO Staroměstská ●
TRAM 17, 18 to Staroměstská

Table Request: Ask to sit in the second section of the dining room, which is further from the front door; large parties should request the Wine Room in the basement.

La Finestra is the sister restaurant of Aromi (see p. 165) and is located in the heart of downtown, just a stone's throw from the Four Seasons Hotel. They offer excellent authentic Italian food in a dark, cozy setting. You won't find any pizza on this menu, but what you *will* find are wonderful antipasti, soup, pasta, meat and fish. Meat is their specialty, and they will bring the various cuts of the day to your table so you can choose what you like. The last time I was there, I had a monstrous steak, which was grilled to perfection. Between courses they serve a delicious sorbet, and the quick, helpful staff doesn't miss a beat. I'm confident you will enjoy a meal here. Be forewarned that reservations are an absolute must, as this is quite possibly the most sought-after restaurant in Prague, so I recommend making them at least several days in advance.

Starters: 180–345 CZK
Main courses: 345–545 CZK
Dessert: 165–195 CZK
Wine: 595–27,500 CZK
Staropramen beer: 45 CZK

SERVING SOUP TO WORKERS AT LUNCHTIME, 1963
(SOURCE: ČTK / CZECH NEWS AGENCY)

Lví Dvůr – Pražské Selátko

CZECH / INTERNATIONAL

U Prašného mostu 6/51,
Prague 1, Hradčany (Map D)
www.lvidvur.cz
TEL 257 530 226
HOURS Daily: 11:00–23:00
METRO Malostranská ●
TRAM 22 to Pražský hrad

Table Request: Ask to sit on the outdoor terrace if the weather allows; if not, try to get a table where you can watch them roast the pig!

I avoided this restaurant for years because I assumed it was simply a tourist trap, as it's located on the grounds of Prague Castle. My assumption was not incorrect – on any visit the majority of guest will almost certainly be tourists – nevertheless, there *are* very good reasons to eat here. They happen to have what is quite possibly the best wiener schnitzel in town (wait till you see it – utterly impressive!) and they're renowned for their suckling pig, which is roasted before your eyes in the main dining room. With a little advance notice, you can even order a whole piglet for 7,000 CZK! Be sure to hang onto your menu long enough to read the interesting history of the building, as well as some historical information about the roasted suckling pig.

Starters: 70–280 CZK
Main courses: 250–590 CZK
Dessert: 90 CZK
Wine: 490–2,900 CZK
Krušovice beer: 70 CZK

Maitrea

INTERNATIONAL / VEGETARIAN

Týnská ulička 6, Prague 1,
Staré Město (Map A)
www.restaurace-maitrea.cz
TEL 221 711 631
HOURS Mon-Fri: 11:30–23:30;
Sat & Sun: 12:00–23:30
METRO Můstek ● ●

DINING

Table Request: I like to sit downstairs, where the atmosphere is more private – but there's really not a bad table in the house.

One of the best vegetarian restaurants in town, Maitrea also happens to be the most beautiful. The interior design can best be described as organic Art Nouveau – reminiscent of the famous Spanish architect Antoni Gaudí – which the website describes as being "in the style of feng shui." The food is excellent and extremely diverse – ranging in style from Asian to Mexican – and even includes vegetarian versions of Czech specialties such as *guláš*, *svíčková* (see p. 156) and roast "duck" with dumplings and cabbage – all of which are made with soy protein. There are also several vegan options, which are clearly marked on the menu. Reservations are absolutely required for lunch and dinner.

They have a second vegetarian restaurant called Lehká Hlava ("Clear Head" | www.lehkahlava. cz), which is located in Old Town at Boršov 2 (Map A), but I simply prefer Maitrea.

Starters: 65–95 CZK
Main courses: 145–160 CZK
Dessert: 65–85 CZK
Wine: 220–480 CZK
Konopné beer (made from hemp!): 40 CZK

■ ■ ■ ■ ■ ■ ■ ■ ■ ■ ■ ■
Nota Bene
(see p. 179)

Although this newcomer (opened in 2012) specializes in Czech craft beer, it also has fantastic food. Worth a trip, even if you're not a beer drinker.

■ ■ ■ ■ ■ ■ ■ ■ ■ ■ ■ ■
PastaCaffé
ITALIAN
Vězeňská 1, Prague 1,
Staré Město (Map A)
www.ambi.cz
TEL 224 813 257
HOURS Mon–Sat: 08:00–22:00; Sun: 10:00–22:00
METRO Staroměstská ●
TRAM 17, 18 to Staroměstská

Table Request: Ask for a banquette along the wall.

At once sleekly Italian and offbeat, this retro 1950s restaurant is perfect for breakfast, lunch or an informal dinner. It's also great for a quick espresso or cappuccino - certain to be one of the best cups of coffee you'll find in town. The menu is limited to salads, paninis and pasta. Frequented by locals and tourists alike, Pastacaffé also happens to be child-friendly, with a large bucket of toys for kids to play with, as well as a changing table in the bathroom.

Starters: 138–188 CZK
Main courses: 165–228 CZK
Dessert: 45–148 CZK
Wine: 288–1,950 CZK
Pilsner beer: 55 CZK

Breakfast: 08:00–11:00; average price 236 CZK

■ ■ ■ ■ ■ ■ ■ ■ ■ ■ ■ ■
Sansho
"FUNKY ASIAN"
Petrská 25, Prague 1,
Nové Město (Map F)
www.sansho.cz
TEL 222 317 425
HOURS Tue–Thurs: 11:30–15:00 & 18:00–22:30;
Fri: 11:30–15:00 & 18:00–23:30; Sat: 18:00–23:00
METRO Florenc ● ○
TRAMS 3, 8, 24 to Bílá labuť or 3 to Těšnov

Table Request: Ask for a table on the sidewalk if the weather is warm; if you're eating inside, ask to sit in the main dining room. Note that indoor tables are communal (with bench seating), so if you want more privacy, request an individual table.

Located off the beaten track on a quiet square, newcomer Sansho opened in 2011 and has quickly become my absolute favorite restaurant in town. The setting is informal yet sophisticatedly chic, with shared tables and a seasonal six-course tasting menu of delectable dishes that are served family-style. The food here is simply sublime, and not only are all ingredients sourced locally, but the sustainably-raised meat comes from the Real Meat Society (see p. 130), which also happens to be owned by Sansho's visionary owner and head chef, Paul Day. And, as if all that wasn't enough, the perfectly-coiffed waiters, dressed in cute plaid shirts, speak perfect English and don't miss a beat. The duck sliders with Hoisin sauce and the pork belly with watermelon salad were two of my favorite items served on a recent visit. If you're not thoroughly stuffed by the end of your meal, don't think twice – say YES to the sticky toffee pudding, as it is simply to die for.

NOTE: The restaurant has no outdoor signage.

Six-course tasting menu: 750 CZK
Dessert: 135 CZK (Sticky Toffee Pudding)
Wine: 380 –3,650 CZK
Kumburak beer: 55 CZK

Terasa U Zlaté studně

INTERNATIONAL

U Zlaté studně 4, Prague 1, Malá Strana (Map B)

www.terasauzlatestudne.cz

TEL 257 533 322

HOURS Daily: 07:00–23:00

METRO Malostranská ●

TRAM 12, 20, 22 to Malostranské náměstí

Table Request: Ask to sit outside on the terrace, next to the railing; if eating inside, request a table next to the window.

The first thing I should say about Terasa U Zlaté studně is that, unless your legs are in spectacular shape, you'll want to take a taxi there, as it is nestled in a little nook high up in the steeply sloped neighborhood of Malá Strana, inside the U Zlaté studně Hotel. They won't win any prizes for best signage (or warmest welcome either); once you're inside the building, just keep heading up and eventually you'll find the rooftop terrace, where you'll be rewarded with one of the most outstanding views of Prague – basically an all-encompassing panorama of the city – which is good, because while the food is certainly fine, it's the view you're really paying for.

Starters: 290–750 CZK
Main courses: 420–1,150 CZK
Dessert: 180–330 CZK
Wine: 800–42,900 CZK
Pilsner beer: 70 CZK

Breakfast: 07:00–11:00; 600 CZK. On a beautiful day when you have a little time to spare, this could be a great option.

U ZLATÉ STUDNĚ (THE GOLDEN WELL), C. 1930

V Zátiší

INTERNATIONAL / CZECH / INDIAN

Betlémské nám./ Liliová 1, Prague 1, Staré Město (Map A)

www.vzatisi.cz

TEL 222 221 155

HOURS Daily: 12:00–15:00 & 17:30–23:00

METRO Staroměstská ●

TRAM 17, 18 to Národní divadlo or Karlovy lázně

Table Request: Ask to sit in the "organic" dining room (not the main dining room), as I find it much prettier and more intimate.

Located on a quiet picturesque square in the heart of downtown, V Zátiší opened in 1991 (just two years after the fall of communism) and was one of the first private restaurants established in Prague. Since then it has become a major destination for food connoisseurs, along with its sister restaurant, Bellevue (see p. 155). A bit more casual than Bellevue (and lacking its magnificent view), V Zátiší serves consistently excellent food and is a place where you will absolutely be dining with locals. The menu can be described as eclectic, as it ranges from International to Czech to even Indian, and this definitely won me over, as there is absolutely something for any palate and everything is delicious. As at Bellevue, ordering is made easy by their pricing structure: all starters, mains and deserts have the same price per category, so there's no need to labor over the dreaded "Can I afford the caviar?" dilemma.

Starters: 295 CZK
Main courses: 695 CZK
Dessert: 245 CZK
Wine: 590 CZK (3 glasses of wine paired to match your order)
Wine: 790–9900 CZK
Pilsner or Budweiser beer: 90 CZK

■ ■ ■ ■ ■ ■ ■ ■ ■ ■ ■ ■ ■ ■

Villa Richter – Terra
CZECH / INTERNATIONAL / GRILL
Staré zámecké schody 6/251, Prague 1, Malá Strana (Map D)
www.villarichter.cz
TEL 257 219 079
HOURS Daily: 11:00–23:00
METRO Malostranská ●
TRAM 12, 18, 20, 22 to Malostranská

Table Request: Ideally, you will want to sit at the open-air terrace, but if that's full or the weather is questionable, ask to be seated on the covered terrace. In either case, request a table that is closer to the view than to the restaurant itself.

Villa Richter – Terra offers a panoramic view of Prague that definitely rivals that of Terasa U Zlaté studně, which is of the most expensive restaurants in town (see p. 164). Nestled among the vineyards of the Prague Castle gardens, just off of the Old Castle Stairs, it's a great choice for lunch or dinner either before or after visiting the castle. They offer a decent selection of Czech wines, and the food, while nothing to write home about, is definitely more than acceptable. The prices are a bargain, especially considering the location and the view: the average meal will cost less than

half what you'd pay at Terasa U Zlaté studně, for example. The one major downside is the service, which is acceptable when business is slow, but terrible when they are busy (which is most of the time), so hopefully you're not in a rush – just sit back and enjoy the view.

NOTE: There are other "Villa Richter" dining options at the same location, including the more upscale Piano Nobile restaurant and a casual wine bar, but Terra is your best bet.

Starters: 89–199 CZK
Main courses: 169–359 CZK
Dessert: 99–129 CZK
Wine: 390–590 CZK (Exclusively Czech)
Pilsner: 55 CZK

Slightly Further Afield

■ ■ ■ ■ ■ ■ ■ ■ ■ ■ ■ ■ ■ ■

Aromi
ITALIAN
Mánesova 78, Prague 2, Vinohrady (Map E)
www.aromi.cz
TEL 222 713 222
HOURS Mon–Sat: 12:00–23:00; Sun: 12:00–22:00
METRO Jiřího z Poděbrad ●
TRAM 11 to Jiřího z Poděbrad
TRAVEL TIME 15 min.

Table Request: In the summer, you'll want to be out on the terrace; if you're sitting inside, ask to sit near a window, preferably in the back corner next to the bookcase.

Aromi is located on a charming, tree-lined street in the residential district of Vinohrady, and they offer excellent authentic Italian food in a warm, cozy setting. You won't find any

pizza on this menu, but what you *will* find is wonderful antipasti, pasta, meat and fish. Fish is their specialty, and the last time I was there, I had the grilled octopus, which was not only grilled to perfection but served in its gloriously monstrous entirety—something you don't see every day. Both helpful and quick, the staff doesn't miss a beat. I'm confident you will enjoy a meal here. If you're staying across the river or in the city center, Aromi is very easy to reach by public transport, but you may simply want to have your hotel arrange for a taxi.

Starters: 325–395 CZK
Main courses: 395–425 CZK
Pasta: 295–385 CZK
Dessert: 155–295 CZK
Wine: 660–11,795 CZK
Stella Artois beer: 55 CZK

■ ■ ■ ■ ■ ■ ■ ■ ■ ■ ■ ■ ■ ■

Radost FX Café
INTERNATIONAL / VEGETARIAN
Bělehradská 120, Prague 2, Vinohrady (Map E)
www.radostfx.cz
TEL 603 193 711
HOURS Daily: 11:00–02:00
METRO Náměstí Míru ● or I. P. Pavlova ●
TRAM 4, 6, 10, 11, 16, 22 to I. P. Pavlova
TRAVEL TIME 10 to 15 min.

Table Request: Ask to sit in the back room, where the seating is comfier and the lounge atmosphere is more fun.

One of the best vegetarian restaurants in town, Radost also happens to be the hippest. The décor is at once charming and funky, and the food is simply terrific. It's perfect for a light supper—or even a

WINDOW AT KAVÁRNA SLAVIA CAFÉ (SEE P. 170), C.1978

DINING

not-so-light one, should you order the huge spinach burger—and it will let you see where all the young hip locals converge. They also serve an excellent brunch on the weekend, including their own highly unique interpretation of a bagel. Should you be traveling with your teenagers or 20-something children, they will definitely thank you for choosing this spot (especially if you give them their own table away from any parental style-cramping).

CASH ONLY

Starters: 135–155 CZK
Main courses: 165–195 CZK
Dessert: 60–85 CZK
Wine: 155–660 CZK
Pilsner or Kozel beer: 40 CZK

Breakfast: 11:00–15:00; average price 220 CZK

CAFÉS / QUICK BITES

I have not included pricing for any of the listings in this section, as they are *all* inexpensive. At virtually any of these listings you can assume the total will be 300 CZK or less; the only exceptions, perhaps, being CukrKávaLimonáda and Lobkowicz Palace Café at the Prague Castle, at either of which your total might reach 400 CZK, depending on what you order.

■ ■ ■ ■ ■ ■ ■ ■ ■ ■ ■ ■ ■
Angelato
Rytířská 27, Prague 1, Staré Město (Map A)
www.angelato.cz
TEL 224 235 123
HOURS Daily: 11:00–21:00
METRO Můstek ● ●

As something of an ice cream connoisseur, I can advise you with confidence that Angelato will satisfy even the most demanding customer. I usually get my cone or cup to go, or take it to one of the informal tables just outside. There are three sizes available and prices start at 35 CZK. Flavors range from the usual classics to locally inspired options such as the marzipan-flavored "Mozart," poppy seeds, and even beer!

CASH ONLY

■ ■ ■ ■ ■ ■ ■ ■ ■ ■ ■ ■ ■
Angels Coffee
Týn 2, Prague 1, Staré Město (Map A)
www.angelscoffee.eu
TEL 723 829 700
HOURS Daily: 08:00–24:00
METRO Můstek ● ● or Náměstí Republiky ●
TRAM 5, 8, 14, 26 to Náměstí Republiky

If you want to sit down for a cup of coffee near Old Town Square but don't enjoy having your toes crushed by swarms of tourists passing by, Angels Coffee is a nice spot to keep in mind. The location is also great if you have kids, as it's tucked away in a courtyard where they'll be able to run around to their hyperactive little hearts' delight while you sip coffee (and try to boost yourself back up to their energy level) without having to worry. Afterwards, pop into nearby Botanicus, a lovely shop filled with all sorts of scented soaps, potpourri and other fragrant goodies.

Au Gourmand

Dlouhá 10, Prague 1, Staré Město (Map A)
www.augourmand.cz
TEL 222 329 060
HOURS Mon–Fri: 08:00–22:00; Sat & Sun: 08:30–22:00
METRO Staroměstská ●
TRAM 17, 18 to Staroměstská

This is a great stop for coffee, cake or a light lunch near the Old Town Square. Formerly a turn-of-the-20th-century butcher shop, it still boasts the original floor mosaic and wall tiles illustrated with animals both before and after their trip to the slaughterhouse (fun!). Apart from anything else, they have the best millefeuille in town. Au Gourmand also has a second location in Old Town (at Rytířská 22), but I like their Flagship store on Dlouhá better.

Bakeshop Praha

Kozí 1, Prague 1, Staré Město (Map A)

www.bakeshop.cz
TEL 222 316 823
HOURS Daily: 07:00–21:00
METRO Staroměstská ●
TRAM 17, 18 to Staroměstská

If you're strolling near Old Town Square and just want a quick bite or a good cup of coffee to go, this is your place. They have fresh baked cookies, brownies, and other treats, as well as delicious BLTs, quiches, bagels and *excellent* lattes. Though there are no tables to sit at, there are stools at a bar-like counter, plus benches outside along the cobblestone sidewalk. Nothing does the trick better when you're super hungover—particularly their ham and cheese croissants, which are extraordinarily high on the grease factor. I highly recommend these, though there's nothing even remotely light or airy about them.

BALOUNKOVA CIKORKA A ŽITNÁ KÁVA zlepší Vaši snídani!

ADVERTISEMENT FOR SUGAR AND COFFEE, C. 1920

Bella Vida Café

Malostranské nábřeží 3, Prague 1, Malá Strana (Map B)
www.bella-vida-cafe.cz
TEL 221 710 494
HOURS Daily: 09:00–21:00
TRAM 6, 9, 12, 20, 22 to Újezd

A charming place for breakfast, lunch or coffee, Bella Vida Café is located in one of the choicest pieces of real estate in the city, which offers lovely views of Kampa Park, Prague Castle, the Charles Bridge, as well as the river. It offers an excellent ham and cheese omelet (always my personal choice), as well as tasty soups, sandwiches, salads, pastas and desserts — all at *very* reasonable prices. If it's warm outside, grab a table on the sidewalk.

Café Louvre

Národní 22, Prague 1, Nové Město (Map A)
www.cafelouvre.cz
TEL 224 930 949, 724 054 055
HOURS Mon–Fri: 08:00–23:30; Sat & Sun: 09:00–23:30
METRO Národní třída ●
TRAM 6, 9, 18, 21, 22 to Národní třída

Café Louvre opened in 1902 and has an illustrious history, having served such greats as Albert Einstein and Franz Kafka. Business was interrupted by the Communists in 1948 and the café did not reopen until 1992. Today you will find a mix of locals and tourists, young and old, indulging in their less-than-fabulous food, which includes offerings for breakfast, lunch, and dinner (and, of course, cake). Also, should you desire, you can even shoot a round of pool in their billiard room, which has five tables and is open all day. The service is typically grumpy and slow, but Café Louvre is worth a visit regardless, if only to stop in and see the space, as it really is a key player in Prague's rich café history.

■■■■■■■ ■ ■ ■ ■ ■
Česká Kuchyně

Havelská 23, Prague 1,
Staré Město (Map C)
www.havelska-koruna.cz
TEL 224 239 331
HOURS Daily: 10:00–20:00
METRO Můstek ● ●

If you *really* want to eat where the locals eat, look no further than this cafeteria where ALL options are well below 100 CZK. When you enter, you will be handed a ticket – don't lose it or you'll need to pay a 500 CZK penalty – and then collect a tray, peruse the various food stations, and select whatever captures your fancy. They offer sweet and savory options, both warm and cold. I definitely recommend indulging in a sweet lunch of *Ovocné knedlíky s tvarohem a máslem* (fruit dumplings with shredded quark cheese and butter), as it is excellent and only 29 CZK; if you fancy something savory, they offer all the Czech classics, including *guláš* and *svíčková* (see p. 156). Pilsner beer is on tap for 36 CZK for a .5 liter glass. After paying, take a seat in one of the many seating areas and enjoy your breakfast, lunch or dinner with *very* few tourists in sight. Shockingly, they have signage in English – bonus!
CASH ONLY

GRAND CAFE ORIENT, C. 1915 (IT LOOKS JUST LIKE THIS TODAY)

■■■■■■■■■■■■■
Country Life

Melantrichova 15, Prague 1,
Staré Město (Map C)
www.countrylife.cz
TEL 224 213 366
HOURS Mon–Thurs: 08:30–19:00; Fri: 08:30–18:00
METRO Můstek ● ●

Should you find yourself hankering for a vegetarian meal or a certified organic peach, Country Life is where you'll want to head. The daily offerings include warm and cold food served in a small, very informal dining area with very cool tables carved from the trunks of trees. During the warm months, be sure to check out the courtyard. While you're there, be sure to hop into their store across the courtyard, where they sell lots of soaps, lotions, oils and candles, some of which are from the Czech Republic (though many others are imported from France).

■■■■■■■■■■■■■
CukrKávaLimonáda

Lázeňská 7, Prague 1,
Malá Strana (Map B)
www.cukrkavalimonada.com/en/
TEL 257 225 396
HOURS Mon–Sat: 09:00–19:00; Sun: 9:30–19:00
METRO Malostranská ●
TRAM 12, 20, 22 to Malostranské náměstí

A charming place for breakfast, lunch or coffee, right in the heart of Malá Strana. CukrKávaLimonáda offers ciabatta sandwiches, frittata, pasta, salads, as well as both sweet and savory crêpes – all at very reasonable prices. They also offer continental breakfast, as well as eggs prepared in various ways, including the very bold and fabulous option of scrambled eggs with shrimp. My favorite is the crêpes, which are made with the very freshest ingredients. Be sure to take note of the painted ceilings!
CASH ONLY

DINING

Grand Café Orient at the House of the Black Madonna

Ovocný trh 19, Prague 1, Staré Město (Map A)

www.grandcafeorient.cz

TEL 224 224 240

HOURS Mon–Fri: 09:00–22:00; Sat &Sun: 10:00–22:00

METRO Můstek ● ● or Náměstí Republiky ●

TRAM 5, 8, 14, 26 to Náměstí Republiky

The original Grand Café Orient opened in 1912 on the first floor of the House of the Black Madonna, which now houses the Museum of Czech Cubisim (see p. 58). Closed since 1925, it was reopened in 2005 after a painstaking renovation (guided by a few surviving plans and photos), and they have succeeded brilliantly in recreating the space. Replicas of the original furniture and brass chandeliers, designed by Czech Cubist designer Josef Gočár, help to conjure up the original atmosphere, and it doesn't take a great deal of imagination or wishful thinking to step back in time to the café's early days – especially when the live pianist performs (Thurs–Sun: 16:00–19:00). This café is more about the experience and echoes of history, however, than getting a latte made to perfection. Not that this seems to be a problem for any of the locals who frequent it, along with some of the savvier tourists. Prices are inexpensive, so if architecture turns you on, I'd definitely put this on your hit list.

CASH ONLY

Grand Hotel Evropa

Václavské náměstí 25, Prague 1, Nové Město (Map A)

www.evropahotel.cz

TEL 224 228 215

HOURS Daily: 12:00–23:00

METRO Muzeum ● ● or Můstek ● ●

TRAM 3, 9, 14, 24 to Václavské náměstí

If you love Art Nouveau style, then a coffee or pre-dinner drink here is a must for you. There's often a piano player in the late afternoon, and it's also a suitable rendezvous spot for a nightcap after a day spent strolling through the city. No matter the weather, sit inside and soak up the magical architecture and old-time ambience of the place.

Hájek

Vodičkova 39, Prague 1, Nové Město (Map C)

www.ovocnysvetozor.cz

TEL 224 946 826, 774 444 874

HOURS Mon–Fri: 08:00–21:00; Sat: 09:00–21:00; Sun: 09:30–21:00

METRO Můstek ● ●

TRAM 3, 9, 14, 24 to Václavské náměstí

Hájek is a Prague institution, beloved by all. Opened in the 1970s under the name Ovocné lahůdky Světozor, they are famed for their *točená ovocná zmrzlina z jahod a banánů*, a banana and strawberry soft-serve sorbet (28 CZK per cone) that is delicious and refreshing. They are also famous for their *ovocné dorty*, which are gelatinous fruit cakes with strawberries (*jahody*), raspberries (*maliny*) or "forest fruits" (*lesní plody*) for 43 CZK per slice; these I could

personally do without, but my Czech staff loves them. They also offer a wide range of *chlebíčky*, open-faced sandwiches that are a staple of Czech cuisine and typically eaten for breakfast or lunch (see p. 156). With an average price of only 24 CZK, I encourage you to try a few! Hájek is iconic and quintessentially Czech, so if you really want to eat where the locals do, add it to your list.

CASH ONLY

NOTE: There are multiple locations all over town, but the one listed above is the original location and has the best old-school vibe.

Jan Paukert Lahůdkářství

Národní 17, Prague 1, Staré Město (Map A)

www.janpaukert.cz

TEL 224 222 615

HOURS Mon–Fri: 09:00–19:00; Sat & Sun: 10:00–18:00

METRO Národní třída ●

TRAM 6, 9, 18, 21, 22 to Národní divadlo

Established in 1916, this wonderful delicatessen claims to have invented *chlebíčky*, open-faced sandwiches that are a staple of Czech cuisine and typically eaten for breakfast or lunch (see p. 156). They offer a wide selection, ranging from *chlebíček s pravým humrem* (lobster) which is the house specialty, to classics such as *chlebíček se šunkou a vejcem* (ham and egg) and *chlebíček s herkulesem* (salami), all of which can be eaten while standing at the small cocktail tables. They also offer a wide assortment of classic Czech salads and baked goods, and there's a very affordable cafeteria in the rear, with standards such as *svíčková na smetaně* (roast beef with whipped cream, cranberries and bread dumplings) to *smažený vepřový řízek* (pork schnitzel).

■ ■ ■ ■ ■ ■ ■ ■ ■ ■ ■ ■ ■ ■
Kavárna Obecní dům
Náměstí Republiky 5, Prague 1, Staré Město (Map A)
www.kavarnaod.cz
TEL 222 002 763
HOURS Daily: 07:30—23:00
METRO Náměstí Republiky ●
TRAM 5, 8, 14, 26 to Náměstí Republiky

This café won't necessarily deliver the best cup of coffee or tastiest piece of cake that the city has to offer, but the setting is *over-the-top fabulous*. Simply put, this café is Art Nouveau at its most dazzling.

NOTE: There are two other restaurants and a bar in this building. The French one on the ground floor has a similarly fabulous interior (which, unfortunately, is too brightly lit much of the time) and serves food that is not only grossly overpriced but also fails to live up to the atmosphere. There's also a wonderful pub in the basement, where inspirations from Czech folklore abound by way of carved wooden booths, folk-art stenciling, and social realist murals. Utterly transporting, the pub is a good option if you're attending a performance in the concert hall and want to try some authentic Czech food either before or afterward. Also in the basement is the American Bar, which, despite its tiny size, is well worth a visit to enjoy a cocktail in its glamorous period interior.

■ ■ ■ ■ ■ ■ ■ ■ ■ ■ ■ ■ ■ ■
Kavárna Slavia
Smetanovo nábřeží 2, Prague 1, Staré Město (Map A)
www.cafeslavia.cz
TEL 224 218 493
HOURS Mon—Fri: 08:00—24:00; Sat & Sun: 9:00—24:00
METRO Národní třída ●
TRAM 6, 9, 17, 18, 22 to Národní divadlo

Perched on an incomparable river location just across from the National Theatre, Kavárna Slavia is the oldest café in Prague, dating all the way back to

HAPPY WORKERS! CZECH DELICATESSEN, 1949
(SOURCE: ČTK / CZECH NEWS AGENCY)

FULL REFRIGERATOR, C. 1961
(SOURCE: DOMÁCNOST 61, MAGAZINE COVER)

1881. The views across the river afforded from this historic Art Deco café are, in a word, *major*. The cake and coffee may not be the best in town, but, as with some of the other cafés I've mentioned in this section, Kavárna Slavia is certainly worth stopping in just to see the space and the amazing location.

■ ■ ■ ■ ■ ■ ■ ■ ■ ■ ■ ■ ■
La Bottega di Finestra
ITALIAN FOOD STORE & BISTRO
Platnéřská 11, Prague 1, Staré Město (Map A)
www.labottega.cz
TEL 222 233 094
HOURS Mon–Fri: 08:00–22:00; Sat: 08:30–22:00; Sun: 08:30–20:30
METRO Staroměstská ●
TRAM 17, 18 to Staroměstská

La Bottega di Finestra has the same owner as La Finestra Cucina (see p. 162), which is just two doors down, and Aromi (see p. 165). Located in the heart of downtown, just a stone's throw from the Four Seasons Hotel, this combination gourmet shop and bistro offers excellent authentic Italian delicacies and is perfect for breakfast or a quick lunch. It's equally prefect for one-stop picnic shopping, as they have terrific cured meats, an extensive cheese selection, fresh fruit, fantastic salads (octopus is my favorite), bottled wine, and even some very delicious profiteroles.

■ ■ ■ ■ ■ ■ ■ ■ ■ ■ ■ ■ ■
Lobkowicz Palace Café at the Prague Castle
Jiřská 3, Prague 1, Hradčany (Map D)
www.lobkowicz.cz
TEL 233 312 925
HOURS Daily: 10:00–18:00
METRO Malostranská ●
TRAM 12, 18, 20, 22 to Malostranská

The location of this café within the gates of the Prague Castle is simply outstanding, and there's probably no better place to take a break from your castle sightseeing. The restaurant features two terraces, each of which offers diners a sweeping view of Prague and is warmed up with heat lamps in the cooler months. There is indoor seating as well, but I wouldn't bother coming unless you plan to eat outdoors. Priced at a premium that reflects the location, the food is, frankly, less than extraordinary. That said, the view alone is worth it; so if the sun is shining, you should definitely stop by for goulash, a wrap sandwich, or soup.

■ ■ ■ ■ ■ ■ ■ ■ ■ ■ ■ ■ ■
Michelské Pekárny
Karmelitská 20, Prague 1, Malá Strana (Map B)
www.pekarny-michle.cz
TEL 257 535 152
HOURS Mon–Fri: 06:30–19:00; Sat & Sun: 08:00–19:00
METRO Malostranská ●
TRAM 12, 20, 22 to Hellichova

This *pekárna* (bakery) is located in the heart of Malá Strana, just down the road from Petřín Hill (see p. 74). Be sure to order a selection of the classic and *very* affordable Czech baked goods, and stock up on their excellent cookies smothered with a mixture of nuts, seeds and raisins – they're my favorite. Additionally, should you wish to bring a picnic to Petřín Hill, there is no better place in the area for one-stop shopping – they offer excellent sandwiches, far more creative than what one typically finds in town, as well as a nice selection of beverages.
CASH ONLY

DINING

T.Z. Cukrárna

Vítězná 14, Prague 1, Malá Strana (Map B)
HOURS Mon–Fri: 10:00–18:00; Sat & Sun: 10:00–17:00
TRAM 6, 9, 12, 20, 22 to Újezd

Step back in time as you walk through the doorway to this small *cukrárna* (sweet shop) at the foot of Petřín hill. Be sure to order a selection of the classic and *very* affordable Czech baked goods, as well as a Turkish coffee (the way coffee was made under communism), which you can then enjoy at one of the small vintage gingham-covered tables. Now you're really in Prague...

CASH ONLY

Slightly Further Afield

Erhart Café

Vinohradská 125, Prague 3, Vinohrady (Map E)
www.erhartovacukrarna.cz
TEL 273 130 574
HOURS Daily: 10:00–19:00;
METRO Jiřího z Poděbrad ●
TRAM 11 to Radhošťská
TRAVEL TIME 15 min.

Located in a Functionalist building from the 1930s, Erhart Café has created a thoughtful interior to reflect this period. Everything is made in-house and they offer some of the best and most creative cakes, confections and chocolates in town. They are the go-to option whenever my friends or I need to purchase a birthday cake; marzipan with pistachio cream is my personal favorite. They offer a wide selection of cakes by the slice, as well as an extensive beverage menu.

CASH ONLY

INDULGING IN A SLICE...OR TWO
(PHOTO BY JAN FISHER, 2012)

LUNCH, 2007
(SOURCE: ČTK / CZECH NEWS AGENCY)

BEER MEISTER, 1969 (SOURCE: ČTK / CZECH NEWS AGENCY)

delicatessen and sweet shop. They offer a wide range of *chlebíčky* (opened-faced sandwiches, see p. 156) and salads, which are meant to be eaten while standing at the long metal tables. They also offer a selection of classic and *very* affordable Czech baked goods and ice cream. So stop in and enjoy your breakfast, lunch or midday snack without another tourist in sight. Additionally, they have a wall filled with an amazing selection of boxed chocolates, which is worth checking out just to see their retro-fabulous approach to merchandising.

CASH ONLY

■ ■ ■ ■ ■ ■ ■ ■ ■ ■ ■
Štrúdl z taženého těsta

Jeseniova 29, Prague 3, Žižkov

TEL 222 590 912

HOURS Mon–Fri: 08:00–12:00 13:00–17:00

Take a taxi and have it wait outside

TRAVEL TIME 10 to 15 min.

Off-the-beaten-track is an understatement for this gem. Walk through a sea of nondescript *paneláky* (Communist-era public housing), and you will literally stumble upon this hole-in-the-wall shop. From these humble origins comes what is easily the best strudel in town. This fabulous and very focused enterprise sells only three items: apple strudel (*jablečný*), cheese strudel (*tvarohový*), and poppy seed strudel (*makový*)—all baked fresh

daily onsite. With the most expensive one ringing in at 48 CZK, I encourage you to try all three, but poppyseed is definitely my personal favorite. Each strudel is about 12 inches in length, and the final step of powdered sugar dusting will be executed while you wait.

CASH ONLY

■ ■ ■ ■ ■ ■ ■ ■ ■ ■ ■
Svatební dorty

Vítězné nám 3, Prague 6, Dejvická (Map D)

www.svatebnidorty.cz

TEL 224 318 616

HOURS Mon–Fri: 06:00–18:30; Sat: 07:00–18:00; Sun: 10:00–17:00

METRO: Dejvická ●

TRAVEL TIME 15 min.

Now this is a dying breed. If you really—and I mean *really*—want to eat where the locals eat, look no further than this old-time

PUBS

There are literally hundreds of drinking establishments in Prague, ranging from sketchy *"herna"* bars where old men gather to play video poker (avoid these!) to fancy nightclubs. But if you really want to experience Czech culture, you'll need to visit a *pivnice* ("beer pub"), as this is where the locals convene, and where you will find the tastiest beer – and some great cheap snacks (see p. 181) as well. Truth be told, I rarely drink alcohol and I'm definitely not a beer fan, so my knowledge of such places is rather limited. However, my friend and editor Scott Ross is a passionate beer enthusiast who has spent quite a bit of time in the local pubs, so I consulted with him on the tips and recommendations that appear below.

First, a few words of basic advice:

A GATHERING OF FARMERS IN THEIR LOCAL PUB, 1951
(SOURCE: ČTK / CZECH NEWS AGENCY)

HOW TO PICK A PUB

Most Prague pubs offer beers produced by one of the three major national brands – Pilsner Urquell, Budvar, or Staropramen – and the house beer will always be displayed on a sign out front. Look for pubs that offer unpasteurized "tank beer" (*pivo z tanku*) – as this is much fresher and more delicious than regular keg beer (see p. 179). If you see lots of locals, you're probably in the right place.

There are also quite a few places around town that either brew their own beer or serve beers from local microbreweries (*minipivovary*). Many of these are worth checking out, even if you're not a beer connoisseur.

For more information on local pubs, visit *www.praguebeergarden.com* and *www.praguepubs.co.uk*.

SERVICE

Before you head out, you should be aware that "real" Czech pubs are notorious for having surly bartenders and slow service, and that this is all part of the experience. Rest assured,

it's not you – they're grumpy with everyone.

PUB ETIQUETTE

- Most good pubs will be super crowded, so it's very common to share tables with others – just be sure to ask before sitting down (even if this means just pointing to the empty chairs and smiling).
- Always set your glass down on a beer mat (coaster) – it's just what's done.
- To toast with friends, raise your glass, say "*na zdraví*" ("to your health"), clink glasses with each person (while making eye contact), and tap the bottom of your glass on the beer mat before drinking.

PAYING THE BILL

In most pubs, the waiter will place a small strip of paper on your table and make marks to keep track of your beer and food orders. Do *not* lose this! I don't know what happens if you do, but it can't be good. When you ask for the bill, your waiter will add it up on the spot and write the total on your slip. If you're with a group, it's very

common to pay separately – just tell your waiter when you ask for the bill.

NOTE: We did not include phone numbers for the most of the pubs listed below, since there is no reason to expect that anyone will answer – or speak English if they do.

■ ■ ■ ■ ■ ■ ■ ■ ■ ■ ■ ■

Klášterní pivovar Strahov

Strahovské nádvoří 301, Prague 1, Hradčany (Map D)
www.klasterni-pivovar.cz
HOURS Daily: 10:00–22:00
METRO Malostranská ●
TRAM 22, 25 to Pohořelec

Located right across the street from the Strahov Monastery Library (see p. 56), this microbrewery makes great *pšeničné* (wheat beer) and also brews the house beer served at the Augustine Hotel (see p. 27). It's a less-smoky alternative to nearby U Černého vola (see p. 177), and you'll have an easier time getting a seat here.

■ ■ ■ ■ ■ ■ ■ ■ ■ ■ ■ ■

Kolkovna

V Kolkovně 8, Prague 1, Staré Město (Map A)
www.kolkovna.cz
HOURS Daily: 11:00–24:00
METRO Staroměstská ●
TRAM 17, 18 to Staroměstská

Located right in the heart of downtown, this Pilsner tank pub is frequented by tourists and locals alike and offers a wide selection of above-average Czech fare – try the sausages from their own smokehouse. The intimate cellar is nice in the winter, but otherwise it's better to eat upstairs, where the air circulation is a bit better.

DINING

Czech Beer: An Introduction

The production – and (copious) consumption – of beer has been an intrinsic part of Czech culture for centuries. The brewing tradition here dates back as far as the 13th century, and even the smallest rural villages always have at least one pub.

Czechs drink more beer than any other nation, at a rate of 132 liters (about 35 gallons) per person in 2010 – which is actually *down* from 2006, when Czechs consumed 163.5 liters (about 43 gallons) per person!

This may be less surprising when you consider that Czech beer is much cheaper than bottled water, soda, or coffee, and is available anywhere you go at any time of day – plus, it's just plain tasty beer.

The Czech Republic's original claim to fame in the beer world is that it was here, in the city of Plzeň (about an hour southwest of Prague), where "pilsner" beer – a hoppy, golden style of lager – was developed in the mid-1800s. With its bright, clear appearance and crisp, refreshing taste, this new style had a huge influence on brewing throughout the region and the rest of the world. Today, the world's most popular beers are variations of the pilsner style.

The largest and most famous Czech brewery is *Pilsner Urquell*, which was founded in Plzeň in 1842. At that time, Plzeň was part of the German-occupied Sudetenland, so the brand name is German for "the Original Beer from Plzeň." However, locals never call it that, preferring instead to use the Czech name, *"Plzeňský Prazdroj"* (which means the same thing), or simply *"Prazdroj"* ("the Original").

There are two other major breweries in the country: *Budvar* (from České Budějovice, about two hours south of Prague), and *Staropramen*, which is brewed right here in town. All three brands make several varieties of decent beer, all of which are different enough from each other to be worth trying

BEER ADVERTISEMENT, C. 1950

while you're here.

Over the past few decades, these three brands have created a virtual monopoly on local pubs by providing owners with free stuff (signs, tablecloths, coasters, etc.) in exchange for an exclusive contract, making it difficult for visitors to sample any of the excellent craft beer produced all across the country. Fortunately, that has changed in recent years, and it's much easier to find pubs serving interesting microbrewery beers all over town.

Most Czech microbreweries (many of which had been in operation for centuries) were shut down under communism, but since 1989 the nation has experienced a huge craft beer revival that continues to grow: As of 2012, there are over 150 breweries in the nation, with more opening all the time. Czech craft beers are some of the best in the world. If you're a beer lover, they are well worth seeking out.

HOP PICKERS, 1930

DINING

NA ZDRAVÍ ("CHEERS!"), C. 1930

Beer by the Numbers

When beers are listed on a pub menu, the listing usually includes not only the name of the brewery and the style, but also a number with a degree sign (11°, 12°, etc.). This number refers to the amount of sugar present in the beer prior to fermentation – NOT the percentage of alcohol in the finished beer. The general rule of thumb, tastewise, is that the higher the number, the "richer" the beer will taste.

This can be confusing to many foreigners, who often assume that the number represents *alcohol percentage*, but most Czech beers are actually between 4%–6% alcohol by volume. There is, however, a correlation between the amount of sugar used in brewing and the resulting beer's alcohol content, so 12° beers will always have slightly more alcohol than 10° or 11° beers.

There's also a price correlation, such that a 12° beer will not only be stronger and heavier tasting than a 10° beer, but will also cost a bit more. This can add up over several beers, in terms of calories and cash, which is why many Czechs will stick with a lighter / cheaper beer for a long night of drinking.

NOTE: Kolkovna is part of a restaurant group that includes several other locations offering essentially the same experience – one of them, Olympia (Vítězná 7, Prague 1, Malá Strana), is convenient if you're in the Malá Strana area.

■ ■ ■ ■ ■ ■ ■ ■ ■ ■ ■ ■ ■ ■

Lokál

Dlouhá 33, Prague 1,
Staré Město (Map A)
http://lokal.ambi.cz/en/
TEL 222 316 265
HOURS Mon–Fri: 11:00–
01:00; Sat: 12:00–01:00; Sun:
12:00–22:00
METRO Náměstí Republiky ●
TRAM 5, 8, 14, 26 to Dlouhá
třída

This pub opened in 2010, but the décor is reminiscent of what Czech pubs looked like in the 1980s, with dim fluorescent lighting, waiters in black vests, and a very authentic paint job. They serve some of the best pilsner in town, and the menu is filled with Czech classics including *svíčková* (see p. 156) and *párky* (hot-dogs). You will also want to check out the bathrooms, as the wallpaper is most memorable. Reservations are absolutely required, as this large space is always packed with locals and savvy tourists – but unlike most bars, they will be able to take your reservation over the phone, so I've included the phone number above.

■ ■ ■ ■ ■ ■ ■ ■ ■ ■ ■ ■ ■ ■

Pivovarský dům

Lípová 15, Prague 2,
Nové Město (Map C)
www.gastroinfo.cz/pivodum
HOURS Daily: 11:00–23:30
METRO I. P. Pavlova ● or
Karlovo náměstí ●

Founded in 1998, this was one of the first "new" microbreweries in town. They offer an outstanding light lager, some questionable flavored beers (although the nettle-flavored beer is somewhat interesting and certainly unique), and acceptable Czech food with an English menu. Mostly frequented by tourists, you will likely need to wait for a table.

U Černého vola

Loretánské náměstí 1, Prague 1, Hradčany (Map D)
HOURS Daily: 09:00–22:00
METRO Malostranská ●
TRAM 22 to Pohořelec

This boisterous, smoky, old-fashioned pub with painted heraldic symbols covering its walls is located right in the heart of the Prague Castle district. Frequented mostly by locals and a few savvy tourists, "At the Black Bull" has Velkopopovický Kozel beer on tap and an English menu of traditional Czech pub snacks. Plan on coming early, as the pub tends to be full for the evening by 18:00.
CASH ONLY

U Dvou koček

Uhelný trh 415/10, Prague 1, Staré Město (Map A)
www.udvoukocek.cz
HOURS Daily: 11:00–23:00
METRO Můstek ● ●
TRAM 6, 9, 18, 22 to Národní třída

Established in 1678, "At the Two Cats" is nothing if not old-school. They serve great unpasteurized (tank) Pilsner and traditional Czech food, but their homebrewed "Světlá Kočka" 12° light lager is the real reason to visit – plus, an accordion player is often on duty! They also sell t-shirts with their fabulous logo, which features two cats nuzzling a beer (170 CZK).

U Medvídků

Na Perštýně 7, Prague 1, Staré Město (Map A)
www.umedvidku.cz
HOURS Mon–Fri: 11:00–23:00; Sat: 11:30–23:00; Sun: 11:30–22:00
METRO Národní třída ●
TRAM 6, 9, 18, 21, 22 to Národní třída

"At the Little Bears" serves unpasteurized (tank) Budvar beer in the sprawling ground-floor pub, but you'll want to head upstairs to the cozy brewpub, where you can sit amongst the brewing equipment and taste the classic "1466" light lager, the delicious "Oldgott" half-dark lager, or the unique "X-33" (billed as 'the strongest beer in the world' at a whopping 12.6% ABV). They also have a gift shop with some interesting beer-related items, located just outside the brewpub.

U Pinkasů

Jungmannovo náměstí 15/16, Prague 1, Nové Město (Map A)
www.upinkasu.cz
HOURS 12:00–24:00
METRO Můstek ● ●
TRAM 6, 9, 18, 22 to Národní třída

This straightforward, traditional restaurant-pub has been serving Pilsner beer since 1843 – longer than anywhere else Prague! The unpasteurized (tank) beer is still flowing here, and the English-speaking waiters, traditional Czech food, and plenty of outdoor seating options make this a great choice if you're near the bottom of Wenceslas Square.

DINING

BARMAN AND WAITER SERVING THE THIRSTY MASSES, 1969
(SOURCE: ČTK / CZECH NEWS AGENCY)

U Tří růží

Husova 10, Prague 1,
Staré Město (Map A)
www.u3r.cz
HOURS Mon–Thurs & Sun:
11:00–23:00; Fri & Sat:
11:00–24:00
METRO Staroměstská ● or
Můstek ● ●
TRAM 17, 18 to Staroměstská

The newest microbrewery
in town, "At the Three
Roses" opened in May 2012
and is conveniently located
right in the heart of Old
Town. The food is thoughtfully prepared and their
beers are terrific. In addition to making delicious
traditional light and half-
dark lagers, they're also
experimenting with non-
Czech styles – their hoppy
American Ale and complex
Belgian-style ale were
unexpected and definitely
worth a taste.

CASH ONLY

Slightly Further Afield

Bašta

Táborská 49, Prague 4,
Nusle
www.ubansethu.cz
HOURS Daily: 11:00–24:00
TRAM 18 to Nuselská radnice
TRAVEL TIME 20–25 min.

This small, homey brewpub
is a worthy destination for
anyone seeking well-made
beer in a quiet, unpretentious setting. There are no
English menus and the
staff speaks very little
English, so ordering food
can be a bit tricky – but
their excellent light and
half-dark lagers make this
place worth seeking out.
Much smaller and less
boisterous than nearby Zlý
Časy (see p. 181), it's a
good choice for a quiet
evening.

CASH ONLY

Beer Point

Mikovcova 4, Prague 2,
Vinohrady (Map C)
www.notabene-restaurant.cz
HOURS Mon–Sat: 17:00–
24:00; closed Saturdays in
summer
METRO I. P. Pavlova ●
TRAM 4, 6, 10, 11, 16, 22 to
I. P. Pavlova

Located just downstairs
from Nota Bene (see next
page), this cellar pub offers
six taps of diverse craft
beers, including hard-to-
find local microbreweries
like Únětický, Matuška, and
Kocour, but not so much
in the way of atmosphere
(the faux-distressed décor
looks a bit… recent), and no
food. So, if the six *different*
taps upstairs at Nota Bene
aren't enough for you (or
you can't get a reservation),
come on down.

CASH ONLY

BEER SERVICE, 1954
(SOURCE: ČTK / CZECH NEWS AGENCY)

DINING

■ ■ ■ ■ ■ ■ ■ ■ ■ ■ ■ ■ ■
Hrom do Police

Moravská 40, Prague 2,
Vinohrady (entrance is on
Chodská) (Map E)
www.hromdopolice.cz
HOURS Mon–Fri: 11:00–
24:00; Sat: 14:00–24:00
SUMMER HOURS Mon–Fri:
11:00–24:00; Sat: 17:00–
24:00
METRO Jiřího z Poděbrad ● or
Náměstí Míru ●
TRAM 10, 16 to Šumavská
TRAVEL TIME 15 min.

This homey pub is note-
worthy in that it serves six
varieties of beer made by
Měšťanský pivovar v Poličce
(located about 2.5 hours
east of Prague). The 11° and
12° *kvasnicové* (unfiltered
"yeast" beers) are both
excellent; if you're feeling
scientific, order one of each
and do a side-by-side
comparison to taste the
difference that a higher
sugar concentration can
make in an otherwise
identical brew. There is an
English menu of tradi-
tional Czech food, and they
also sell bottles to go,
which are worth picking
up just for the fabulous
labels.
CASH ONLY

■ ■ ■ ■ ■ ■ ■ ■ ■ ■ ■ ■ ■
Nota Bene

Mikovcova 4, Prague 2,
Vinohrady (Map C)
www.notabene-restaurant.cz
TEL 721 299 131
HOURS Mon–Fri: 11:00–
23:00; Sat: 12:00–23:00
METRO I. P. Pavlova ●
TRAM 4, 6, 10, 11, 16, 22 to I.
P. Pavlova

Opened in 2012, this
newcomer has the local
beer cognoscenti *buzzing*
about their frequently
rotated craft beer selection

Fresh Beer Is Best

When packaging beer for sale in kegs and bottles,
breweries around the world routinely *pasteurize*
beer – heating it to kill off any bacteria that may
be present, which also kills the healthy living
yeast that are part of fresh beer. While this is
effective in increasing shelf life, it changes the
"natural" taste of the beer, resulting in a very
different product. Fortunately, it's possible to taste
unpasteurized beer from all three of the major
breweries (Pilsner Urquell, Budvar, and
Staropramen) – just seek out one of the many
"tank beer" (*pivo z tanku*) pubs around town,
which are specially set up for this purpose. At
these pubs, the beer is stored in temperature-
controlled tanks that are equipped with refillable
plastic bags. Pressure is then created inside the
tank, squeezing the bag and forcing the beer
through pipes and tubes to the tap (unlike kegs,
which use carbon dioxide to generate pressure,
thereby infusing the beer with extra carbonation).
The result is creamy, delicious, and worth seeking
out. The tanks are refilled every two weeks, so
no matter when you visit, the beer will taste fresh.

A Pivo By Any Other Name...

Almost all of the beer you'll encounter here will be
some kind of *ležák* ("lager"). The most common is
světlý ("light"), but *polotmavý* ("half-dark") and
tmavý ("dark") are also common. Several
microbreweries now make *pšeničné* (wheat beer,
similar to a German hefeweizen). Less common is a
uniquely Czech style called *kvasnicové* – an
unfiltered "yeast beer" that is absolutely worth
seeking out (you can sample some at Hrom do
Police; see entry at left).

and great locally sourced
food. All of the meat comes
from the sustainably
focused Real Meat Society
(see p. 130); the rabbit
pâté and hamburger I
sampled on a recent visit
were both excellent. There
is no English menu, but

the waiters speak English
and will guide you through
the limited selections.
Overall, this place is
outstanding and highly
recommended.
Reservations required.
CASH ONLY

DINING

BREWERY WORKERS WITH BEER BARRELS, 1953

Plan Your Own Beer Adventure

Why not plan a trip to visit a few local breweries? To do so, you will definitely want to get your hands on a newly updated 2012 "Pivovary České republiky" map, which lists EVERY brewery in the Czech Republic and comes with a highly informative booklet. You can order it online and have it shipped to you (*www.kartografie.cz/tituly-pro-verejnost/pivovary-ceske-republiky*), or simply pick up a copy at a bookstore here in town.

Another indispensable resource for anyone seeking a deep understanding of Czech beer – and the breweries that make it – is the **Good Beer Guide to Prague & the Czech Republic** (CAMRA Books, 2007). Author Evan Rail is renowned as an expert on this topic, and the book is chock-full of useful information and spot-on beer reviews. You can pick up a copy on Amazon or at local bookshops.

Pivo a Párek

Korunní 105, Prague 3,
Vinohrady (Map E)
HOURS 10:00–22:00
METRO Jiřího z Poděbrad ●
TRAM 10, 16 to Perunova
TRAVEL TIME 15 to 20 min.

Conveniently located right at the #10 and #16 tram stops, this somewhat random little hole-in-the-wall is more of a beer shop that also offers food than a proper pub. As the name ("Beer and Sausage") implies, they offer a diverse array of craft beer and grilled sausages – all hand-chosen by the friendly owner. Head outside to the garden to enjoy your snack, and when you're through you can grab a few bottles to go.
CASH ONLY

Pivovarský klub

Křižíkova 17, Prague 8, Karlín
www.gastroinfo.cz/pivoklub
HOURS Daily: 11:30–23:30
METRO Florenc ● ●

A destination for local beer lovers since 2005, this pub serves their own beers (brewed at Pivovarský Dům – see p. 176), as well as a frequently changing selection from other local microbreweries. They also have a very extensive selection of bottled beer that you can take home.

Richter Brewery

Pivovar U Bulovky
Bulovka 17, Prague 8, Libeň
www.pivovarubulovky.cz
HOURS Mon–Thurs: 11:00–23:00; Fri: 11:00–24:00 Sat & Sun: 12:00–24:00
METRO Palmovka ● then
TRAM 10, 24, 25 to Bulovka
TRAM 10, 24, 25 to Bulovka
TRAVEL TIME 20–25 min.

This cozy brewpub is a bit out of the way, but it's a worthy destination for anyone seeking a real local experience, great craft beer, and surprisingly good food. The owner is from Germany, and the Bavarian-style beers and food menu reflect this influence. Be sure to try the spaetzle!

CASH ONLY

■ ■ ■ ■ ■ ■ ■ ■ ■ ■ ■ ■ ■ ■

U Sadu

Škroupovo náměstí 5, Prague 3, Žižkov (Map E)
www.usadu.cz
HOURS Mon–Thurs: 08:00–02:00; Fri: 08:00–04:00; Sat & Sun: 09:00–4:00
METRO Jiřího z Poděbrad ●
TRAM 11 to Jiřího z Poděbrad
TRAVEL TIME 15 min.

Open since 1929, U Sadu offers unpasteurized (tank) Pilsner Urquell, a decent selection of beers from local microbreweries, and even some Belgian ales available in bottles. Their food is actually quite good – particularly the pork knee, ribs, and cheese-filled potato pancakes – and the kitchen stays open until 02:00! They have great outdoor picnic tables and the main indoor seating area features an eclectic assortment of vintage objects. Overall, this is just a nice, basic neighborhood pub. What more do you need?

■ ■ ■ ■ ■ ■ ■ ■ ■ ■ ■ ■ ■ ■

Zlý Časy

Čestmírova 5, Prague 4, Nusle
www.zlycasy.eu
HOURS Mon–Thurs: 11:00–23:30; Fri: 11:00–01:00; Sat: 17:00–01:00; Sun: 17:00–23:00
TRAM 11, 18 to Náměstí Bratří Synků
TRAVEL TIME 20 min.

Beer Snacks

These classic savory snacks go great with beer and are typically priced well under 100 CZK, so why not try several?

Nakládaný hermelín: Pickled Camembert cheese with onions and peppers served with rye bread.

Utopenec (literally, "drowning man"): A thick pork sausage pickled with onions and peppers and served cold with rye bread.

Pivní sýr: "Beer cheese" is a semi-soft cheese served with chopped white onions, paprika, and mustard. Mash them all up with a fork, together with a splash of beer from your glass, and then spread the mixture on rye bread. Fun!

Topinky s česnekem: Fried rye bread with garlic – often served with a raw clove of garlic for you to rub on the bread. Also fun!

Klobásy: Traditional grilled sausages served with mustard and a slice of rye bread.

Škvarkové sádlo: Lard with cracklings – shockingly, also served with rye bread. Only for the brave.

BEER SNACKS L TO R: NAKLÁDANÝ HERMELÍN (PICKLED CAMEMBERT), UTOPENEC (PICKLED SAUSAGE) & TLAČENKA S CIBULÍ (HEAD CHEESE WITH ONIONS)

DINING

With 24 taps of local craft beer to choose from, this otherwise-not-so-enticing pub is a mecca for those seeking variety over atmosphere. The downstairs pub area is rather cramped and noisy, and it can be hard to find an open table, but if you're a die-hard beer hound willing to make the trek, you'll be rewarded with a well-curated selection of beers you won't find elsewhere in town.

CASH ONLY

Neznámý pohled na Prahu z Riegrových sadů.

VIEW FROM RIEGROVY SADY, C. 1930

BEER GARDENS

Beer gardens are a long-standing part of Czech culture – but not in the same way as in Germany: You won't find any lederhosen or oompah bands here, but what you *will* find are very pleasant, relaxing scenes where groups of (mostly young) locals come – often with their dogs – to hang out, drink beer, eat grilled sausages, and enjoy the great outdoors. Two of the best beer gardens in town are in Letenské sady up on Letná Hill and in Riegerovy sady in the Vinohrady neighborhood – both of which are slightly outside the center of downtown, but worth making the trek. These parks are perfectly safe at night; just use your head.

Letná Park
Letenské sady, Prague 7, Holešovice (Map F)
(see p. 73)
HOURS Daily: 11:00–23:00 (May–Sept)

Visit in the daytime to catch the amazing view of the river, bridges, and spires of the city. People will be spilling over from the picnic tables onto nearby grassy lawns, hanging out and drinking beer every day (and evening) of the week when the weather is nice. Just behind the beer garden is a slightly fancier place (meaning glass glasses), where you can get a real meal – I'm particularly fond of the grilled chicken, corn on the cob, and potatoes. Yum!

NOTE: Letná Park is huge! To find the beer garden, enter the park from the National Technical Museum (see p. 59) and the beer garden will soon be visible on your left.

Riegrovy sady
Riegrovy sady 28, Prague 2, Vinohrady (Map E)
www.restauraceriegrovysady.cz
TEL 222 717 247
HOURS Daily: 12:00–24:00 (Apr–Oct)
METRO Jiřího z Poděbrad ●
TRAM 11 to Vinohradská tržnice

This park also has a nice sweeping view of the city, but not from the beer garden. It's just a low-key spot where you can grab a nice juicy *klobása* sausage, a cold beer and a game of foosball against the locals. Complete with a big screen projector, it's also a cool place to be during televised sports games. Bring your dog along and you'll fit right in.
CASH ONLY

"PRAGUE: GARDEN CITY" (POSTCARD, C. 1970)

NOTE: The beer garden is found in the northeast corner of the park.

BARS

The listings in this section are for drinking establishments that do not specialize in beer; instead, they offer a more of a "regular" bar atmosphere that may appeal more to the younger set (that is, hipsters in their 20s and 30s) than the more traditional (i.e., beer-focused) pubs listed above. As is the case with pubs, this is not really my area of expertise, but the recommendations below come from trusted local sources, and I'm sure you'll have fun at any of them.

If you're looking for nightclub recommendations, see p. 198–199.

■ ■ ■ ■ ■ ■ ■ ■ ■ ■ ■ ■
Nová Scéna Café
Národní 4, Prague 1, Nové Město (Map A)
www.cafenona.cz
TEL 775 755 147
HOURS Mon–Fri: 09:00–24:00; Sat & Sun: 11:00–24:00
closed July–August
METRO Národní třída ●
TRAM 6, 9, 17,18, 21, 22 to Národní divadlo

Hidden away up a fabulous flight of green marble stairs, this inner-circle café is primarily frequented by a young, hip and creative local crowd. There is often interesting live music – a rollicking gypsy-folk ensemble was tearing it up on a recent visit – and the view of Národní třída from the wall-to-wall windows is memorable. Although it's open all day, the scene really starts in the evening.

■ ■ ■ ■ ■ ■ ■ ■ ■ ■ ■ ■
U Sudu
Vodičkova 10, Prague 1, Nové Město (Map C)
www.usudu.cz
TEL 222 232 207
HOURS Mon–Thurs: 09:00–04:00; Fri & Sat: 10:00–05:00; Sun: 11:00–04:00
METRO Karlovo náměstí ● or Národní třída ●
TRAM 3, 9, 14, 24 to Lazarská

Holy fire hazard, batman! This wine bar (which recently also started serving beer) spirals deep into the bowels of the earth. Stride confidently into the deceptively small first chamber, make a right, and then keep going downstairs—there's a bar on almost every level. The youngish, rather 'alternative' crowd here drinks, chats, and smokes way into the wee hours.
CASH ONLY

A Guide to Czech Liquor

Slivovice: This strong plum brandy is perhaps the most traditional drink in the Czech Republic – consumed by the shot to commemorate, well, just about anything. It's best chilled (as the cold masks the strong alcohol burn), but never served with ice. R. Jelínek is the most popular brand, available all over town – as well as at the airport.

Becherovka: This sweet herbal liqueur from Karlovy Vary with a secret recipe of 22 herbs can be consumed straight up in a shot, as the locals do, or with tonic water, ice, and a slice of lemon (called a *Beton*, this is my personal favorite). Also widely available, and you can't miss it at the airport, either.

Zelená: This green, peppermint-flavored liqueur is another popular option for shots and is also used in mixed drinks. Božkov is a popular brand; they also make a range of other flavors.

Fernet: This bitter liqueur is often compared to Jägermeister, as it has a similarly herbal flavor. Like Becherovka, it is usually consumed straight up in a shot, but can also be mixed with tonic water and served over ice (this is called a *Bavorák*).

Absinthe: Although it's not uniquely Czech, you will see lots of absinthe for sale in the local shops. Known as "the green fairy," this highly alcoholic beverage (up to 70% ABV) has a strong anise flavor and was the drink of choice among 19th-

POURING BECHEROVKA AT THE KARLOVY VARY FILM FESTIVAL, 1968 (SOURCE: ČTK / CZECH NEWS AGENCY)

century artists, writers and poets, including Van Gogh, Hemingway, and Baudelaire. It also has a reputation for causing hallucinations and madness. Drink at your own risk....

Ultramarin

Ostrovní 32, Prague 1, Nové Město (Map C)
www.ultramarin.cz
TEL 224 932 249
HOURS Mon–Fri: 11:00–02:00; Sat & Sun 12:00–02:00
METRO Národní třída ●
TRAM 6, 9, 18, 21, 22 to Národní třída

Also a restaurant with pretty good food (served until 01:00) and a surprisingly large Thai menu, Ultramarin serves cocktails that are outstanding. Their Bloody Mary, easily the best I've had in this country, is mixed with theatrical flair. Head downstairs to the cellar bar, which comes complete with a live DJ and a foosball table.

Vzorkovna

Bartolomějská 13, Prague 1, Staré Město (Map C)
TEL N/A
HOURS Daily 15:00– 23:00
METRO Národní třída ●
TRAM 6, 9, 18, 21, 22 to Národní třída

This recently-opened, multifunctional bar space (the name means "showcase") features artwork and music from young artists in a setting that is as close to the East Village in New York City that you're likely to find here. I went on a Thursday evening and found it packed with young, hip, art-school types rocking out to a live band. In addition to serving beers from the award-winning Únětický brewery, they also offer a limited, daily-changing menu of food sourced within 10km of Prague, and smoked meats, cheeses, and fresh milk are delivered daily and available for purchase – love that! The maze-like space is festooned with second-hand sofas in cozy nooks, so it's a great date spot. CASH ONLY

DINING

■ ■ ■ ■ ■ ■ ■ ■ ■ ■ ■ ■ ■

Bukowski's

Bořivojova 86, Prague 3, Žižkov (Map E)

TEL 774 530 680

HOURS Daily: 18:00–03:00

TRAM 5, 9 and 26 to Husinecká

TRAVEL TIME 15 to 20 min.

Named for a famously hard-drinking author and poet, Bukowski's is a good old-fashioned bar, serving good Old Fashioned cocktails (and other tasty beverages) to a discerning crowd of 30-something locals and expats. Located on a gritty street in Žižkov, the casual, low-key atmosphere and good music make this a great neighborhood alternative for the "grown up" kids.

CASH ONLY

■ ■ ■ ■ ■ ■ ■ ■ ■ ■ ■ ■ ■

Fraktal

Šmeralova 1, Prague 7, Bubeneč (Map F)

www.fraktalbar.cz

TEL 777 794 094

HOURS Daily: 11:00–24:00

METRO Hradčanská ●

TRAM 1, 8, 15, 25, 26 to Letenské náměstí

TRAVEL TIME 15 min.

Sandwiched between two of Prague's most fabulous parks – Stromovka and Letná (see p. 73) – this neighborhood joint is very cool. Czechs and expats alike enjoy the slightly gritty atmosphere and interesting design of this popular restaurant and bar. The food is delish — try the hamburger, one of the best in Prague. Don't bring your mom.

CASH ONLY

WINE BARS

Czech wines are not particularly well renowned, probably because they lack the edgy minerality one associates with excellent vintages. There are exceptions, but they're rare. Most local wines taste more like someone's grandfather made them at home in the family cellar, resulting in a very sour, *grapey* taste. White wines from Moravia here tend to be the more interesting and successful, as the Czech Republic does not get enough annual sunshine to develop red grapes properly. That said, it's always fun to go local, so I've recommended the two best wine bars I know featuring Czech wines.

Many of the wines you see on bar or restaurant wine lists are not available at local shops, since most of the Czech vineyards are very small and have a limited annual output. If you want to own something you've tried, the wisest choice would be to ask the bar or restaurant if you can purchase a bottle or two, as this will often be the only way to acquire it.

■ ■ ■ ■ ■ ■ ■ ■ ■ ■ ■ ■ ■

Bokovka

Pštrossova 8, Prague 1, Nové Město (Map C)

www.bokovka.com

TEL 721 262 503

HOURS Mon–Sat: 16:00–01:00

METRO Karlovo náměstí ● or Národní třída ●

TRAM 3, 6, 18, 22, 24 to Karlovo náměstí; 6, 9, 18, 22 to Národní třída

Bokovka is a small, very local wine bar, well off the beaten track. The atmosphere isn't particularly charming, but they offer wines from very small Czech vineyards that you won't find elsewhere. They only offer five wines by the glass, and the most interesting wines are

WINE CELLAR, 1966
(SOURCE: ČTK / CZECH NEWS AGENCY)

DINING

Interview with Wei-Hai Chu: A Night on the Town

Local entrepreneur Wei-Hai Chu is a long-term expatriate from the US (born in the Netherlands) who has lived in Prague for nearly a decade. Not only is he a savvy businessman, but he also really knows how to have a good time. Wei-Hai is renowned for his nights on the town, and his knowledge of restaurants and bars is not only extensive but always spot-on, so I thought he'd be the ideal person to offer a few suggestions for places to add to your agenda for a perfect evening on the town ... as well as the morning after.

Karen: What's your all-time favorite restaurant to bring visitors from out of town?

Wei-Hai: If I'm after a fancy night out, *Alcron* is the place. The food is consistently exceptional, especially the fish, and the intimate Art Deco-inspired dining room is a real knockout. When I want something a bit more understated, my new favorite is *Kofein*, a great little tapas bar in the Vinohrady neighborhood.

Karen: After dinner, I know you're a fan of hitting the bars for a drink or two. Where do you like to start the evening, stop in the middle, and finish up?

Wei-Hai: My favorite starting point is *Kozička*, although not all of my friends agree. I can best describe Kozička as smoky, with a relaxed atmosphere, a good-looking crowd, and a very chill vibe. One favorite second stop is *Tretters* – but I prefer to go on weekdays, as it's too busy on the weekends. The music is always great, and the cocktails are excellent (but not as good as *Bugsy's*, which definitely has the best cocktails in town). It's also worth noting that Tretters is well known as a resource for 'ladies of the night' – it will be very clear who they are. For dancing, *James Dean* is an excellent choice – check out the scene downstairs – and although the concept is very American, it's quite well done and always a fun time. When it comes to after-hours party locations, *Le Clan* is the go-to spot, but you don't want to show up before 3am. It's dark, mysterious, and seedy – very reminiscent of New York City's downtown scene after-hours scene in the 1980s.

Karen: How does the Czech bar scene different from that in the United States??

Wei-Hai: Although in many ways I actually view the two scenes as similar, there are definitely distinct differences. The most

CELEBRATION, 1947
(SOURCE: ČTK / CZECH NEWS AGENCY)

important difference is that going out in Prague is rather affordable: for 1,000 CZK you can definitely have a very fun night on the town, and for 2,000 CZK you can have a *really* great evening – and even be able to treat your friends to a round or two! This ability to indulge without going broke creates a very different atmosphere. Needless to say, as a result, there is far more debauchery in Prague. It must also be mentioned that it's still possible to smoke in Prague bars and, as we all know, that is a huge difference!

■ ■ ■ ■ ■ ■ ■ ■ ■ ■ ■ ■

Alcron

Radisson Blu Alcron Hotel, Štěpánská 40, Prague 1, Nové Město (Map C)
www.alcron.cz
HOURS Mon–Sat: 12:00–14:30 17:30–22:30

Kofein

Nitranská 9, Prague 3, Vinohrady (Map E)
www.ikofein.cz
HOURS Mon-Fri: 11:00–24:00; Sat & Sun: 17:00–24:00
TRAVEL TIME 10–15 min.

Kozička Restaurant

Kozí 1, Prague 1, Staré Město (Map A)
www.kozicka.cz
HOURS Mon-Fri: 12:00–04:00; Sat: 18:00–04:00; Sun: 19:00–03:00

Tretter's Cocktail Bar

V Kolkovně 3, Prague 1, Staré Město (Map A)
www.tretters.cz
HOURS Mon–Sat: 19:00–03:00; Sun: 19:00–02:00

Bugsy's Bar

Pařížská 10, Prague 1, Staré Město (Map A)
www.bugsysbar.cz
HOURS Daily: 19:00–02:00

James Dean

V Kolkovně 1, Prague 1, Staré Město (Map A)
www.jamesdean.cz
HOURS Daily: 08:00–04:00 (restaurant); 21:00–06:00 (club); kitchen open until 23:00

Le Clan

Balbínova 23, Prague 2, Vinohrady (Map E)
www.leclan.cz
HOURS Tue–Sun: 02:00–10:00

served by the bottle, so plan to settle in for the evening as the locals do (starting at 20:00; if you go earlier, no one will be there), and try a few bottles. They also offer nibbles, including cheeses, meats and nuts. A recent evening there, including two bottles of wine, water and lots of snacks came to 1,000 CZK – a real bargain. The menu is not in English, but the staff is always happy to assist.
CASH ONLY

■ ■ ■ ■ ■ ■ ■ ■ ■ ■ ■ ■

Dům vína U Závoje

Havelská 25, Prague 1, Staré Město (Map A)
www.uzavoje.cz
TEL 226 006 111
HOURS Daily: 11:00–24:00
METRO Můstek ● ●

Dům vína U Závoje is perfectly charming, and it's obvious that the staff not only love wine, but are genuinely enthusiastic about working there. They even insist on serving wines in appropriately shaped glasses, a first for me in the Czech Republic! Dům vína U Závoje has an extensive list of wines by the glass – including over 50 Czech wines – allowing for far greater experimentation than usual. An added bonus is that they have a wine store in the same complex, so you can purchase a bottle or two to home with you.

Looking to buy a bottle? See p. 142 for wine shop listings.

Also, for more information on Czech wine, see the interview on the following page.

DINING

187

Interview with Bohuslav Uher: Czech Wine

For years, simply out of ignorance, I've always advised visitors to avoid Czech wines, as I personally had none to recommend (I'm not a big drinker). But as this was hardly sufficient advice for my readers, I decided to interview Bohuslav Uher, the former assistant restaurant manager of Essensia restaurant at the Mandarin Oriental Hotel in Prague, so that you can benefit from some insider's tips on what to order and / or buy.

Karen: Where is your favorite place in Prague to enjoy a glass of wine?

Bohuslav: I always like Dům vína U Závoje in the Old Town (see p. 142). They offer a wide selection of wines by the glass, which is nice when you would like to try something new. At the same location, they also have a wine shop where you can buy the bottle immediately, and the prices are reasonable. Several times a month they offer wine tastings; their food is excellent; and they have the best cheese shop in town.

Karen: What are your favorite wine stores in Prague?

Bohuslav: In addition to Dům vína U Závoje, I've been buying wines for years at Monarch Wine Cellar, also located in the Old Town.

Karen: Which Czech winemaker is your favorite?

Bohuslav: My favorite is Tanzberg; they produce only top quality wines, including sparkling, and their presentation—often a handicap of Czech wineries—is very smart. Another one I like is Sonberk; their straw and ice wines are really unique.

GRAPE HARVESTING, 1963
(SOURCE: ČTK / CZECH NEWS AGENCY)

Karen: What should someone keep in mind when they visit a wine store and there's no one to assist them? What should they look for?

Bohuslav: Buying ordinary Czech table wines is a waste of money. If you don't know the Czech market, buy only wines with special attributes. For example: late harvest (*pozdní sběr*); selection of grapes (*výběr z hroznů*); selection of berries (*výběr z bobulí*); ice (*ledové*); and straw (*slámové*) wines. In terms of local grape varieties, among whites, Pálava (a cross between Gewurztraminer and Müller Thurgau) is very interesting, and I also recommend Welsch Riesling. Among reds, I would suggest trying the André variety (a cross between the St. Laurent and Blaufrankisch grapes).

Wine Shop Recommended by Bohuslav:

■ ■ ■ ■ ■ ■ ■ ■ ■ ■ ■ ■ ■

Monarch Wine Cellar
Na Perštýně 15, Prague 1, Staré Město (Map A)
www.monarch.cz
TEL 224 239 602
HOURS Mon–Sat: 15:00–24:00
METRO Národní třída ●
or Můstek ● ●
TRAM 6, 9, 18, 22 to Národní třída

DINING

Entertainment

NATIONAL THEATRE, C. 1930

CONCERT VENUES

Many of the venues listed below are impressive not only for their performances but also for their architectural merit. Whether you prefer opera, ballet, orchestral music or jazz, ticket prices tend to be quite affordable, offering great bang for your buck and a lovely night out on the town. Hence, I must encourage you to fit in a visit to at least one of these venues while you're in town.

Opera & Ballet

All three theatres listed below offer performances of opera and ballet, with nightly performances (usually starting at 19:00) and weekend matinees. The schedules vary, so check their websites for details.

■ ■ ■ ■ ■ ■ ■ ■ ■ ■ ■ ■

National Theatre
Národní divadlo
Národní 2, Prague 1, Nové Město (Map C)
www.nationaltheatre.cz
TEL 224 901 111
HOURS Daily: 10:00–18:00
TICKETS 560–1,100 CZK
METRO Národní třída ●
TRAM 6, 9, 17,18, 21, 22 to Národní divadlo

Majestically overlooking the Vltava River, the National Theatre was inaugurated in June of 1881, and ever since then it has remained a true symbol of national pride. Indeed, Czechs both rich and poor voluntarily dug into their own pockets to pay for this magnificent building after the Hapsburg Empire refused to fund it. Then, on August 12 of the same year, the building was ravaged by fire. All that remained were the outside walls. Remarkably, within 47 days of the catastrophe, enough money was collected to rebuild the theatre, and work was completed in less than two years. The theatre was re-inaugurated on November 18, 1883 with a performance of Bedřich Smetana's opera, *Libuše*, which he composed especially for the occasion.

FOR A PRIVATE TOUR Contact Mrs. Kovářová (m.kovarova@narodni-divadlo.cz
TEL 224 901 506.
ENTRANCE FEE: 3,000 CZK for groups up to 9 people.

State Opera
Státní opera

Legerova 75, Prague 1,
Vinohrady (Map C)
www.opera.cz
TEL 224 901 780
HOURS Mon–Fri: 10:00–
18:00; Sat & Sun: 10:00–
12:00 & 13:00–17:30
TICKETS 300 CZK–1,250 CZK
METRO Muzeum ● ●
TRAM 11 to Muzeum

Built in 1888, the State Opera house suffers from a rather unfortunate location, as it is immediately adjacent to the one major highway running through town. Not only is all the pavement and whizzing traffic less than picturesque, it makes the building quite difficult to access. As a result I would recommend a visit to one of the other two opera houses listed here over this one. Should these be all booked, however, or should you find the State Opera's program simply of greater interest, you won't be sorry you made the effort, at least not once you're safely inside. The largest theatre in Prague, it's graced by an opulent Neo-Rococo interior, and the quality of the productions here is consistently high.

FOR A PRIVATE TOUR Contact Mrs. Kovářová (m.kovarova@narodni-divadlo.cz
TEL 224 901 506.
ENTRANCE FEE: 3,000 CZK for groups up to 9 people.

Estates Theatre
Stavovské divadlo

Ovocný trh 1, Prague 1,
Staré Město (Map C)
www.estestheatre.cz
TEL 224 902 322
HOURS Daily: 10:00–18:00
TICKETS 660 CZK–1,320 CZK
METRO Můstek ● ●
TRAM 5, 8,14, 26 Náměstí Republiky

Built in the 1780s, the Estates Theatre is my favorite of the National Theatre's several venues, as it is by far the smallest and most intimate. I also love the light blue velvet chairs! Mozart had many connections to this theatre, the most famous being that *Don Giovanni* premiered here in 1787. It also happens to be one of only two opera houses in Europe that remain preserved more or less as they would have been during the composer's time.

FOR A PRIVATE TOUR Contact Mrs. Bruderová (v.bruderova@narodni-divadlo.cz
TEL 224 901 506.
ENTRANCE FEE: 4,200 CZK for groups up to 9 people.

Concert Halls (Classical Music)

Obecní dům
The Municipal House

Náměstí Republiky 5, Prague 1, Nové Město (Map A)
www.obecnidum.cz
TEL 222 002 101
HOURS Daily: 10:00–20:00
TICKETS 500 CZK–1,300 CZK
METRO Náměstí Republiky ●
TRAM 5, 8, 14, 26 to Náměstí Republiky

The Prague Symphony, founded in 1934, utilizes the main auditorium at Obecní dům, Smetana Hall, for their concerts (see p. 64 for more info on this great building).

BALLET PERFORMANCE AT NATIONAL THEATRE, 1959

Rudolfinum

Alšovo nábřeží 12, Prague 1,
Staré Město (Map A)
www.ceskafilharmonie.cz
www.galerierudolfinum.cz
TEL 227 059 227 (concert tickets)
TEL 227 059 309 (exhibitions)
HOURS Tue, Wed, Fri–Sun: 10:00–18:00; Thurs: 10:00–20:00
TICKETS 150 CZK–1,500 CZK
METRO Staroměstská ●
TRAM 17, 18 to Staroměstská

This Neo-Renaissance masterpiece was built from 1876–1884 and is surely one of the most striking and recognizable buildings along the river embankment (even serving as the backdrop to the opening of Tom Cruise's first *Mission: Impossible* movie). The interior is equally fabulous. Home to the world-famous Czech Philharmonic (its first concert here was directed by none other than Antonín Dvořák), it features a magnificent main hall, as well as a smaller space for chamber concerts, an exhibition space featuring rotating art exhibitions, and a café.

NOTE: The box office is also open one hour before each concert, but will only sell tickets for performances on the same day.

Other Classical Music Venues

Church of St. Nicholas
Kostel sv. Mikuláše

Malostranské náměstí 25, Prague 1, Malá Strana (Map B)
www.stnicholas.cz
TEL 257 534 215
HOURS Daily: 09:00–18:00
TICKETS 450 CZK Adults; 300 CZK Children; 10 & under Free
METRO Malostranská ●
TRAM 12, 20, 22 to Malostranské náměstí

This is one of Prague's most celebrated churches, with a stunning Baroque interior and exceptional acoustics. Mozart played the organ here in 1787, which you can easily imagine while closing your eyes as you take in one of the many organ recitals or choral concerts given here – most days at 18:00.

CASH ONLY

Chapel of Mirrors
Zrcadlová kaple

Klementinum, Mariánské náměstí, Prague 1, Staré Město (Map A)
www.klementinum.com
TEL 222 220 879
HOURS March: 10:00–16:00; Apr-Oct: 10:00–17:00; Nov–Jan: 10:00–16:00
TICKETS 450–600 CZK
METRO Staroměstská ●
TRAM 17, 18 to Staroměstská or Karlovy lázně

This pink marble (and marbleized wood!) chapel,

VIEW OF THE PRAGUE CASTLE FROM THE RUDOLFINUM, C. 1920

decorated with frescoes illustrating passages from the Ave Maria prayer, features a vast early Baroque organ with exceptional sound, making it a wonderful venue for music. The only way to gain access to this over-the-top space is by buying a ticket to one of their concerts, but it's well worth it. Concerts usually start at 17:00 and 20:00.

CASH ONLY

Other Music Venues (Jazz, Rock, Etc.)

▪ ▪ ▪ ▪ ▪ ▪ ▪ ▪ ▪ ▪ ▪ ▪ ▪ ▪

Jazz Dock – Jazz & Blues Bar & Café
(see entry in box on right)

▪ ▪ ▪ ▪ ▪ ▪ ▪ ▪ ▪ ▪ ▪ ▪ ▪ ▪

U Malého Glena
Karmelitská 23, Prague 1, Malá Strana (Map B)
www.malyglen.cz
TEL 257 531 717
HOURS Mon–Fri: 11:00–02:00; Sat & Sun: 11:00–03:00
METRO Malostranská ●
TRAM 12, 20, 22 to Malostranské náměstí

This jazz joint is tiny, so definitely make a reservation – and don't chat too loudly during the performance. The quality of the acoustics produced within this small arched-stone venue has been compared to the great clubs of New Orleans. Great place for an intimate handholding date, but equally appropriate to bring your mom.

NOTE: Music starts at 21:30 (you must be there by 21:15 to claim a reservation).

Interview with Glenn Spicker: Prague's Jazz Scene

Glenn Spicker, the owner of U Malého Glena (see entry at left), has lived in Prague for 20 years. He's been booking jazz and blues shows for purists seven nights a week for the past 16 years, so he seemed like the perfect person to make jazz recommendations for my readers.

Karen: When you're not taking in a show at your own venue, what's your favorite jazz joint in town and why?

Glenn: Jazz Dock is the new place to go. It's very well designed and the space is literally on the water. Like any venue, the quality of their acts varies, so although the club is awesome you need to check out the program on their website (which includes an English option) and ask around before you go. They occasionally have some music that's pretty far from jazz; on the other hand, they seem to have lots of money, so they can – and frequently do – offer some great world class jazz artists. Table reservations are absolutely recommended, and they offer a limited dinner menu that's more than acceptable.

Karen: Is there anything that makes the Prague jazz scene unique?

Glenn: The fact that there are quite a few clubs, with prices that tend to be very reasonable, has certainly been beneficial in terms of creating a scene. Plus, just the aura of jazz in the former Communist bloc has always been exciting. It developed (to some extent) as dissident music in Prague.

Karen: What Czech jazz band or vocalist do you think an English speaker would get the biggest kick out of?

Glenn: Miriam Bayle, for sure! Yvonne Sanchez is also fun to catch, if you're in mood for the Latin bossa nova sound, and Olga Škrancová can really sing as well.

▪ ▪ ▪ ▪ ▪ ▪ ▪ ▪ ▪ ▪ ▪ ▪ ▪ ▪

Jazz Dock – Jazz & Blues Bar & Cafe
Janáčkovo nábřeží 2, Prague 5, Smíchov
www.jazzdock.cz
TEL 774 058 838
HOURS Mon–Thurs: 15:00–04:00; Fri & Sat: 13:00–04:00; Sun: 13:00–02:00 (April–September) Mon–Fri: 17:00–04:00; Sat: 15:00–04:00; Sun: 15:00–02:00 (October–March)
TICKETS start at 120 CZK; 90 CZK for Seniors and 24 and under
METRO Anděl ●
TRAM 6, 9, 12 and 20 to Arbesovo náměstí

■ ■ ■ ■ ■ ■ ■ ■ ■ ■ ■

Palác Akropolis
Kubelíkova 27, Prague 3,
Žižkov (Map E)
www.palacakropolis.cz
TEL 296 330 911
HOURS Daily: 19:00–05:00
METRO Jiřího z Poděbrad ●
TRAM 11 to Jiřího z Poděbrad
TRAVEL TIME 15–20 min.

This place has it all – café, gallery and main stage (a smattering of big name bands play here), as well as both medium and small DJ rooms. Every night you can find at least one of these open, and quite often all three are in full effect – each with a different danceable vibe. The understatedly trippy décor is not to be missed. Definitely one of the best-known (and loved) spots in the gritty neighborhood of Žižkov.
CASH ONLY

CINEMAS

Thankfully, movies here are shown in their native language with subtitles in Czech. If a movie is dubbed, which is usually the case only for children's films, it will be clearly marked.

■ ■ ■ ■ ■ ■ ■ ■ ■ ■ ■

Cinema City
Slovanský dům
Na Příkopě 22, Prague 1,
Nové Město (Map A)
www.cinemacity.cz
TEL 255 742 021
TICKETS 179 CZK Adults; 129 CZK Children under 12
METRO Náměstí Republiky ● or Můstek ● ●

This multiplex is located in a downtown shopping arcade, close to the Obecní dům (Municipal House – see p. 64). They show only first-run features – generally a month or two after their U.S. release – and even offer ham-flavored popcorn…. Need I say more?!

■ ■ ■ ■ ■ ■ ■ ■ ■ ■ ■

Cine Star Anděl
Radlická 1E, Prague 5,
Smíchov
www.goldclass.cz
TEL 251 115 111
TICKETS 339 CZK
METRO Anděl ●
TRAM 4, 6, 7, 9, 10, 12, 14, 16, 20 to Anděl

OK, let me paint the scene: first, imagine the most super-comfortable La-Z-Boy recliner you've ever lounged in, including a foot rest, of course; second, put a table by your side where a waiter delivers drinks, finger food or popcorn; last, you sit back and enjoy a first-run feature film in the most deluxe setting ever. "Gold Class" brings movie viewing to a whole new level, I have to say, and I definitely encourage you to enjoy life on the other side, should you manage to fit in a movie during your visit to Prague. The setting and the price, at 339 CZK per ticket (less than double the cost of a regular movie ticket), make it very hard to go back to standard movie viewing! Reservations are recommended, as this theater only has 24 seats; if you wish, though, it's also possible to rent the entire theater!

Czech Films with English Subtitles on DVD

Three things to keep in mind, should you decide to purchase a DVD in Prague: **1.** Ask the store assistant to double-check that it has English subtitles. **2.** The DVD will only work in the U.S. if you have a "universal" system that plays both European and American DVDs, as the two are formatted differently. **3.** They are not cheap! The following recommended titles, for instance, range in price from 449 to 559 CZK.

Closely Watched Trains (Ostře sledované vlaky)
Jiří Menzel, 1966
(1967 Oscar for best Foreign Film)
Set at a village railway station in Nazi-occupied Czechoslovakia, this movie concerns a bumbling young dispatcher who longs to lose his virginity. Utterly oblivious to the war unfolding around him, he embarks on a journey of sexual awakening at his sleepy depot. One of the most beloved films of the Czech New Wave, it is based on a novel written by the famous Czech author Bohumil Hrabal (see p. 94).

The Hop Pickers (Starci na chmelu)
Ladislav Rychman, 1964
The Czech equivalent of *West Side Story*, this is a story of young love, set in the hop fields of Bohemia. One of my personal favorites.

ENTERTAINMENT

LUCERNA CINEMA FOYER (COURTESY OF LUCERNA)

I Served the King of England
(Obsluhoval jsem anglického krále)
Jiří Menzel, 2006

In this film, by the same director as *Closely Watched Trains* — and also based on a book written by Bohumil Hrabal (see p. 94) — the life and ambitions of the protagonist (a waiter-turned-millionaire-turned-prisoner) provide unique insight into the tumultuous history of the Czech nation.

Limonádový Joe
(Limonádový Joe aneb Koňská opera)
Oldřich Lipský, 1964

Central Europe has an odd fascination with the American west, and this 1964 musical send-up of Hollywood westerns pays homage to the "Spaghetti Western" style. Karel Gott ("The Golden Voice of Prague") is the singing voice of the lead character, Joe.

Little Otik *(Otesánek)*
Jan Švankmajer, 2000

Švankmajer is, without a doubt, the master of surrealist animation. Here he brings to life the classic folktale, *Der Struwwelpeter*, about a childless couple whose longing for a child transforms a tree root into a gnarly and insatiable baby.

Arthouse Cinemas

■ ■ ■ ■ ■ ■ ■ ■ ■ ■ ■ ■ ■ ■

Kino Světozor

Vodičkova 41, Prague 1,
Nové Město
(Map C)
www.kinosvetozor.cz
TEL 224 946 824
TICKETS 100–120 CZK
METRO Můstek ● ●
TRAM 3, 9, 14, 24 Václavské náměstí

Conveniently located in the city center, this cinema boasts one Czech film with English subtitles every day. Seeing depictions of Czech life on the silver screen is a great way to experience the culture, since it's unlikely that you'll ever get invited into someone's *panelák* apartment. You can also pick up a Světozor T-shirt for a unique souvenir.

■ ■ ■ ■ ■ ■ ■ ■ ■ ■ ■ ■ ■ ■

Lucerna Cinema

Vodičkova 36, Prague 1,
Nové Město (Map C)
www.lucerna.cz
TEL 224 216 972
TICKETS 120 CZK
METRO Můstek ● ●
TRAM 3, 9, 14, 24 to Václavské náměstí

The oldest continually operated movie theatre in Europe, the Lucerna Cinema opened in 1909. It was here that the very first "talkie" premiered in Europe. With its glamorous velvet curtain, gilt chandeliers and balcony, this auditorium will absolutely take you back to the golden age of cinema. Even if you're not up for a movie, it's worth a visit just to check out the building (Lucerna Palace, see p. 70).

LUCERNA CINEMA INTERIOR, PERIOD PHOTO (COURTESY OF LUCERNA)

Slightly Further Afield

Kino Aero

Biskupcova 31, Prague 3,
Žižkov
www.kinoaero.cz
TEL 271 771 349
TICKETS 100 CZK
TRAM 9, 10, 16, 19 to
Biskupcova; 1, 9, 16 to Ohrada
TRAVEL TIME 20 min.

Definitely go early to this little cinema, located nowhere near the beaten path, and rejoice in the fact that they serve beer instead of popcorn! The theater itself is 1970s auditorium-style, and the crowd is a healthy mix of the young and the simply film-savvy. Be sure to check for English subtitles in Czech and foreign films. Art films and classics often appear on the schedule.

NIGHTCLUBS

Nightclubs in Prague are always lots of fun, but I must admit they not really my scene, as I am a bit of a homebody. To create a list of must-hit locations, I decided to consult a few of my trusted night-owl friends, and we came up with this list...

If you're looking for bar recommendations, see p. 183–185.

Lucerna Music Bar

Vodičkova 36, Prague 1,
Nové Město (Map C)
www.lucerna.musicbar.cz
TEL 224 217 108
HOURS Daily: 20:00–03:00
METRO Můstek ● ●
TRAM 3, 9, 14, 24 to Vodičkova

Featuring 80s and 90s music on the weekends, this is where people go to dance. They also project music videos above the dance floor, so there are many levels of entertainment. Lucerna also hosts bands and events, so check the website to see what's going on.

Nebe

Křemencova 10, Prague 1,
Nové Město (Map C)
www.nebepraha.cz
TEL 608 644 784
HOURS Mon & Tue: 18:00–02:00; Wed & Thurs: 18:00–04:00; Fri & Sat: 18:00–05:00
METRO Karlovo Náměstí ● or Národní třída ●
TRAM 3, 4, 6, 10, 16, 18, 22, 24 to Karlovo náměstí

Full of hipster study-abroad students and open late, this joint is fully international. DJs spin tracks of indie, 80s or techno, depending on the night. Lots of comfy couches for maximum schmoozability. This bar's ambience will even impress those from Los Angeles and NYC. You'll find young boys experimenting with their sexuality and chicks with brand new asymmetrical "Euro Haircuts." Kitschy (yet beautiful) oil paintings of the Virgin and Child adorn the walls as a nod to the name *Nebe* – meaning "heaven" in Czech.

Roxy and Roxy NOD

Dlouhá 33, Prague 1,
Staré Město (Map A)
www.roxy.cz
TEL 602 691 015
HOURS Daily: 20:00–Late
METRO Náměstí Republiky ●
TRAM 5, 8, 14, 26 Dlouhá třída

A decrepit old theater turned all-night techno dance party, Roxy also hosts touring live bands of all sorts (rock, ska, punk, reggae – you name it). The chill-out room, located downstairs, comes complete with a large polar bear sculpture, as well as ice cubes to sit on. You can also take the staircase from the entrance on the left up to *Roxy NOD* (daily: 12:00–Late) where you'll find an ever-changing art gallery, featuring contemporary young artists and perhaps a theatrical or musical performance. Free Wi-Fi, too.

Zlaté časy

Vladislavova 1, Prague 1,
Nové Město (Map C)
www.zlatecasy.cz
TEL 224 948 170
HOURS Mon–Wed: 11:00–24:00; Thurs: 11:00–02:00; Fri: 11:00–04:00; Sat: 17:00–04:00
METRO Karlovo Náměstí ● or Národní třída ●
TRAM 3, 9, 14, 24 to Lazarská

Fair warning: aptly named "Golden Times," Zlaté časy is nothing less than a Czech disco. Don't expect the barmen to speak English, but do expect a scantily costumed professional dancer or two on the weekends. At some point the DJ will probably break into a medley of Czech hits that you've never heard, as the locals go wild on the dance floor. It's awesome.

Slightly Further Afield

■ ■ ■ ■ ■ ■ ■ ■ ■ ■ ■ ■ ■ ■

Cross Club
Plynární 23, Prague 7, Holešovice (Map F)
www.crossclub.cz
HOURS Mon–Thurs: 18:00–04:00; Fri & Sat: 18:00–06:00
METRO Nádraží Holešovice ●
TRAM 5, 12, 15 to Nádraží Holešovice
TRAVEL TIME 15–20 min.

Huge blinking robotic sculptures adorn the walls and ceilings – need I say more? In an industrial part of town (easily accessible by metro), this club is pretty darn gritty. Expect throbbing techno, drum & bass, maybe even punk or experimental – and try your best not to look like a tourist.

■ ■ ■ ■ ■ ■ ■ ■ ■ ■ ■ ■ ■ ■

Radost FX
(see p. 165)

This is where the beautiful people go clubbing, so it can be a bit of a meat market – which is ironic, since it also happens to be a delicious vegetarian restaurant. Fabulously upholstered couches and an opulent theme prevail. Yummy nachos and other meals are served till 04:00 in the upstairs lounge.

PRAGUE NIGHTCLUB, C. 1978
(SOURCE: PRAGUE HOUSE OF PHOTOGRAPHY)

CZECH CROONER KAREL GOTT ("THE GOLDEN VOICE OF PRAGUE"), C. 1972 (SOURCE: WWW.KARELGOTT.NET)

ENTERTAINMENT

Who Better to Ask About Czech Hockey than a Former Player?

Jiří Fiala was interviewed in 2007 for the first edition of this book. Sadly he passed away in 2008, but his interview remains both relevant and interesting, so I have decided to reprint it here...

Jiří Fiala
AGE: 49
TEAM: HC Slavia, 1974–1977
POSITION: Defense
HOBBY: Mushroom-picking

Karen: What makes Czech hockey different from North America's NHL?

Jiří: The Czech leagues play excellent hockey, but they're not at the same level of play as the NHL. There's more emphasis on passing, positioning and setting up plays to score than in the NHL, where such fancy play will often be stopped short by thundering body checks. Czech hockey is played on an international-size rink — the kind used throughout Europe — that's wider and longer than an NHL ice rink, and as a result, NHL hockey is much faster. Czech hockey leagues earn much more money from sponsorship than ticket sales or TV broadcasts, so the players' uniforms, the ice surface, the boards surrounding the ice, and even the team names often have sponsor's names and logos plastered

JIŘÍ FIALA, AFTER A SUCCESSFUL DAY OF MUSHROOM-PICKING AT HIS CHATA, C. 1980

all over them — but the players' salary is peanuts compared to what the NHL pays.

Karen: Sports teams always have personalities. How would you describe HC Slavia versus HC Sparta?

Jiří: Under communism, HC Sparta was owned by one of the biggest companies in the country, and this allowed the team to have far greater benefits, including salary, travel, and even better uniforms. However, they also had a lot

ENTERTAINMENT

POND HOCKEY, 1972 (JIŘÍ FIALA IS SECOND FROM LEFT)

more pressure on them due to this management structure. As a result, in general, I would describe the players as tougher.

HC Slavia, during this period, was a club team; the players played as a hobby, just for the love of the game. As a result, the team was much more laid-back. There was no management and no money. Today, I'm certain it's very different, as they are now owned by a large company, just like HC Sparta is.

Karen: Crazy fans always make a game much more fun. Which Prague team has the most intense fans?

Jiří: HC Sparta, no question!

Karen: What's your favorite Prague arena to see a game at?

Jiří: O2 Arena. This was where the Hockey World Championship was played in 2004. In fact, it was built for the occasion, and it's far more deluxe than all of the other local arenas.

Karen: What is your favorite team in the Czech Republic and why?

Jiří: HC Slavia, silly! Gotta stay loyal to my team.

SPORTS

Of the two national pastimes in the Czech Republic – mushroom picking and hockey – the latter is unquestionably the more riveting; so taking in a local game with Czech fans in their element could be great fun. While not as popular as hockey, soccer (or football, as they call it here) also has a very strong following. Here's all you need to know to get into the game:

Ice Hockey

• • • • • • • • • • • • • •

HC Slavia
02 Arena
Českomoravská 2345/17,
Prague 9, Libeň
www.hc-slavia.cz
TEL 266 121 122
TICKETS 100–260 CZK
METRO Českomoravská ●
TRAVEL TIME 10–15 min.

HC Slavia plays in the largest indoor rink in the Czech Republic, built for the 2004 World Ice Hockey Championships.

• • • • • • • • • • • • • •

HC Sparta
TIP Sport Arena
Za elektrárnou 419/1, Prague 7, Bubeneč (Map F)
www.hcsparta.cz
TEL 266 727 443

TICKETS 115–195 CZK
METRO Nádraží Holešovice ●
TRAM 5, 12, 14, 15, 17 to Výstaviště
TRAVEL TIME 15–20 min.

The local rival of HC Slavia.

Football (Soccer)

• • • • • • • • • • • • • •

SK Slavia
SYNOT Tip Arena
U Slavie 1540/2a, Prague 10, Vršovice
www.slavia.cz
TEL 731 126 104
TICKETS 150–550 CZK
METRO Strašnická ●, then
TRAM 7 to Slavia
tram 6, 7, 22, 24 to Slavia
TRAVEL TIME 20–25 min.

The local underdog.

• • • • • • • • • • • • • •

AC Sparta
Milady Horákové 98, Prague 7, Bubeneč (Map F)
www.sparta.cz
TEL 296 111 400
TICKETS 130–400 CZK
METRO Hradčanská ●
TRAM 1, 8, 15, 25, 26 to Sparta
TRAVEL TIME 15–20 min

As the defending champs, AC Sparta has the largest following.

BOATING ON THE VLTAVA RIVER, C. 1871

BOATING

One wonderfully relaxing alternative way to see Prague is from the deck of your own privately rented boat on the Vltava River. Here are a few ways to do just that...

River Tours

■ ■ ■ ■ ■ ■ ■ ■ ■ ■ ■ ■ ■
Prague Inspirations, s. r. o.
Nekázanka 11, Prague 1, Nové Město (Map C)
www.cruise-prague.cz
TEL 774 278 473
METRO Můstek ● ●
TRAM 3, 9, 14, 24 to Jindřišská

This company allows you to rent boats of various sizes for private cruises along the river.
My two favorites are:

Chroust: This tugboat, built in Dresden in 1896, is

small, quirky and perfect for a picnic, as the onboard seating is situated is around a table. So be sure to stop at La Bottega di Finestra (see p. 171) to pick up some snacks on your way to the dock. The maximum is 10 passengers, and they offer hot and cold beverages.

COST: 2,500 CZK per hour, not including beverages, minimum of 1 hour (but I recommend 2).
CASH ONLY

Elbis: A replica of a 19th-century Australian steamboat built in 2002, this boat has a cabin that can accommodate up to 25, and a sun deck for 20. Compared to the *Chroust*, your experience on the *Elbis* will certainly be a bit more deluxe, as they offer hors d'oeuvres, a bar with hot and cold drinks, and a WC

with full plumbing (as opposed to a dry chemical toilet).

COST: 790 CZK per person for 1 hour, minimum charge of 15,000 CZK.
CASH ONLY

Rowboats & Paddle Boats

■ ■ ■ ■ ■ ■ ■ ■ ■ ■ ■ ■ ■
Slavic Island
Slovanský ostrov
Prague 1, Staré Město (Map C)
www.slovanka.net
HOURS Daily: 11:00–22:00 (Apr–Oct)
COST PER HOUR 150 CZK (paddle / row boat); 400 CZK (small boat with engine); 600 CZK (speedboat).
METRO Národní třída ● or Karlovo náměstí ●
TRAM 6, 9, 17,18, 22 to Národní divadlo

If the *Chroust* and the *Elbis* sound like too much of a commitment, or if you prefer to be not just the captain of your own ship, but also the source of *horsepower*, then renting a rowboat or paddle boat for an hour or two on the Vltava might be just the ticket. On a sunny spring or summer afternoon, I have to say, it's one of my favorite pastimes. I prefer the paddleboats.

CASH ONLY

NOTE: ID required.

Boat to Troja Chateau and Prague Zoo

■ ■ ■ ■ ■ ■ ■ ■ ■ ■ ■ ■

Prague Steamboat Company
Pražská paroplavební společnost
Rašínovo nábřeží, Prague 2, Nové Město (Map C) (Between Palackého and Jiráskův Bridge)
www.paroplavba.cz
TEL 224 930 017 | 224 931 013
HOURS Daily May–Oct
departs: 09:00, 12:00 & 15:30
returns: 10:30, 13:30 & 17:00
TICKETS 150 CZK Adults;
80 CZK Children; 3 and under Free
METRO Karlovo Náměstí ●
TRAM 3, 4, 7, 10, 16, 17, 21 to Palackého náměstí

If you're planning on visiting the Troja Chateau (a 17th-century Baroque palace) or the Prague Zoo (see p. 208), one very scenic and fun way to get there is a 75-minute boat ride on the Vltava. It's approximately a five-minute walk from the landing dock to either destination.

Rent Your Very Own Tram (Seriously!)

Travelling by tram is one of the best ways to see Prague, so why not rent your own private vintage (c. 1951) tram? With 26 seats, there's plenty of room for all your family and friends to come along. Prices start at 3,800 CZK per hour and the ride can commence at any tram stop you wish. Refreshments and entertainment (an accordion player) are available upon request and are also quite affordable. This totally unique activity is certain to be a hit with young and old alike.

■ ■

Dopravní podnik hlavního města Prahy
www.dpp.cz/en/rental-of-historical-trams-and-the-urban-mass-transit-museum
TEL 296 124 902
PRICES start at 3,800 CZK per hour.

ROČNÍK VI. ČÍSLO 27   5 Kčs

Mladý TECHNIK

RYCHLE, SPOLEHLIVĚ A BEZPEČNĚ
JE NÁZEV NAŠÍ REPORTÁŽE O NOVÉM TYPU TRAMVAJE

MLADÝ TECHNIK MAGAZINE COVER, 1952

ENTERTAINMENT

HELICOPTER RIDES

No time to spare, but still want to visit a castle in the Bohemian countryside? Flying by helicopter is an ideal solution for traveling when you don't have hours to spend driving (or if you just have a hankering to wear that cool headset!). Possible destinations include a fairy-tale visit to Český Krumlov, a spa treatment in Karlovy Vary, or a round of golf at Karlštejn Castle, to name only a few.

▪ ▪ ▪ ▪ ▪ ▪ ▪ ▪ ▪ ▪ ▪ ▪ ▪ ▪

V.I.P. Helicopter Czech
www.helicopter.cz
TEL 731 150 142
cost starts at 20,000 CZK
Helicopters accommodate 1–5 passengers

Reservations should be made 14 days in advance, including payment by bank transfer or cash. However, two days in advance is often possible, based on availability. From Prague, helicopters depart from Prague Airport or Letňany. The company also charters airplanes within the Czech Republic and Europe. Visit their website to see a complete list of their fleet. Email Marek Krátký, director, for price quotes (vip@helicopter.cz); his English is excellent.

HOT AIR BALLOONING

If you're seeking the MOST exciting and all-inclusive view of the city, Balloon Center Prague should be definitely be added to your must-hit list. However, if seeing the oh-so-picturesque Czech countryside is your goal, I can think of no better or more relaxing way to do so than by hot air balloon. Either way, you're sure to have a memorable experience.

▪ ▪ ▪ ▪ ▪ ▪ ▪ ▪ ▪ ▪ ▪ ▪ ▪ ▪

Balloon Center Prague
Balon Centrum Praha
Cihelná 2b, Prague 1, Malá Strana (Map B)
www.baloncentrum.cz
TEL 773 650 522
HOURS Daily: 10:00–21:00 (May–Oct)
TICKETS 800 CZK (15 minute ride)
METRO Malostranská ●
TRAM 12, 18, 20, 22 to Malostranská

A hot air balloon flight over Prague's historic center is thrilling and memorable – but not for the faint of heart! The balloon in question is attached to a fixed cable – so you don't need to worry about floating away – and rises 80 meters (about 265') above the Charles Bridge, providing a gorgeous panoramic view of Prague and beyond. I went with my editor and we both loved it, although I will admit I was a bit nervous at the time. A word to the wise: be prepared for the jolt you'll feel when the balloon reaches maximum height – and for the fact that it can get a bit windy up there – and you'll be just fine. The operation is very professional, and safety is clearly a priority – they even provide you with a walkie-talkie so that you can communicate with them if you wish to end your ride early. Note that children up to 40 kilos (about 90 lbs.) can ride for FREE, if they are brave enough to want to! I recommend that you (or your hotel concierge) call ahead to confirm flight schedules, as the operation is, of course, highly dependent on wind and weather conditions.

▪ ▪ ▪ ▪ ▪ ▪ ▪ ▪ ▪ ▪ ▪ ▪ ▪ ▪

Ballooning CZ
www.ballooning.cz
TEL 222 783 995 | 739 318 121
OPEN Daily
COST 4,800 CZK per person weekdays; 5,300 CZK per person weekends & holidays Balloons accomdate 1–7 passengers.

The balloon departs from Konopiště (see p. 55), very close to the castle, and the flight will slowly float over this beautiful area of southern Bohemia for roughly one hour, though preparation takes an additional 30 minutes. If the balloon is booked for a single group, other launch sites are possible. Flights are available year-round, but only in favorable weather (dry with 5km of visibility and little wind). Morning launches must take place no later then two hours after sunrise and evening launches must take place no later than two hours before sunset. Flights over the city of Prague are not possible.

NOTE: Reservations must be made 14 days in advance, including payment by bank transfer or cash.

EASTER GREETINGS, 1919 (SOURCE: J. WENIGA)

FESTIVALS & HOLIDAY CELEBRATIONS

Easter Monday
Velikonoce
MARCH / APRIL

Although Easter is certainly observed as a religious holiday here, you'll find very few Czechs at church services. Instead they generally participate in a bizarre pagan ritual called *pomlázka*, in which Czech men beat women with willow sticks decorated with colorful ribbons in order to keep them fertile during the year to come. The women retaliate by throwing cold water over their male tormentors. Peace is finally restored when the women present the men with shots of *slivovice* (home-made brandy, see p. 184) and hand-painted eggs. Called *kraslice*, these eggs are hand-decorated using various techniques – including the application of straw, thread, crochet work, wax, grass pulp, batik, and dyes applied with onionskins – to achieve a precise decorative motif. Small masterpieces, all of them. Manufaktura (see p. 101) is the best local source for painted eggs.

Burning of the Witches
Pálení čarodějnic
APRIL 30

Marking the death of winter and the birth of spring, bonfires are lit throughout the country-side (and occasionally in Prague) to purge the land of evil winter spirits and keep witches at bay. Although it's illegal to light fires within Prague's city limits, an unofficial (though sanctioned) celebration is held on Petřín Hill (see p. 74).

May Day / Labor Day
Svátek Práce
MAY 1

While this celebration may not be what it once was, you'll find plenty of Communists out in Letná Park (see p. 73) making a valiant effort to keep the party alive – the Communist party, that is, which is currently supported by 17% of the Czech population (up from 12% in 2006 – not sure what to say about that...). The celebration is still going strong in the countryside; one parade I saw near my country house featured a float with an enormous head of Lenin made from papier-mâché, and teenage girls with pompoms leading the way.

Prague Spring
Pražské jaro
MAY 12 TO JUNE 3
Rudolfinum
Náměstí Jana Palacha,
Prague 1, Staré Město
(Map A)
www.festival.cz
TEL 257 312 547
METRO Staroměstská ●
TRAM 17, 18 to Staroměstská

MAY DAY AT LETNÁ PARK, MAY 1, 1986
(SOURCE: ČTK / CZECH NEWS AGENCY)

This internationally prestigious music festival is, bar none, the biggest arts event of the year in the Czech Republic. The event dates back to 1946 and traditionally begins on May 12, the anniversary of Bedřich Smetana's death, with a procession from his grave in Vyšehrad all the way to the Obecní dům (Municipal House – see p. 64), where the composer's *Má vlast* ("My Country") is performed in the presence of the president. The festival finishes on June 3 with a performance of Beethoven's *Ninth Symphony*. Tickets sell out fast, so if you're planning a trip to Prague during this time, you'll want to purchase tickets in advance, either online or through your hotel. Tickets go on sale December 12 (yes, every year!).

EVE OF ST. NICHOLAS, 1947
(SOURCE: ČTK / CZECH NEWS AGENCY)

Prague International Marathon
LATE MAY
www.pim.cz

Runners from all over the world come to brave the cobblestones and traverse the Charles Bridge. If you'd like to join in, or simply observe, check their website for exact dates.

Fringe Festival Prague
LATE MAY / EARLY JUNE
www.praguefringe.com

This weeklong festival, which began in 2001, offers the best in theatre, cabaret, music, comedy and dance from around the world. In 2012, there were 41 companies from 19 countries. The

BLUDGEONING CARP FOR CHRISTMAS DINNER, 1936
(SOURCE: ČTK / CZECH NEWS AGENCY)

participating venues lean toward the intimate, and most performances run about one hour.

World Festival of Puppet Art
LATE MAY / EARLY JUNE
www.wap-prague.org

The World Festival of Puppet Art is a weeklong international festival organized by the puppeteer's world body, UNIMA, which is based in Prague and founded in 1996. Last year's festival had participants from 26 countries, including

206

China, India, Russia and South Africa. The competition is juried, providing participants and audiences an opportunity to see great performances, both traditional and innovative, of this unique craft.

Tanec Dance Festival
JUNE
www.tanecpha.cz

Tanec is an international festival of modern dance that takes place over a period of three weeks at venues throughout the city. Past festivals have introduced Bill T. Jones and Merce Cunningham to Czech audiences. The event

is often used as a platform for world premieres, and has attracted participants from all over the world, including Finland, Israel, Mexico and Taiwan.

Anniversary of the Velvet Revolution
Sametová Revoluce
NOVEMBER 17
Václavské náměstí, Prague 1, Nové Město (Map C)

This holiday commemorates the demonstrations in Wenceslas Square that began the Velvet Revolution in 1989. Candles are lit and flowers are laid, but overall it tends to be pretty understated.

Eve of St. Nicholas
Mikuláš
DECEMBER 5
Should you happen to pass a trio dressed as an angel, a devil and a saint on this night, fear not. You're not crazy, but simply happen to be in Prague on the eve of St. Nicholas – one of my personal favorite holidays. The costumed trio visits small children (and large ones, like me), with the angel handing out sweets to children who have been good and the devil handing out coal and potatoes to those who have been bad – giving children a useful indication of what is to come on Christmas day! Should you happen to be in Prague with children during this time, ask your hotel concierge to arrange a visit for them. Yes, the trios are actually available for hire, and the hotel should be able to take care of this.

Christmas
Vánoce
DECEMBER 24

Czechs celebrate Christmas on the night of the 24th. Festivities include a meal of fish soup, fried carp, potato salad, *vánočka* (sweet bread similar to challah), and cookies. Only after the meal are children allowed to open their presents…which, by the way, have been delivered by Baby Jesus (*Ježíšek*), not Santa Claus.

CHRISTMAS, C. 1960

CIRKUS BEROUSEK, 2006

KIDS

As I'm really a kid a heart, I've listed a few of my favorite things to do that are, more often than not, thought of as kids' activities.

Circus & Zoo

■ ■ ■ ■ ■ ■ ■ ■ ■ ■ ■ ■

Cirkus Berousek
www.berousek.cz/program.php
TEL 607 222 220
ENTRANCE FEE 200–350 CZK Adults; 150–200 CZK Children

Have your hotel concierge find out if this wonderful circus happens to be in town during your visit. It's a one-ring show that is bound to charm young and old alike, as it includes lots of acrobats, animals and clowns. The highlight during my last visit was an act featuring bears riding motorcycles. Without even reserving tickets in advance, I was able to get front row seats for 350 CZK per ticket. Needless to say, the horses, elephants and camels were perhaps closer than some would like, but the four-year-old next to me and I were both

definitely in our element! You'll want to bring plenty of cash, as you're certain to be cajoled by your child into buying them popcorn, cotton candy and very cool multi-color circus lights that play an annoyingly catchy tune. During intermission, you can take a ride on a camel in the ring, and, for a small fee, have a Polaroid picture taken as a keepsake.

CASH ONLY

NOTE: It's possible to order tickets online, and I would recommend having your concierge take care of this to ensure that you get the best possible seats.

Slightly Further Afield

■ ■ ■ ■ ■ ■ ■ ■ ■ ■ ■ ■ ■

Prague Zoo
U Trojského zámku 3, Prague 7, Troja
www.zoopraha.cz
TEL 296 112 111
HOURS Daily: 09:00–17:00 (Mar); 09:00–18:00 (Apr, May, Sept, Oct); 09:00–19:00 (Jun–Aug); 09:00–16:00 (Nov–Feb)
ENTRANCE FEE 200 CZK Adults; 150 CZK Children; 100 CZK Dogs; 3 and under Free
MAP 5 CZK (Get it!)
METRO Nádraží Holešovice ● bus 112 to Zoologická zahrada
NOTE: I recommend taking either a taxi (see p. 17) or a boat (see p. 203).
TRAVEL TIME 15–20 min by taxi; 75 min by boat

Lions and tigers and flying chairs – oh my! Prague has a great zoo, and if you've got youngsters traveling with you, it's a great destination (especially if you travel by boat to get there – see p. 203). The zoo is big enough that it'll be difficult to fit it all in during one visit; be certain to get a map when you buy your tickets, so you can be sure to hit the exhibitions that interest you most. I'm a big fan of the petting zoo, where 5 CZK gets you a handful of nibbles to feed the goats and sheep. They also offer pony rides (20

KIDS, C. 1925

BOOK COVER, C. 1930

PETŘÍN HILL VIEWING TOWER, C. 1940

CZK), a miniature tram ride (10 CZK), and even a kiddie pool – so if your little ones love the water, you'll want to bring a change of clothes. But without question, my favorite attraction here is the Flying Chairs ride (20 CZK; free for children under 6), which is tranquil on the way up, picturesque on the way down, and offers a stunning panoramic view of Prague – I was completely enchanted and went on it three times!

Parks & Playgrounds

- - - - - - - - - - - - -
Children's Island
Dětský ostrov
Vltava River, Prague 1, Malá Strana; Entrance on Janáčkovo nábřeží (Map B)
TRAM 4, 7, 10, 14, 16 to Zborovská; 6, 9, 12, 20 to Arbesovo náměstí

A wonderful little riverside oasis where your little ones can run around, which also includes an enclosed

playground. Thankfully, there are lots of benches where you can relax as you take in the exceptional location and view.

- - - - - - - - - - - - -
Petřín Hill Mirror Maze
Petřínské sady bludiště
Petřín Hill Viewing Tower
Petřínské sady rozhledna
(Map B)
www.petrinska-rozhledna.cz
HOURS Daily: Apr–Sept: 10:00–22:00; Oct & Mar: 10:00–20:00; Nov–Feb: 10:00–18:00
ENTRANCE FEE 100 CZK Adults; 50 CZK Children; 6 & under 20 CZK

Wonderfully tourist-free, the Mirror Maze is housed in a mock-Gothic castle built for the 1891 Prague Jubilee. This hall of distorting mirrors is an opportunity for great hilarity among both young and old. You can take a funicular (cable car) up using standard tram tickets, and the view is excellent. If you're up for it, you can also climb up the mini Eiffel Tower, also built for the Jubilee, which

VINTAGE POSTCARD, C. 1920

TRANSPORT HALL, NATIONAL TECHNICAL MUSEUM
(PHOTO COURTESY OF NTM)

has a viewing gallery 53 meters (170 ft.) off the ground. The park at Petřín, in general, is very peaceful, so if your wee ones enjoy walking, this is a wonderful place to spend a few hours.

CASH ONLY

Mini-Train Ride

Children's Train
Dětský Vláček
Slovanský ostrov, Prague 1, Nové Město (Map C)
www.cesky-lvicek.cz
TEL 602 379 860
HOURS Daily: 10:00–12:00 & 14:00–18:00 (April–October)
TICKETS 10 CZK (5 minute ride)
METRO Národní třída ●
TRAM 6, 9, 17,18, 21, 22 to Národní divadlo

Why not treat your child to a ride in a scaled down replica of an 1841 train? The Czech Lion (Český Ivíček) travels along its 53-meter (about 175') track at 3km per hour, and at only 10 CZK per ride, it is certain your little ones will want to indulge in at least a few go-rounds. The train is located on the picturesque Slavic Island (*Slovanský ostrov*) which also has a playground and paddle boat rental (see p. 202). Ages 3 to 10.

Museums

The National Museum
Národní muzeum
(see p. 58)
Closed the 1st Tuesday of every month.

Closed for renovation; due to reopen June 2015.

At the National Museum, it's most likely the zoological collection that children will find most mesmerizing.

National Technical Museum
Národní technické muzeum
(see p. 59)

This museum is tons of fun. The Transport Hall, filled to the brim with Czech-made vehicles, is sure to be a hit with the whole family.

Toy Museum
Muzeum hraček
(see p. 60)

This museum, with an interesting collection of toys dating back over 150 years, is certain to be a winner with kids of all ages.

▪ ▪ ▪ ▪ ▪ ▪ ▪ ▪ ▪ ▪ ▪
Public Transport Museum
Muzeum městské hromadné dopravy
(see p. 60)

A wonderful hands-on experience for young and old alike, this museum features historic trams and buses, several of which you can even climb into and explore. Super fun! You can even take "Nostalgic Tram Line No. 91," which features vintage trams dating back to 1875. This special tramline is in operation from April through November on Saturdays, Sundays and holidays from 12:00 to around 17:35. The cost is 35 CZK per ride. See their website (www.dpp.cz/en/nostalgic-tram-line-no-91/) for more information.

THE #17 TRAM, C. 1956
(PHOTO BY ERICH EINHORN)

Theatre

▪ ▪ ▪ ▪ ▪ ▪ ▪ ▪ ▪ ▪ ▪
New Stage of the National Theatre
Nová Scéna Národní divadlo
Národní 4, Prague 1, Nové Město (Map C)
www.novascena.cz
www.laterna.cz
TEL 224 931 482
HOURS Mon–Fri: 09:00–18:00; Sat & Sun: 10:00–18:00
TICKETS 210–680 CZK
METRO Národní třída ●
TRAM 6, 9, 17,18, 21, 22 to Národní divadlo

As a tourist in Prague, it will not take long for you to become aware of the presence of several different "Black Light Theatre" groups offering performances all around town. Not being a fan of this type of spectacle myself, I avoided these shows for years, but in writing this book I felt obliged to see of any were worthy of recommendation. Now, while I still firmly believe that most of these should be avoided like the plague, it turns out that performances by the Laterna Magika ensemble at the New Stage of the National Theatre are actually quite worthy – especially if you're traveling with children from ages 5–16. Their multimedia performance is quite intriguing and does not present a language barrier for non-Czech speakers. Of the various programs in their repertoire, my favorite is "Wonderful Circus," which has been in continuous production since 1977; I love the fabulous vintage film clips they have incorporated into it.

The theatre itself, completed in 1983, is an offshoot of the National Theatre located next door. The Brutalist-style building, reminiscent of an ice cube, is seen by many locals as one of the dreariest examples of Communist architecture. I shared that opinion when I first moved to Prague, but I now have a great appreciation for the building – especially the interior, with its massive light fixtures – as well as for the very cool Nová Scéna Café, located on the third floor (see p. 183).

ENTERTAINMENT

211

Resources

TRAVEL ADVERTISEMENT,
C. 1930

ČSA AIRLINE CABIN, 1940
(PHOTO COURTESY OF CZECH AIRLINES)

IMPORTANT TELEPHONE NUMBERS

■ ■ ■ ■ ■ ■ ■ ■ ■ ■ ■ ■ ■

Czech Country Code: +420
Emergency: 112
Ambulance: 155
Emergency Road Service:
1230, 1240

AIRLINES

■ ■ ■ ■ ■ ■ ■ ■ ■ ■ ■ ■ ■

www.csa.cz
www.easyjet.com
www.skyeurope.com
www.smartwings.net

BICYCLE RENTAL

■ ■ ■ ■ ■ ■ ■ ■ ■ ■ ■ ■ ■

City Bike
Královorská 5, Prague 1,
Staré Město (Map A)
www.citybike-prague.com
TEL 776 180 284
HOURS Daily: 09:00–19:00
(Apr–Oct)
METRO Náměstí Republiky ●
TRAM 5, 8, 14, 26 to
Náměstí Republiky
PRICES Start at 300 CZK for
2 hours.

■ ■ ■ ■ ■ ■ ■ ■ ■ ■ ■ ■ ■

Praha Bike
Dlouhá 24, Prague 1,
Staré Město (Map A)
www.prahabike.cz
TEL 732 388 880
HOURS Daily: 09:00–20:00
METRO Náměstí Republiky ●
TRAM 5, 8, 14, 26 to Dlouhá
třída
PRICES Start at 200 CZK for
2 hours.

■ ■ ■ ■ ■ ■ ■ ■ ■ ■ ■ ■ ■

**ILIKEEBIKE -
Electric Bike Rental**
Vlašská 15, Prague 1,
Malá Strana (Map B)
www.ilikeebike.com
TEL 604 474 546
HOURS Daily: 09:00–19:00
METRO Malostranská ●
TRAM 12, 20, 22 to
Malostranské náměstí
PRICES Start at 590 CZK for
a half-day.

COMPUTER REPAIR

■ ■ ■ ■ ■ ■ ■ ■ ■ ■ ■ ■ ■

**Počítačová
Pohotovost**
Lublaňská 19, Prague 2,
Vinohrady (Map C)

www.pocitacovapohotovost.cz
TEL 224 262 826; 603 757 677
HOURS Daily: 24/7
METRO I.P. Pavlova ●
TRAM 4, 6, 10, 11, 16, 22 to
I.P. Pavlova

If your computer malfunctions and panic begins to set in, take a deep breath and call this firm—you will be in good hands. My friend Raul needed to pay them a visit when his Apple laptop went on the blink during his visit here. We found this place after the Apple store proved completely incapable of doing anything but trying to sell him new products. They work on both PCs and Macs, and are the authorized repair firm for Lenovo (formerly IBM).

CREDIT CARD COMPANIES

■ ■ ■ ■ ■ ■ ■ ■ ■ ■ ■ ■ ■

Master Card / Visa:
+001 880 826 2181
American Express:
222 800 222
Diners Club:
255 712 712

CZECH TOURISM

■ ■ ■ ■ ■ ■ ■ ■ ■ ■ ■ ■ ■ ■ ■

www.czech.cz

This is the official foreign ministry website for the Czech Republic. It includes general information about the country, but most importantly, it includes entry requirements. Definitely double-check this site before traveling to the Czech Republic, as requirements vary within the European Union.

www.czechtourism.com

This website covers not only Prague but also the entire Czech Republic. It's not especially easy to navigate but it can be a very helpful resource.

www.praguewelcome.cz

If you're traveling to Prague, this is the best website to utilize as a resource. It's easy to navigate and offers excellent information on Prague, particularly concerning cultural events.

www.praguecard.biz

If you're a die-hard sightseer, the four-day card that this website offers could be an excellent investment: It provides free admission to over 50 museums and attractions, including the Prague Castle. They also offer two-day and three-day options. Visit their website to see what destinations are included and where the card can be purchased.

COST (4 DAY CARD): 1,200 CZK Adults; 850 CZK Students

DEPARTMENT STORES

■ ■ ■ ■ ■ ■ ■ ■ ■ ■ ■ ■ ■ ■ ■

Marks & Spencer

Václavské nám. 36, Prague 1, Nové Město (Map C)
www.marks-and-spencer.cz
TEL 224 237 503
HOURS Mon–Fri: 8:30–20:30; Sat: 10:00–20:00; Sun: 10:00–20:00
METRO Muzeum ● ● or Můstek ● ●
TRAM 3, 9, 14, 24 to Václavské náměstí

This British department store specializes in clothing and shoes for men, women, and children; they also have a grocery store and café.

■ ■ ■ ■ ■ ■ ■ ■ ■ ■ ■ ■ ■ ■ ■

VAN GRAAF

Václavské nám. 17, Prague 1, Nové Město (Map C)
www.vangraaf.com
TEL 296 304 200
HOURS Daily:10:00–21:00
METRO Můstek ● ●
TRAM 3, 9, 14, 24 to Václavské náměstí

This fashion emporium offers over 200 top brands of clothing and accessories.

EMBASSIES

■ ■ ■ ■ ■ ■ ■ ■ ■ ■ ■ ■ ■ ■ ■

British Embassy

Thunovská 14, Prague 1, Malá Strana (Map B)
www.ukinczechrepublic.fco.gov.uk
TEL 257 402 111 (emergencies 257 402 255)
HOURS Mon–Fri: 09:00–17:00
METRO Malostranská ●
TRAM 12, 20, 22 to Malostranské náměstí

PORTER ASSISTING AN ELEGANT TRAVELER (SOURCE: DEPOSITPHOTOS.COM)

Canadian Embassy
Muchova 6, Prague 6,
Dejvice (Map D)
www.canadainternational.
gc.ca/czech-tcheque
TEL 272 101 800
HOURS Mon–Fri: 08:30–12:30
& 13:30–16:30
METRO Hradčanská ●

Irish Embassy
Tržiště 13, Prague 1,
Malá Strana (Map B)
www.irishembassy.cz
TEL 257 530 061 / 064
HOURS Mon–Fri: 09:30–12:30
& 14:30–16:30
METRO Malostranská ●
TRAM 12, 20, 22 to
Malostranské náměstí

U.S. Embassy
Tržiště 15, Prague 1,
Malá Strana (Map B)
www.usembassy.cz
TEL 257 022 000
HOURS Mon–Fri: 08:00–16:30
METRO Malostranská ●
TRAM 12, 20, 22 to
Malostranské náměstí

EXPAT-ORIENTED INFO
(And General Information
that May Prove Useful to
Temporary Visitors)

expats.cz
www.expats.cz

This website is the Holy
Grail for local expats, and
you'll find information
on anything and every-
thing here, including
restaurants, movie listing,
employment opportu-
nities, and even online
dating. Just an all-around
excellent resource.

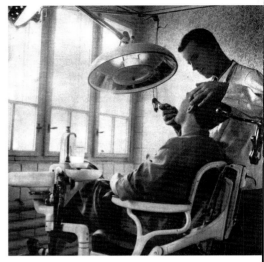

DENTAL CARE, 1953

prague.tv
www.expats.cz

This website also primarily
serves the expatriate
community and has
excellent, easy-to-navigate
listings of cultural events
and cinema showtimes.

Prague Stay
www.prague-stay.com/
lifestyle/

This website is a great
resource for planning your
trip to Prague, or to utilize
while you are here, as the
site offers excellent reviews
that are, for the most part,
right on the mark.

GAY-ORIENTED TRAVEL INFO

Prague Saints
Polská 32, Prague 2,
Vinohrady (Map E)
www.praguesaints.cz
info@praguesaints.cz

TEL 222 250 326
HOURS Daily: 19:00–04:00
METRO Jiřího z Poděbrad ●
tram 11 to Jiřího z Poděbrad

This organization
specializes in gay-oriented
travel info, and their
website offers one-stop
shopping for planning and
enjoying your stay in
Prague.

GOLF COURSES

Karlštejn Golf Resort
Běleč 272, 267 27 Liteň
www.karlstejn-golf.cz
TEE TIMES: 7:00–21:00
TRAVEL TIME 30 min.

Albatross Golf Resort
Sokolská 162, 267 16 Vysoký
Újezd
www.albatross.cz
TEE TIMES: Tue–Sun: 07:30–
21:00; Mon: 8:30–21:00
TRAVEL TIME 30 min.

HEALTH CARE

Dentists

American Dentist in Prague (Dr. Eric)

Pštrossova 10, Prague 1, Nové Město (Map C)

www.americandentist.cz

TEL 773 505 773

HOURS Mon, Wed & Thurs: 09:00–17:00; Tue: 09:00–19:00

METRO Národní třída ●

TRAM 6, 9, 17,18, 21, 22 to Národní divadlo or 14 to Myslíkova

Doctors & Clinics

Canadian Medical Care

Veleslavínská 1, Prague 6, Veleslavín

www.cmcpraha.cz

TEL 235 360 133 (After hours & weekends: 724 300 301)

HOURS Mon, Wed, Fri: 08:00–18:00; Tue & Thurs: 08:00–20:00; Sat: 09:00–14:00

METRO Dejvická ●

TRAM 20, 26, 36 to Nádraží Veleslavín

Centrum Cestovní Medicíny (Center for Travel Medicine)

Havelská 14, Prague 1, Staré Město (Map A)

www.centrumcestovni mediciny.cz

TEL 222 094 121

HOURS Mon–Thurs: 08:00–12:00 & 12:30–18:00; Fri: 08:00–12:00 & 12:30–15:00

METRO Můstek ● ●

Should you be traveling from Prague to India, Afghanistan, or any other exotic or war-torn location that requires vaccinations, this is your best bet.

Polyclinic at Národní

Poliklinika Na Národní

Národní 9, 3rd Floor, Prague 1, Staré Město (Map A)

www.poliklinika.narodni.cz

TEL 222 075 120 (Emergency: 777 942 270)

HOURS Mon–Fri: 08:30–17:00

METRO Národní třída ●

TRAM 6, 9, 17, 18, 22 to Národní divadlo

Obstetrics & Gynaecology

OG Medical Centre Elena Figurová, MD

Vodičkova 30, 4th & 5th Floor, Prague 1, Nové Město (Map C)

www.oggroup.cz

TEL 224 220 037

HOURS Mon–Thurs: 07:30–18:30; Fri: 07:30–16:30

METRO Můstek ● ●

TRAM 3, 9, 14, 24 to Václavské náměstí

Hospitals

Motol Hospital

V Úvalu 84, Prague 5, Motol

www.fnmotol.cz

TEL 224 431 111 (emergencies, adults: 224 438 590) (emergencies, children: 224 433 652)

HOURS Daily: 24 hours

METRO Anděl ● (exit Na Knížecí) then Bus 167 to Nemocnice Motol

TRAM 4, 6, 7, 9, 10, 12, 14, 16, 20 to Anděl

Take a taxi (see p. 17).

This hospital is dedicated to the treatment of foreigners.

Na Homolce Hospital

Roentgenova 2, Prague 5, Motol

www.homolka.cz

TEL 257 271 111

HOURS Daily: 24 hours

METRO Anděl ● (exit Na Knížecí), then Bus 167 to Nemocnice Motol

TRAM 4, 6, 7, 9, 10, 12, 14, 16, 20 to Anděl

Take a taxi (see p. 17).

This happens to be my hospital of choice.

NURSE WEIGHING A NEWBORN BABY AT THE ŠKODA AUTO COMPANY HOSPITAL, 1982 (SOURCE: ČTK / CZECH NEWS AGENCY)

Pharmacies (open 24 hours)

▪ ▪ ▪ ▪ ▪ ▪ ▪ ▪ ▪ ▪ ▪ ▪ ▪

Pharmacy U sv. Ludmily
Belgická 37, Prague 2,
Vinohrady (Map E)
TEL 222 519 731
METRO Náměstí Míru ●
TRAM 4, 10, 16, 22 to
Náměstí Míru

▪ ▪ ▪ ▪ ▪ ▪ ▪ ▪ ▪ ▪ ▪ ▪ ▪

Pharmacy U Palackého
Palackého 5, Prague 1,
Nové Město (Map C)
TEL 224 946 982
METRO Můstek ● ●
TRAM 3, 9, 14, 24 to Václavské
náměstí

Opticians

▪ ▪ ▪ ▪ ▪ ▪ ▪ ▪ ▪ ▪ ▪ ▪ ▪

GrandOptical
28. Října 5, Prague 1,
Staré Město (Map C)
www.grandoptical.cz
TEL 224 238 371
HOURS Daily: 09:00–20:00
METRO Můstek ● ●

If you happen to lose or
break your glasses while in
Prague, you'll be happy to
have this address. They'll
give you new glasses in one
hour.

Veterinarian

▪ ▪ ▪ ▪ ▪ ▪ ▪ ▪ ▪ ▪ ▪ ▪ ▪

Panda Veterinary Clinic
Panda Vetrinární klinika
Krkonošská 8, Prague 2,
Vinohrady (Map E)
www.veterinarniklinikapanda.com
TEL 222 725 345
HOURS Mon–Fri: 08:30–
21:00; Sat: 09:00–13:00;
Sun: 16:00–19:00
METRO Jiřího z Poděbrad ●
TRAM 11 to Jiřího z Poděbrad
Take a taxi (see p. 17).

VETERINARY TREATMENT, C. 1950

This is my personal vet. If
your little munchkin is
traveling with you and
happens to be a bit under
the weather, this is where
you'll want to go. Best of
all, they speak decent
English.

JEWISH INTEREST

▪ ▪ ▪ ▪ ▪ ▪ ▪ ▪ ▪ ▪ ▪ ▪ ▪

www.kehilaprag.cz
This website has informa-
tion on everything you
might want to know about

TWINS, C. 1915

the current Jewish community in Prague. (For a tour guide specializing in Judaic tours, see listing for PragueWalkers, p. 220.)

KIDS

Baby Sitting: Agentura Pohoda
www.agenturapohoda.cz
TEL 737 282 627
RATES 160–210 CZK per hour

This agency offers babysitting, with a minimum of two hours. Their services have been utilized by any number of international film stars, embassies and multinational corporations, so you can feel confident that your little tyke will be in good hands.
CASH ONLY

NOTE: Prices listed are based on one child; review their excellent website for a complete price list.

Kids in Prague
www.kidsinprague.com

This website is a great resource if you have children aged 0–11. It includes a list of playgrounds and child-friendly restaurants, as well as a section for "useful information" that is indeed extremely useful.

MOTORCYCLE RENTAL

Motorbike Ventures
Lovosická 856, Prague 9, Prosek
www.motorbikeventures.com
TEL 777 031 441
METRO Prosek ●

Longing to hit the open road, but left your hog back home? These are the go-to guys in town, who can set you up with a cool bike or take you on a tour to locations around the country.

NEWS

The Prague Post
www.praguepost.com

The Prague Post is the major English language newspaper in Prague, and their website is a helpful tool for cultural listings, as well as real estate (should you fall in love with the city and decide to stay a while).

Prague Daily Monitor
www.praguemonitor.com

A daily summary of Czech news in English.

POLICE STATIONS

STARÉ MĚSTO
Bartolomějská 14, Prague 1, Staré Město (Map A)
TEL 974 851 700
HOURS 24 hours
METRO Národní třída ●
TRAM 6, 9, 18, 22 to Národní třída

MALÁ STRANA
Vlašská 3, Prague 1, Malá Strana (Map B)
TEL 974 851 730
HOURS 24 hours
METRO Malostranská ●
TRAM 12, 20, 22 to Malostranské náměstí

NOVÉ MĚSTO
Jungmannovo náměstí 9, Prague 1, Nové Město (Map C)
TEL 974 851 750
HOURS 24 hours
METRO Můstek ● ●

VINOHRADY
Šafaříkova 12, Prague 2, Vinohrady (Map E)
TEL 974 852 720
METRO Náměstí Míru ● or I. P. Pavlova ●
TRAM 4, 10, 16, 22 to Náměstí Míru

POST OFFICE

www.ceskaposta.cz
This website from the Czech Post Office has useful information about shipping, which might come in handy if you've been extraordinarily indulgent and purchased far too much to carry home.

PRIVATE DRIVER

Mike's Chauffeur Service
www.mike-chauffeur.cz
info@mike-chauffeur.cz
TEL 241 768 231
MOBILE 602 224 893

If you decide to take a day trip to Český Krumlov, Karlovy Vary, Telč, or even a short trip to Nelahozeves (see p. 55), this might prove to be a useful contact. Mike can also take you to your next destination outside the Czech Republic, be it Budapest, Dresden, Salzburg, or Vienna, with stops along the way. His website is easy to use and includes standard pricing, though he's also able to quote a price for custom itineraries. A list of his vehicles and the number of passengers each can accommodate is also on the site.

SERVICE WORKER, 1971 (SOURCE: ČTK / CZECH NEWS AGENCY)

your tour, so you'll want to confirm the exact price once you finalize your itinerary.

CASH ONLY

■ ■ ■ ■ ■ ■ ■ ■ ■ ■ ■ ■ ■ ■
PragueWalker
www.praguewalker.com
katerina@praguewalker.com
TEL 603 181 300

This organization offers a wide range of tours to consider taking during your visit. Owner Kateřina Svobodová wrote her Charles University thesis on Jewish burial customs, so if this is an area of interest to you, she's an excellent choice for a guide. They also offer several tours to the countryside. Prices start at 600 CZK per hour for 1 to 6 people.

CASH ONLY

While his fleet is not as current, chic, or comfortable as cars available at any of the hotels I've suggested, using his services instead of your hotel's for a day trip will save you a bundle of crowns.

PRIVATE TOUR GUIDES

If you're traveling alone or in a small group, there's no better way to see the city and learn its lore and legends than with a private tour guide. I find it very cumbersome to travel with groups, as they never seem to travel at the right pace for me—I always feel guilty if I'm holding everyone up by wanting to pop into a store to check out a few items. But with a private tour, you will be the master! The four guides listed below will customize unique tours to meet your specifications. Payment in cash is required, whether CZK or EUR.

NOTE: **Fees do *not* include entry fees to museums and exhibitions!**

■ ■ ■ ■ ■ ■ ■ ■ ■ ■ ■ ■ ■ ■
Personal Prague Guide
www.personalpragueguide.com
sarka@me.com
TEL 777 225 205

The owner of this firm, Šárka Pelantová, has a terrific website that clearly outlines the various tours and services she can provide for you. In addition to various Prague tours, they offer several to the countryside as well. They have a team consisting of many guides, each with a specialty of some kind (art, music, Jewish history, etc.). Šárka's father, Milan Pelant, has taken several of my friends on tours and has received rave reviews – the stories about his personal experience as a member of the Velvet Revolution in 1989 are fascinating. Prices start at 400 CZK per hour; however, the price increases with the number of people on

■ ■ ■ ■ ■ ■ ■ ■ ■ ■ ■ ■ ■ ■
Arts & Music Travel
Miloš Čuřík
arts.music@volny.cz
TEL 603 475 754

Miloš is my go-to guide in Prague. His wealth of Prague knowledge is utterly impressive and one could best describe him as a historical generalist with a specialization in art and music. Prices start at 800 CZK per hour; however, they vary based on the length of your tour, so you'll want to confirm the exact price once you finalize your itinerary. A complete price list is available upon request.

■ ■ ■ ■ ■ ■ ■ ■ ■ ■ ■ ■ ■ ■
Pathways through Europe
www.pathwaysthrough
europe.com

Tereza Rafoth specializes in small group tours for walkers and bikers. She also happens to be very passionate about food, and she offers a very unique Prague food tour – as well as picnics made to order. Her English is exceptional (I actually did not realize she was Czech the first time we met); she lived in the US for several years and is married to an American. Her standard half-day Prague walking tour costs 4,625 CZK and there is no limit to the number of people.

SHOPPING MALL

PALLADIUM
Náměstí Republiky 1, Prague 1, Nové Město (Map A)
www.palladiumpraha.cz
TEL 225 770 250
HOURS Sun–Wed: 09:00–21:00; Thurs–Sat: 09:00–22:00
METRO Můstek ● ● or Náměstí Republiky ●
TRAM 5, 8, 14, 26 to Náměstí Republiky

This centrally located shopping mall offers 170 shops and 30 restaurants and bars (including two Starbucks), so there's something here for everyone.

TELEPHONE SERVICE PROVIDERS

Vodafone
www.vodafone.cz

T-Mobile
www.t-mobile.cz

O2
www.o2.com

TICKET AGENCIES

www.ticketpro.cz
One-stop shopping for any cultural or sporting event ticket in town, including theatre, ballet, sports, music, and even social events.

www.czechopera.cz
An excellent website that allows you to see what performances will be offered at all the major venues in town; it also lets you order tickets online.

ESCALATOR AT MUZEUM METRO STATION, 1980
(PHOTO BY JAROSLAV VEBR)

TRANSPORTATION

www.dpp.cz/en
This website is a great resource that tells you everything you ever wanted to know about the Prague municipal transport system, including its history, and also includes a handy journey planner.

www.cd.cz
If you'll be traveling by train, this is a great resource for all kinds of useful information.

www.metroweb.cz
This website has lots of information about the Prague metro system, including maps, historical images, future development plans, and even MP3 recordings of all your favorite metro announcements.

TRAVEL INSURANCE

www.worldnomads.com
This is an easy way to buy travel insurance before you leave home. It was recommended to me by two friends, Daniel Noll and Audrey Scott, who write the great travel blog *www.uncorneredmarket.com*.

www.squaremouth.com
This travel insurance company offers many affordable options.

WEATHER

www.prague.ic.cz/prague-weather.htm
Get your 12-day weather forecast here.

CONVERSION TABLES

Currency

$1 = 20 CZK **€1 = 25 CZK**

CZK	$	€
1 CZK	0.05	0.04
5	0.25	0.20
10	0.50	0.40
20	1.00	0.80
50	2.50	2.00
100	5.00	4.00
200	10.00	8.00
300	15.00	12.00
400	20.00	16.00
500	02.00	20.00
600	30.00	24.00
700	35.00	28.00
800	40.00	32.00
900	45.00	36.00
1,000	50.00	40.00
1,500	75.00	60.00
2,000	100.00	80.00
2,500	125.00	100.00
3,000	150.00	120.00
3,500	175.00	140.00
4,000	200.00	160.00
4,500	225.00	180.00
5,000	250.00	200.00
10,000	500.00	400.00
15,000	750.00	600.00
20,000	1000.00	800.00

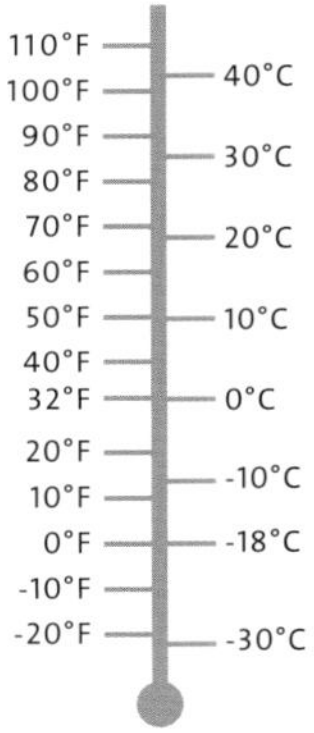

Women's Clothes

CZ	UK	USA
32	4	2
34	6	4
36	8	6
38	10	8
40	12	10
42	14	12
44	16	14
46	18	16
48	20	18

Women's Shoe Sizes

CZ	UK	USA
35	2.5	5
36	3.5	6
37	4	6.5
38	5	7.5
39	6	8.5
40	6.5	9
41	7	9.5
42	7.5	10

Men's Shirts

CZ	UK	USA
35	14	14
36/37	14 ½	14 ½
38	15	15
39/40	15 ½	15 ½
41	16	16
42/43	16 ½	16 ½
44	17	17
45	17 ½	17 ½

Men's Shoe Sizes

CZ	UK	USA
38	5	5.5
39	6	6.5
40	6.5	7
41	7.5	8
42	8	8.5
43	9	9.5
44	9.5	10
45	10.5	11
46	11.5	12

Temperature

32°F = 0°C

TO CONVERT F° TO C°
Subtract 32 and
multiply by ⁵⁄₉ (.555)

TO CONVERT C° TO F°
Muliply by 1.8
and add 32

110°F	
100°F	40°C
90°F	
80°F	30°C
70°F	
60°F	20°C
50°F	10°C
40°F	
32°F	0°C
20°F	
10°F	-10°C
0°F	-18°C
-10°F	
-20°F	-30°C

COUNTING IN PRAGUE, 1963 (SOURCE: ČTK / CZECH NEWS AGENCY)

COUNTING CURRENCY (SOURCE: DEPOSITPHOTOS.COM)

a 44 dní kolem světa

Jak 15 letý skaut překonal
Phileasa Fogga

Maps

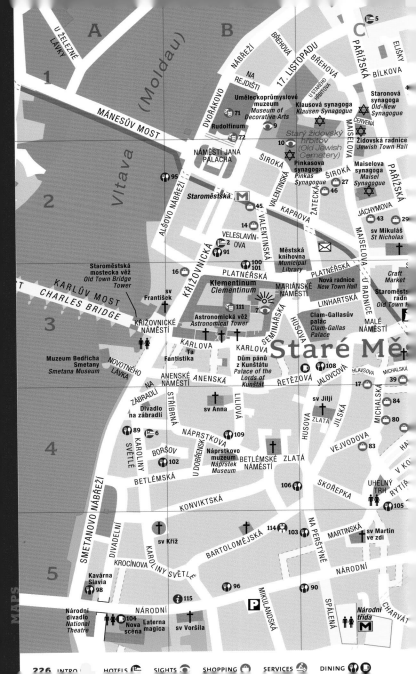

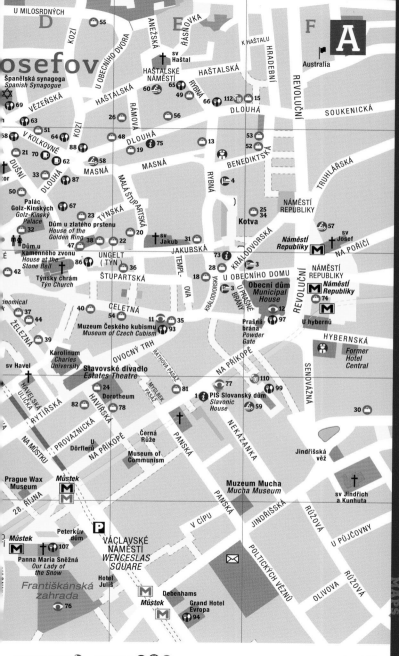

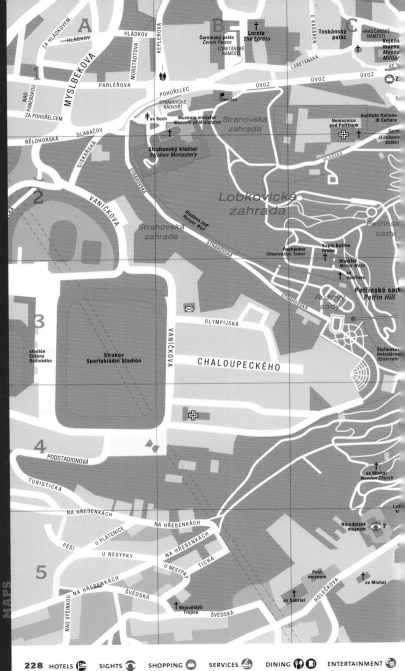

ZA HLÁDKOVEM
HLÁDKOV
HLÁDKOV
KEPLEROVA

Černínský palác
Černín Palace
LORETÁNSKÉ
NÁMĚSTÍ

†
Loreta
The Loreto

U KASÁREN
Toskánský
palác
†

HRADČANSKÉ
NÁMĚSTÍ
Vojens
muzeu
*Museu
Militar*

1

NAD
PAMENSKOU

MYSLBEKOVA

MORSTADTOVA

PARLÉŘOVA

POHOŘELEC

LORETÁNSKÁ

ÚVOZ

ÚVOZ

ÚVOZ

KE H

2:

Š

ZA POHOŘELCEM

STRAHOVSKÉ
NÁDVOŘÍ

█Sweden

*Strahovská
zahrada*

Nemocnice
pod Petřínem

Instituto Italiano
di Cultura

BĚLOHORSKÁ

DLABAČOV

DISKAŘSKÁ

† sv Roch

†

Muzeum miniatur
Museum of Miniatures

Germ
(Lobkovic
palác)

Strahovský klášter
Strahov Monastery

VLAŠSKÁ

*Lobkovické
zahrada*

VANÍČKOVA

2

*Strahovská
zahrada*

Hladová zeď'
Hunger Wall

STRAHOVSKÁ

*Petřínsk
sady*

Rozhledna
Observation Tower

Kaple Božího
hrobu
†

Bludiště
Mirror Maze

† sv Vavřinec

STRAHOVSKÁ

*Růžový
sady*

Petřínské sad
Petřín Hill

3

stadión
Evžena
Rošického

Strahov
Spartakiádní Stadión

VANÍČKOVA

✉

OLYMPIJSKÁ

CHALOUPECKÉHO

Štefánikova
Hvězdárna
Observato

✚

4

PODSTADIONOVÁ

TURISTICKÁ

† sv Michal
Wooden Church

NA HŘEBENKÁCH

NA HŘEBENKÁCH

Le
kl

PĚŠÍ

U PLÁTENICE

NA HŘEBENKÁCH

TICHÁ

Národopisné
muzeum

👁 7

5

U NESYPKY

U NESYPK

Post
muzeum

† sv Michal

NAD VYŠÍNKOU

NA HŘEBENKÁCH

ŠVÉDSKÁ

† Nejsvětější
Trojíce

† sv Gabriel

HOLEČKOVA

ŠVÉDSKÁ

nádvoří

D
III nádvoří

Královský palác
Royal Palace
Jižní zahrady
(South Gardens)

Lederburský palác

Thun
sv Kajetán –Hohenštejnský palác **14**
NERUDOVA
Morzinský palác
Romania
Lichtenštejnský palác
Hudební pavilón

Britain **43**
Sněmovna

D
Poland
VALDŠTEJNSKÁ
M Malostranská

Valdštejnský palác
Wallenstein Palace
Valdštejnská jízdárna

F

B

KLÁROV

VALDŠTEJNSKÉ NÁMĚSTÍ
P
Valdštejnská zahrada

LETENSKÁ

MÁNESŮV MOST

13

THUNOVSKÁ
dům Smiřických
sv Tomáš
28

Vojanovy sady

SEMINÁŘE

LETENSKÁ

ŠPETISLAVOVA USA
44 **46**
Schönbornský palác
VLAŠSKÁ **47**
32 **45**
TRŽIŠTĚ
Ireland

sv Mikuláš
St Nicholas **16**
MALOSTRANSKÉ NÁMĚSTÍ
41
P **P**

JOSEFSKÁ

sv Josef

U LUŽICKÉHO
Kafka Museum **34**
40
Havel Library
35

MOSTECKÁ

Vrtbovský palác
Vrtbovská zahrada **12** **42**

15 **33**
PROKOPSKÁ
NERUDOVA
Japan
Denmark

MALTÉZSKÉ NÁMĚSTÍ
Grand Priory
Panna Maria pod řetězem
VELKOPŘEVORSKÉ NÁM.
Buquoyský palác
France

DRAŽICKÉHO NÁMĚSTÍ MIŠEŇSKÁ
22 **17** **23**

SASKÁ

ornská rada

Panna Maria Vítězná
9

36

KARMELITSKÁ

HARANTOVA
HARANTOVA

České Museum Hudby
Nostický palác **6**
29
19

Lichtenštejnský palác
Lichtenstein Palace

NA KAMPĚ

KARLŮV MOST
CHARLES BRIDGE

Staroměstská mostecka věž
Old Town Bridge Tower

Muzeum Bedřicha Smetany
Smetana Museum

Staroměstská mostecka věž
Little Quarter Bridge Tower
Malostranská mostecka věž

1

á Strana

HELLICHOVA

HELLICHOVA
39
Finland
Norway

eminářská zahrada

Kampa

Museum Kampa **10**

NOVOTNÉHO LÁVKA

áha ailway
U LANOVÉ DRÁHY

VŠEHRDOVA

sv Jan Křtitel na Prádle
ŘÍČNÍ
ŘÍČNÍ

30

KAROLINY SVĚTLÉ

K.H. Mácha

27 **37** **18**
VÍTĚZNÁ

SERIKOVA

DIVADELNÍ

SMETANOVO NABŘEŽÍ

KROCIN-OVA

red' all

ÚJEZD

31

MOST LEGIÍ

Kavárna Slavia
Národní scéna
Nova scéna

PLASKÁ
ZBOROVSKÁ

Střelecký ostrov

Národní divadlo
National Theatre
Laterna magica

MĚLNICKÁ
PETŘÍNSKÁ

JANÁČKOVO NABŘEŽÍ

OSTROVNÍ

ROŠICKÝCH

NÁMĚSTÍ KINSKÝCH
Portugal

VODNÍ

Goethe-Institut

NA STRUZE

Žofín

25

ELIŠKY PEŠKOVÉ

V JIRCHÁŘÍCH

MALÁTOVA **24**

ŠÍTKOVA

sv Vojtěch

ZUBATÉHO
ŠTEFANÍKOVA

PAVLA
ARBESOVO NÁMĚSTÍ

26

HOLEČKOVA

KROFTOVA

ZBOROVSKÁ

SEMČÍCE

48

JANÁČKOVO NABŘEŽÍ

Dětský ostrov

Slovanský ostrov

Hlahol
Výstavní síň Mánes

MASARYKOVO NABŘEŽÍ

VOJTĚŠSKÁ

VIKTORA HUGA

PRESLOVA

KOŘENSKÉHO

V BOTANICE
JIRÁSKŮV MOST

JIRÁSKOVO NÁMĚSTÍ
NÁPLAVNÍ

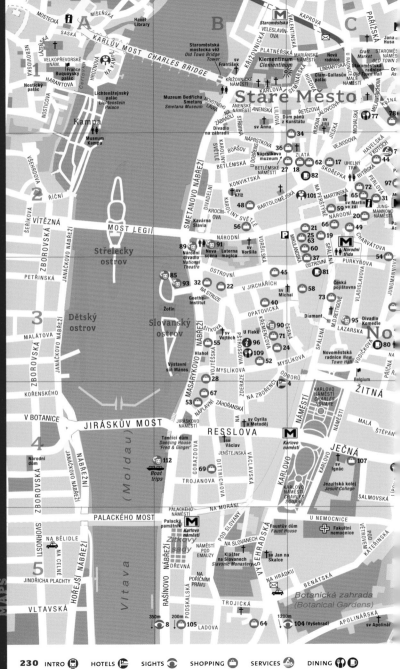

D · E · F · C

Kotva
NÁMĚSTÍ REPUBLIKY
Muzeum Prahy
Prague Museum

Dům u zlatého prstenu
sv Jakub
NÁMĚSTÍ REPUBLIKY
sv Josef
NA PŘÍKOPĚ
Banka legii
NA PORIČI
76
Divadlo Archa
6
11

Nové Město

České kubismu
um of Czech Cubism
O OBECNÍHO DOMU
Obecní dům
Municipal House
NÁMĚSTÍ REPUBLIKY
V CELNICI
NÁMĚSTÍ REPUBLIKY
NA FLORENCI

Prašná brána
Powder Gate
Lidový dům
American Center for Trade & Culture
Florenc
MM
Florenc
Bus Station
Praha Florenc

Stavovské divadlo
Estates Theatre
Dorotheum
PIS Slovanský dům
Slavonic House
39
HYBERNSKÁ
Former Hotel Central
3
Café Arco
43
DLÁŽDĚNÁ
HYBERNSKÁ

Train Station
Masarykovo nádraží

51
Černá Růže
92
SENOVÁŽNÉ NÁMĚSTÍ
JINDŘIŠSKÁ
BOLZANOVA

Museum of Communism
68
Muzeum Mucha
Mucha Museum
Jindřišská věž
Jubilejní synagoga
30
Vrchlického sady
WILSONOVA
HUSITSKÁ
SEIFERTOVA

sv Jindřich a Kunhuta
V CÍPU
VÁCLAVSKÉ NÁMĚSTÍ
WENCESLAS SQUARE
102
JINDŘIŠSKÁ
10
POLITICKÝCH VĚZŇŮ
OLIVOVA
RŮŽOVÁ
U PŮJČOVNY
OPLETALOVA

Train Station
Hlavní nádraží
1
ITALSKÁ

14
16
Můstek
Debenhams
Grand Hotel Evropa
15
British Council
Hlavní nádraží
M

12
79
86
46
98
Lucerna
29
Hotel Jalta
KUNĚTICKÁ
LICHNICKÁ
ITALSKÁ

38
87 88
Černé divadlo
VÁCLAVSKÉ NÁMĚSTÍ
WENCESLAS SQUARE
OPLETALOVA
WASHINGTONOVA
WILSONOVA
ŠPANĚLSKÁ
HELÉNSKÁ
NA SMETANCE

42
9
47
STĚPÁNSKÁ
75
Památník Wenceslas Monument
83
41
M
M
Muzeum
13
94
103
Smetanovo divadlo
(Státní opera Praha)
Prague State Opera
LEGEROVA
DIVADLA
Riegrovy sady
Vinohrady

Město
VE SMEČKÁCH
KRAKOVSKÁ
MEZIBRANSKÁ
Národní muzeum
National Museum
VINOHRADSKÁ
BALBÍNOVA
MÁNESOVA
POLSKÁ
LETENSKÁ
POLSKÁ

ŽITNÁ
Čelakovského sady
ŠKRÉTOVA
RUBEŠOVA
ŘÍMSKÁ
BALBÍNOVA
ITALSKÁ
MÁNESOVA
BLANICKÁ
VINOHRADSKÁ

sv Longin
V TŮNÍCH
HÁLKOVA
SOKOLSKÁ
LEGEROVA
MIKOVCOVA
VOCELOVA
108 110
ŘÍMSKÁ
IBSENOVA
ANNY
SIBIŘSKÁ
ŘÍMSKÁ

JEČNÁ
NÁMĚSTÍ
I.P. PAVLOVA
M
I.P. Pavlova
JUGOSLÁVSKÁ
LONDÝNSKÁ
Náměstí Míru
Divadlo na Vinohradech
NÁMĚSTÍ MÍRU
sv Ludmila
SLEZSKÁ
SAZAVSKÁ

TYLOVO NÁMĚSTÍ
BĚLEHRADSKÁ
KORUNNÍ
BLANICKÁ

KE KARLOVU
NA BOJIŠTI
U kalicha
RUMUNSKÁ
LUBLAŇSKÁ
RUMUNSKÁ
AMERICKÁ
BELGICKÁ
FRANCOUZSKÁ
SAZAVSKÁ

TYRŠOVA
LUBLAŇSKÁ
BĚLEHRADSKÁ
LONDÝNSKÁ
URUGUAYSKÁ
VARŠAVSKÁ
AMERICKÁ
BUDEČSKÁ

KE KARLOVU
FÜGNEROVO NÁMĚSTÍ
113
KOUBKOVA
BRUSELSKÁ
ZÁHŘEBSKÁ
JANA MASARYKA

MAPS

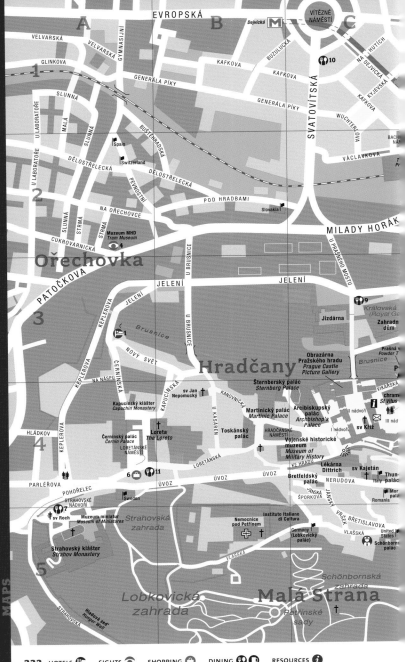

EVROPSKÁ

Dejvická **M**

VÍTĚZNÉ NÁMĚSTÍ

A   B   C

NA HUTICH

VELVARSKÁ

VELVARSKÁ

GYMNASIJNÍ

BUZULUCKÁ

KAFKOVA

NA DEJVICKÁ

🍴 10

GLINKOVA

1

GENERÁLA PÍKY

KAFKOVA

KYJEVSKÁ

BUŠTĚHRADSKÁ

SLUNNÁ

U LABORATOŘE

GENERÁLA PÍKY

KAFKOVA

SVATOVÍTSKÁ

WUCHTEROVA

MALÁ

SLUNNÁ

Spain

VÁCLAVKOVA

BACHI NÁ

U LABORATOŘE

DĚLOSTŘELECKÁ

Switzerland

BUŠTĚHRADSKÁ

DĚLOSTŘELECKÁ

PEVNOSTNÍ

T Pr

2

NA OŘECHOVCE

POD HRADBAMI

SLUNNÁ

STRMÁ

STRMÁ

STRMÁ

Slovakia

MILADY HORÁK

CUKROVARNICKÁ

Muzeum MHD
Tram Museum
4

U BRUSNICE

U PRAŠNÉHO MOSTU

PATOČKOVA

Ořechovka

JELENÍ

JELENÍ

🌳 9

Královská
(Royal Ga

KEPLEROVA

JELENÍ

Jízdárna

Zahradn
dům

3

Brusnice

U BRUSNICE

Prašná
Powder T

KEPLEROVA

NOVÝ SVĚT

Hradčany

Obrazárna
Pražského hradu
Prague Castle
Picture Gallery

Brusnice

P

ČERNÍNSKA

NA NÁSPINSKA

KAPUCÍNSKA

sv Jan
Nepomucký

KANOVNICKÁ

Šternberský palác
Sternberg Palace

VIKÁŘSKÁ

chrám
St Vítus

HLÁDKOV

Kapucínský klášter
Capuchin Monastery

U KASÁREN

Martinický palác
Martinic Palace

Arcibiskupský
palác
Archbishop's
Palace

II nádvoří

sv Kříž

III nád

4

KEPLEROVA

Černínský palác
Černín Palace

Loreta
The Loreto

Toskánský
palác

HRADČANSKÉ
NÁMĚSTÍ

I nádvoří

LORETÁNSKÉ
NÁMĚSTÍ

Vojenské historické
muzeum
Museum of
Military History

KE HRADU

HLÁDKOV

6 🏛 11

LORETÁNSKÁ

Lékárna
Dittrich

sv Kajetán

Thun-
palác

PARLÉŘOVA

POHOŘELEC

ÚVOZ

ÚVOZ

ÚVOZ

Bretfeldský
palác

NERUDOVA

Italy

Mor
palá

STRAHOVSKÉ
NÁDVOŘÍ

Sweden

JÁNSKÝ
VRŠEK

Romania

sv Roch
7

Muzeum miniatur
Museum of Miniatures

Strahovská
zahrada

Nemocnice
pod Petřínem

Instituto Italiano
di Cultura

Germany
(Lobkovický
palác)

VLAŠSKÁ

BŘETISLAVOVA

United
States
Schönborn
palác

5

Strahovský klášter
Strahov Monastery

VLAŠSKÁ

VLAŠSKÁ

Schönbornská
zahrada

STRAHOVSKÁ

Hladová zeď
Hunger Wall

Lobkovická
zahrada

Malá Strana

Petřínské
sady

MAPS

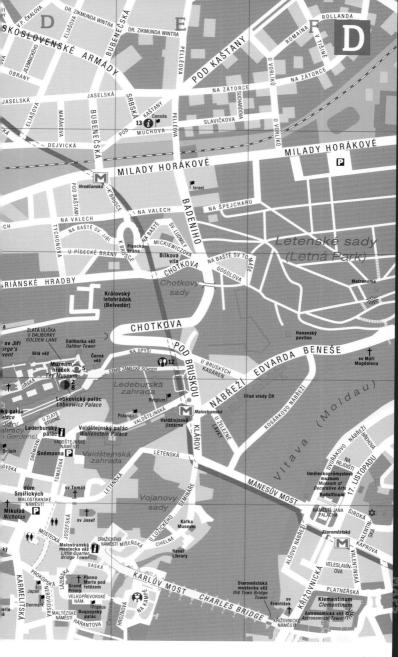

D E F D

DR. ZIKMUNDA WINTRA
DR. ZIKMUNDA WINTRA
ROLLANDA
ROMAINA
V TIŠINĚ
V.P. ČKALOVA
ELIÁŠOVA
JELÍNKOVA
BUBENEČSKÁ
PELLÉOVA
POD KAŠTANY
U VORLÍKŮ
NA ZÁTORCE
NA ZÁTORCE
OBRANY
JASELSKÁ
SRBSKÁ
KAŠTANY
NA ZÁTORCE
SUCHARDOVA
JASELSKÁ
MARÁKOVA
ELIÁŠOVA
BUBENEČSKÁ
POD
MUCHOVA
13 ℹ Canada
PELLÉOVA
SLAVÍČKOVA
U VORLÍKŮ
DEJVICKÁ

MILADY HORÁKOVÉ P

CH
MILADY HORÁKOVÉ
Hradčanská Ⓜ
POD BAŠTAMI
K BRUSCE
NA VALECH
Israel
NA ŠPEJCHARU

NA VALECH
TYCHONOVA
NA BAŠTĚ SV. JIŘÍ
K BRUSCE
NA VALECH
BADENIHO
SV. LUDMILY
NA BAŠTĚ SV. TOMÁŠE

Letenské sady
(Letná Park)

Písecká
brána
MICKIEWICZOVA
Bílkova
vila
Metronome

ARIÁNSKÉ HRADBY
U PÍSECKÉ BRÁNY
CHOTKOVA
GOGOLOVA

Královský
letohrádek
(Belvedér)
Chotkovy
sady
Hanavský
pavilon

a
ZLATÁ ULIČKA
U DALIBORKY
GOLDEN LANE
CHOTKOVA
POD BRUSKOU
NÁBŘEŽÍ EDVARDA BENEŠE
sv Maří
Magdaléna

sv Jiří
orge's
vent
Daliborka věž
Dalibor Tower
Bílá věž
Černá
věž
NA OPYŠI
Muzeum
hraček 5
Toy Museum
2
8
STARÉ ZÁMECKÉ SCHODY
ℹ 12
U BRUSKÝCH
KASÁREN
Úřad vlády ČR
Vltava (Moldau)

ký palác
Lobkovický palác
Lobkowicz Palace
Ledeburská
zahrada
Belgium
Malostranská Ⓜ
KOSÁRKOVO NÁBŘEŽÍ
JIRSKÁ

Jiřní
rahrady
n Gardens)
Britain
U ZLATÉ
STUDNĚ
Lederburský
palác
Valdštejnský palác
Wallenstein Palace
Poland
VALDŠTEJNSKÁ
Valdštejnská
jízdárna
U ŽELEZNÉ
LÁVKY

VALDŠTEJNSKÉ
NÁM.
Sněmovní P
Valdštejnská
zahrada
LETENSKÁ
DVOŘÁKOVO NÁBŘEŽÍ
17. LISTOPADU
NÁBŘEŽÍ

OVSKÁ
TOMÁŠSKÁ
LETENSKÁ
MÁNESŮV MOST
NA
REJDIŠTI
Umělecko-
průmyslové
muzeum
Museum of
Decorative Arts
Rudolfinum

dům
Smiřických
MALOSTRANSKÉ
NÁMĚSTÍ
sv Tomáš
Vojanovy
sady
SEMINÁŘSKÉ
NÁMĚSTÍ JANA
PALACHA
VALENTINSKÁ

Mikuláš
Nicholas P
ky
JOSEFSKÁ
sv Josef
U LUŽICKÉHO
Kafka
Museum
Staroměstská Ⓜ
ŠIROKÁ
KAPROVA
VALENTINSKÁ

MOSTECKÁ
Malostranská
mostecká věž
Little Quarter
Bridge Tower
DRAŽICKÉHO
NÁMĚSTÍ MÍŠEŇSKÁ
CIHELNA
Havel
Library
ALŠOVO NÁBŘEŽÍ
VELESLAVÍNOVA
PLATNÉŘSKÁ

PROKOPSKÁ
LÁZEŇSKÁ
NEBOVIDSKÁ
SASKÁ
KARLŮV MOST
Staroměstská
mostecká věž
Old Town Bridge
Tower
KŘIŽOVNICKÁ
Klementinum
Clementinum

Japan
KARMELITSKÁ
MALTÉZSKÉ
NÁMĚSTÍ
Panna
Maria pod
řetězem
Grand
Priory
VELKOPŘEVORSKÉ
NÁM.
NA KAMPĚ
CHARLES BRIDGE
sv
František
Astronomická věž
Astronomical Tower

aria
Denmark
Buquoyský
palác
France
HROZNOVA
KŘIŽOVNICKÉ
NÁMĚSTÍ
HARANTOVA

MAPS

Černá Růže
✝
Museum of Communism

PANSKÁ
NEKÁZANKA

Jindřišská věž

SENOVÁŽNÉ NÁMĚSTÍ

JINDŘIŠSKÁ
BOLZÁNOVA
SEIFERTO

C

A
B

Muzeum Mucha
Mucha Museum

V CIPU
PANSKÁ
JINDŘIŠSKÁ
RŮŽOVÁ

✝ sv Jindřich a Kunhuta

JERUZALÉMSKÁ

Jubilejní synagoga

Vrchlického sady

OPLETALOVA

WILSONOVA

1

U PŮJČOVNY

Nové Město

✉
M
Debenhams
Grand Hotel Evropa

POLITICKÝCH VĚZŇŮ
OLIVOVA
RŮŽOVÁ
OPLETALOVA

M
Hlavní nádraží

Train Station
Hlavní nádraží
ℹ️🚂

ITALSKÁ

Můstek

KUNĚTICKÁ

Lucera
P

Černé divadlo

Hotel Jalta

OPLETALOVA

British Council

WASHINGTONOVA

Vrchlického sady

P

ŠPANĚLSKÁ
LICHNICKÁ
ITALSKÁ

ŠTĚPÁNSKÁ

VÁCLAVSKÉ NÁMĚSTÍ
WENCESLAS SQUARE

Památník Wenceslas Monument

Muzeum
M

LEGEROVA
DIVADLA

WILSONOVA

Smetanovo divadlo (Státní opera Praha)
Prague State Opera

ŠPANĚLSKÁ
NA SMETANCE
HELENSKÁ

Riegro sady

VE SMEČKÁCH
KRAKOVSKÁ
MEZIBRANSKÁ

Národní muzeum
National Museum

23 🛍️
BALBÍNOVA
MÁNESOVA
11 🛍️

VINOHRADSKÁ

POLSKÁ

ITALSKÁ

Vinoh

3
ŽITNÁ

LEGEROVA

Čelakovského sady
ŠKRÉTOVA
RUBEŠOVA
ŘÍMSKÁ

LETENSKÉ

MÁNESOVA
PO

15 🛍️

VINOHRADSKÁ

SOKOLSKÁ
LEGEROVA

MIKOVCOVA
VOCELOVA

LONDÝNSKÁ
BALBÍNOVA
ITALSKÁ

ŘÍMSKÁ
ANNY

5 🛍️
6 🛍️
BLANICKÁ
ŘÍMSKÁ
14 🛍️

V TŮNÍCH
HÁLKOVA

JEČNÁ
KATEŘINSKÁ

NÁMĚSTÍ I. P. PAVLOVA
M *I.P. Pavlova*

🍴 25

JUGOSLÁVSKÁ

UBESNOVA
ŠUBERTOVA

M
Náměstí Míru

Divadlo na Vinohradech
✝ sv Ludmila

Vir

SLEZSKÁ

4

1 🏛️
Vila Amerika (Muzeum Antonína Dvořáka
Dvořák Museum)

NA BOJIŠTI

U kalicha

LUBLAŇSKÁ

BĚLEHRADSKÁ

TYLOVO NÁMĚSTÍ

9 🛍️

NÁMĚSTÍ MÍRU

KORUNNÍ

SÁZAVSKÁ

RUMUNSKÁ

SOKOLSKÁ
LEGEROVA

RUMUNSKÁ

LUBLAŇSKÁ
TYRŠOVA

BĚLEHRADSKÁ
LONDÝNSKÁ

ℹ️ 30

AMERICKÁ
BELGICKÁ
URUGUAYSKÁ

BLANICKÁ

SÁZAVSKÁ
MORAVS

FUGNEROVO NÁMĚSTÍ

KOUBKOVA

BRUSELSKÁ

VARŠAVSKÁ
AMERICKÁ

FRANCOUZS
ZÁHŘEBSKÁ

KE KARLOVU

5

WENZIGOVA
BOŽENY NĚMCOVÉ

LUBLAŇSKÁ

BĚLEHRADSKÁ
LONDÝNSKÁ

ŠAFAŘÍKOVA
U ZVONAŘKY
ZÁHŘEBSKÁ

ZÁHŘEBSKÁ

JANA MASARYKA
AMERICKÁ

VARŠAVSKÁ

MÁCHOVA

MA

Muzeum policie
Police Museum

3 🏛️

17 🎭

🎭 31

JANA MASARYKA

KOPERNÍKOVA

ŠMILO

MAPS

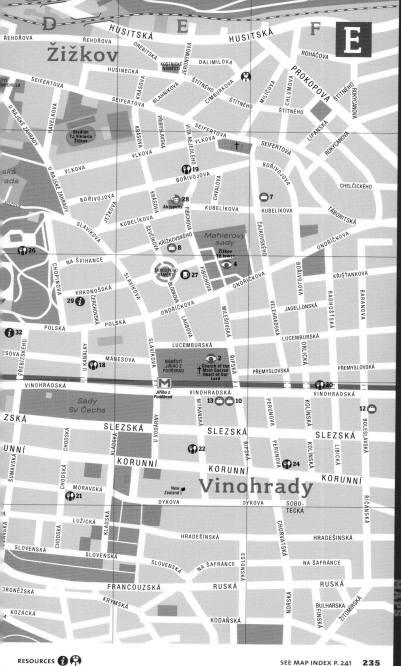

A   B   C

1

Stromovka Park

Divadlo globe

Panorama L. Marolda

Místodržitelský letohrádek

Planetarium

NÁMĚSTÍ POD KAŠTANY

Russia

Bubeneč

2

ROMAINA ROLLANDA

NA ZÁTORCE

V TIŠINĚ

NAD KRÁLOVSKOU OBOROU

NAD KRÁLOVSKOU OBOROU

ZAJÍCE

HAVANSKÁ

ČECHOVA

ŠMERALOVA

U AKADEMIE

GERSTNEROVA

UMĚLECKÁ

OVENECKÁ

SOCHAŘSKÁ

MALÍRSKÁ

U STUDÁNKY

KAMENICKÁ

KAMENICKÁ

STRO

Sportovní hala TJ Sparta ČKD Praha

KORUNOVAČNÍ

JANA

SLÁDKOVA

KERAMICKÁ

ČECHOVA

VELETRŽNÍ

HAŠKOVA

HEŘMANO

NA VÝŠINÁCH

U LETENSKÉ VODÁRNY

LETENSKÉ NÁMĚSTÍ

11  **7**

MILADY

HORÁKOVÉ

3

Stadión Sparta Praha

U SPARTY

14

MILADY HORÁKOVÉ

P

P

P

NAD ŠTOLOU

JIREČKOVA

OVENECKÁ

DOBROVSKÉHO

U LETENSKÉHO SADU

KAMENICKÁ

LETOHRADSKÁ

MILADY HO

10

LETOHRADSKÁ

Letenské sady (Letná Park)

4

3

Metronome

Národní technické muzeum National Technical Museum **5**

LETENSKÝ TUNEL

KOSTELNÍ

12

Praha Expo 58

NÁB

NÁBŘEŽÍ EDVARDA BENEŠE

ŠTEFÁNIKŮV MOST

5

sv Máří Magdalena

CECHŮV MOST

Vltava   (Moldau)

NÁMĚSTÍ CURIEOVÝCH

NA FRANTIŠKU

NA FRANTIŠKU

NÁBŘEŽÍ LUDVÍKA S

DVOŘÁKOVO NÁBŘEŽÍ

BŘEHOVA

17. LISTOPADU

BŘEHOVA

NA REJDIŠTI

PAŘÍŽSKÁ

DUŠNÍ

KOZÍ

U MILOSRDNÝCH

sv Šimon a Juda

BÍLKOVA

Anežský klášter St Agnes's Convent

MALÁ KLÁŠTERSKÁ

RÁSNOVKA

KLÁŠTERSKÁ

RÁSNOVKA

HRADEBNÍ

REVOLUČNÍ

NOVO-

MLÝNSKÁ

NOVÉ MLÝNY

Poštovní muzeum Postal Museum

POŠTOVNÍ

Josefov

DUŠNÍ

Španělská synagoga Spanish Synagogue

U OBECNÍHO DVORA

HAŠTALSKÁ

sv Haštal

HAŠTALSKÉ NÁMĚSTÍ

RYBNÁ

HAŠTALSKÁ

Australia

sv Kliment

KLIMENTSKÁ

SOUKEN

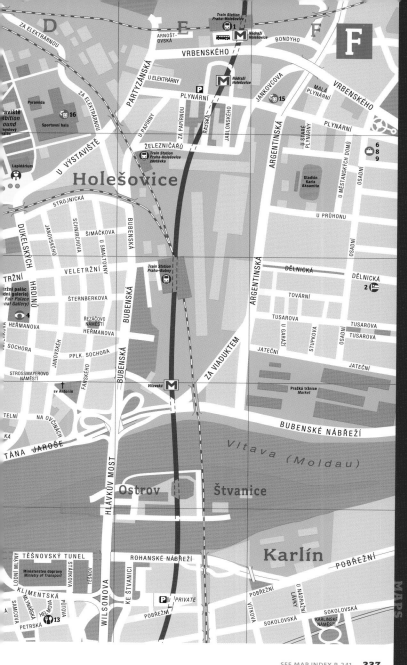

D E F F

ZA ELEKTRÁRNOU

Train Station
Praha–Holešovice
1

ARNOŠT-
OVSKÁ

Nádraží
Holešovice

VRBENSKÉHO

BONDYHO

VRBENSKÉHO

PARTYZÁNSKÁ

U ELEKTRÁRNY

Nádraží
Holešovice

JANKOVCOVA

MALÁ
PLYNÁRNÍ

ZA ELEKTRÁRNOU

PLYNÁRNÍ

15

Pyramida

16

Sportovní hala

U PAPÍRNY

ZA PAPÍRNOU

RAŠSKÁ

JABLONSKÉHO

PLYNÁRNÍ

U STARÉ
PLYNÁRNÍ

U MĚSTANSKÝCH DOMŮ

OSADNÍ

6
8
9

avistě
ibition
ound
ný slový
atál

ŽELEZNIČÁŘŮ

Train Station
Praha-Holešovice
zastávka

ARGENTINSKÁ

Stadión
Karla
Aksamita

U VÝSTAVIŠTĚ

Holešovice

STROJNICKÁ

U PRŮHONU

Lapidárium

DUKELSKÝCH

JANOVSKÉHO

SCHNIRCHOVA

ŠIMÁČKOVA

U SMALTOVNY

BUBENSKÁ

OSADNÍ

OSADNÍ

VELETRŽNÍ

TRŽNÍ

HRDINŮ

Train Station
Praha–Bubny

ARGENTINSKÁ

DĚLNICKÁ

DĚLNICKÁ

2

ržní palác
dní galerie
Fair Palace
nal Gallery)

ŠTERNBERKOVA

BUBENSKÁ

TOVÁRNÍ

4

ŘEZÁČOVO
NÁMĚSTÍ

TUSAROVA

TUSAROVA

HEŘMANOVA

HEŘMANOVA

U GARÁŽÍ

STUPKOVA

OSADNÍ

TUSAROVA

SOCHORA

JANOVSKÉHO

PPLK. SOCHORA

FAŘSKÉHO

JATEČNÍ

JATEČNÍ

STROSSMAYEROVO
NÁMĚSTÍ

BUBENSKÁ

ZA VIADUKTEM

sv Antonín

Vltavská

Pražská tržnice
Market

TELNÍ

NA OVČÍNÁCH

KÁ

BUBENSKÉ NÁBŘEŽÍ

TÁNA JAROŠE

Vltava (Moldau)

HLÁVKŮV MOST

Ostrov

Štvanice

Karlín

POBŘEŽNÍ

TĚŠNOVSKÝ TUNEL

ROHANSKÉ NÁBŘEŽÍ

ŠTÁRKOVA

Ministerstvo dopravy
Ministry of Transport

TĚŠNOV

POBŘEŽNÍ

U NÁDRAŽNÍ
LÁVKY

KLIMENTSKÁ

MLYNÁŘSKÁ

PLÚTOVA

KE ŠTVANICI

PRIVATE

POBŘEŽNÍ

VÍTKOVA

SOKOLOVSKÁ

A

SAMCOVA

HELMOVA

WILSONOVA

POBŘEŽNÍ

SOKOLOVSKÁ

KARLINSKÉ
NÁMĚSTÍ

PETRSKÁ

13

MAPS

MAPS

POSTCARD BY BOHUMÍR JARONĚK, C. 1915

VÁCLAVSKÉ NÁMĚSTÍ (POSTCARD), C. 1900

MAPS

Hotels

Romantik hotel
U raka **1** A3

Sights

Lobkowicz Palace...... **2** D4
Prague Castle **3** C4
Public Transport
Museum.............. **4** A2
Toy Museum **5** D3

Shopping

Hračky Houpací Kůň... **6** A4

Dining

Klášterní pivovar
Strahov **7** A5
Lobkowicz Palace Café
at the Prague Castle... **8** D4
Lví Dvůr – Pražský
Hrad................. **9** C3

Svatební dorty **10** C1
U Černého vola........ **11** A4
Villa Richter - Terra **12** E3

Resources

Canadian Embassy.... **13** E1

Sights

Dvořák Museum /
Villa Amerika **1** A4
Church of the
Most Sacred Heart of
our Lord **2** E3
Police Museum **3** A5
Žižkov TV Tower **4** E3

Shopping

AAA Antiques Art
Auctions.............. **5** C3
Bazar P & J............ **6** C3
Bohemian Retro....... **7** F2
Drdova Gallery........ **8** E2
Dům porcelánu **9** B4
Koralky **10** E4

Korallo................ **11** C3
Pavel Truhlář **12** F4
Pour Pour **13** E4
Robinson **14** C3
Rooya................ **15** B3
U Krále Železnic....... **16** C3

Services

Pure Spa @
Hotel Le Palais **17** B5

Dining

Aromi **18** D3
Bukowski's **19** E2
Erhart Café **20** F4
Hrom do Police........ **21** D4
Kofein **22** E4

Le Clan **23** B3
Pivo a Párek........... **24** F4
Radost FX Café........ **25** B4
Riegrovy sady **26** D2
U Sadu **27** E3

Entertainment

Palác Akropolis........ **28** E2

Resources

Panda Veterinary
Clinic **29** D3
Pharmacy U sv.
Ludmily.............. **30** B4
Police Station
Vinohrady **31** B5
Prague Saints **32** D3

Intro

Nádraží Holešovice
(Train Station)........ **1** E1

Hotels

Sir Toby's Hostel...... **2** F3

Sights

Letná Park **3** A4
National Gallery....... **4** D3
National Technical
Museum.............. **5** B4

Shopping

BenDOX at DOX........ **6** F2
Dog Town............. **7** B3
DOX................. **8** F2
DOX by Qubus........ **9** F2
Hunt Kastner
Artworks **10** C3

Dining

Fraktal............... **11** B3
Letná Park **12** C4
Sansho **13** D5

Entertainment

AC Sparta Stadium **14** A3
Cross Club **15** F1
HC Sparta Stadium **16** D1

PRAHA. Kostel sv. Mikuláše

MALOSTRANSKÉ NÁMĚSTÍ
AND CHURCH OF ST. NICHOLAS,
1934

Index

INDEX

INDEX

Boxed Info

247

INDEX

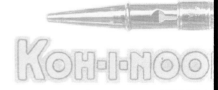

KOPIERSTIFTE

NOTES

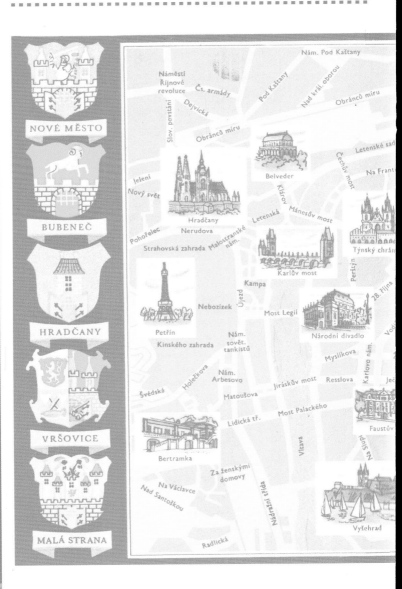

PRAGUE MAP, 1957

250